Connecticut Schoolhouses
Through Time

Melinda K. Elliott

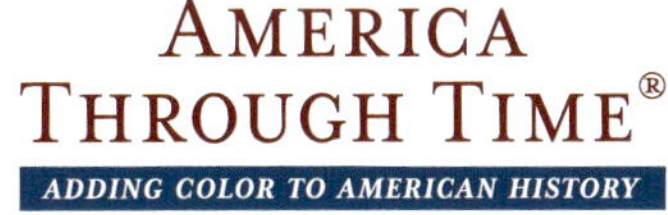

The book is dedicated to all who love old schoolhouses

America Through Time is an imprint of Fonthill Media LLC
www.through-time.com
office@through-time.com

Published by Arcadia Publishing by arrangement with Fonthill Media LLC
For all general information, please contact Arcadia Publishing:
Telephone: 843-853-2070
Fax: 843-853-0044
E-mail: sales@arcadiapublishing.com
For customer service and orders:
Toll-Free 1-888-313-2665

www.arcadiapublishing.com

First published 2017

ISBN 978-1-63500-056-6

Typeset in Mrs Eaves XL Serif Narrow
Printed and bound in England

Contents

Acknowledgments

This book would not have been possible without the help of dozens of historical societies, their members, and many other historical groups. To acknowledge all the contributors of information and photographs is impossible in this limited space. I truly appreciate the time you took to meet or communicate with me. The organizations that have allowed the use of their photographs are listed below the captions. Please know that I really enjoyed getting to know so many schoolhouse enthusiasts, and value your stories and input.

Another wonderful source of photographs was the Connecticut History Illustrated (connecticuthistoryillustrated.org), Connecticut State Library, which provides digital historical images of the state, along with oral histories and maps.

Included are several 100-year-old postcards or photographs from my extensive personal collection. Someday I will find a way to use my 500+ images in one place.

All of the contemporary color photographs were taken by myself or my husband, Ray. Even though Connecticut is a small state, we spent many enjoyable hours travelling to schoolhouses to get just the right picture for each page.

Every effort has been taken to verify the accuracy of all the information included in the book, and each source had to be weighed carefully. Please accept my regrets over any detail that is incorrect.

Thank you, a hundred times over, to every single person that contributed to this book in whatever capacity, to my family for the disruption in the normal routines, and to my very supportive, patient husband.

INTRODUCTION

The fact that you can visit an old schoolhouse in Connecticut is almost a miracle. The school buildings had a life expectancy of 20 years, according to former state historian, Christopher Collier. Despite of the odds, Connecticut still has a number of schoolhouses standing that were built as early as 1740.

The very first place of education for Connecticut children was at home or at a Dames school. The scholars met in a teacher's home to learn the basics of reading, as required by law. When the towns grew to 50 families, a school was supposed to be built, which was often in the middle of town. In the frontier farming communities, sending a child to school was not always feasible because of the long distance to walk, and the amount parents had to pay for their children to attend.

By the mid-1700s, schoolhouses were set up in various areas of a town. Occasionally, these buildings were used as a moving school, where one teacher would visit each school for a few weeks and then move on to the next school. Some of these buildings were constructed to be used only for a month.

Around the Revolutionary War, more schoolhouses were built in a variety of styles and materials, with district borders allowing children to walk two miles or less to school. The normal school term was for four months from November through March. Later, a four-month summer session was added.

By 1830, many of the schoolhouses were run down. One school surveyor reported that out of 103 schools examined, only 31 were in good repair and a mere three schools had an outhouse. The awareness of the deplorable conditions brought an explosion of new school construction, and many old schools were renovated. By 1852, there were 1,642 active schoolhouses, with one teacher for each building, teaching all the students from 1st to 8th grades.

It wasn't until 1899 that a state-wide compulsory attendance law ordered all students between ages seven and sixteen to be in school. For the first time, this included girls. The school year was set at 180 days, with the students required to spend only 60 days in class.

As the transportation and roads improved, and modern educational ideas prevailed, the one- and two-room schoolhouses were closed in favor of brand new modern buildings where all the town's students could attend with a designated room and teacher for each grade.

The law stated that an unused schoolhouse was to revert to the ownership of the last known landowner's family. If not available, the buildings were to be sold at auction, with the proceeds going to the Consolidated School building expenses. A schoolhouse could stay as it was, if used for public educational purposes.

Many of the old schoolhouses were carted away to be used as houses, garages, chicken houses, or for church purposes. Several schoolhouses became the local library and others were left along the side of the road, neglected until they rotted away.

The 1976 United States Bicentennial brought a revived interest in American history, and a wave of nostalgia encouraged towns to restore one- and two-room schoolhouses to preserve them for the following generations.

As you travel along Connecticut backroads, you are still able to see the old schoolhouses in varying conditions—some falling apart, some made into homes that proudly bear a sign stating it was once a schoolhouse, along with many that have been restored and made into museums by historical societies.

Look around and find an old restored schoolhouse in your area, then make a point to go visit it. I can assure you that you will be welcomed to step back into time and for a moment become a scholar in the olden days.

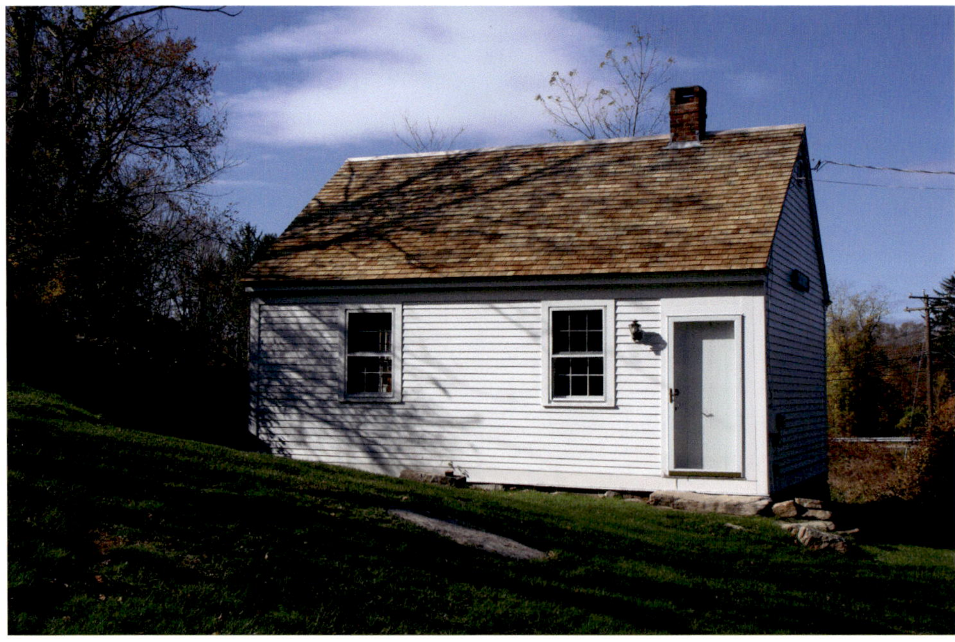

c. 1829 Road District Schoolhouse, Stonington, CT.

1

EARLY SCHOOLS, PRE-1800

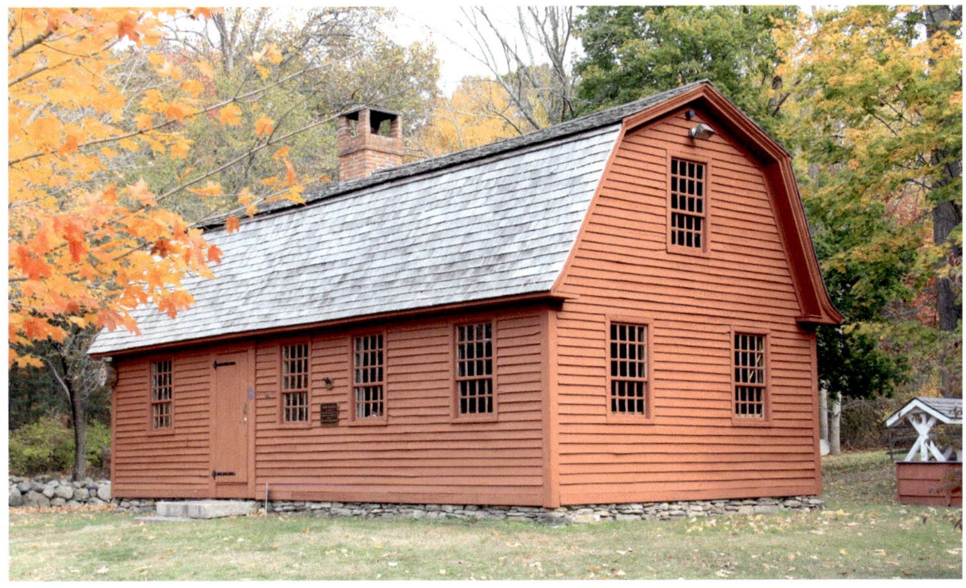

The schoolhouses in this chapter were all built before 1800, and still exist due to caring communities who saved a piece of their local history.

The earliest schoolhouses in Connecticut were simple structures that were easy to make and often considered temporary buildings, little more than a shed. As the importance of schooling increased, the schoolhouses were built with a thought of permanence, with stronger structures.

Schoolhouses constructed of wood or brick with a gambrel roof was a popular style in the southeastern side of the state. The Jordan Schoolhouse, pictured above, is a good example of that style. It was built about 1740, and stands today in the Jordan Village in Waterford.

By the 1780s, each Connecticut town had several school districts with a one-teacher schoolhouse in each district, under the watchful eye of the church. The buildings reflected the style and available building materials of the immediate community. Schools were built where the largest concentration of children lived. The locations were rarely ideal, with schools built in the middle of the road, or on a piece of land unsuitable for any other purpose. Some districts were fortunate to have a parent or patron donate a piece of land to be used for a schoolhouse.

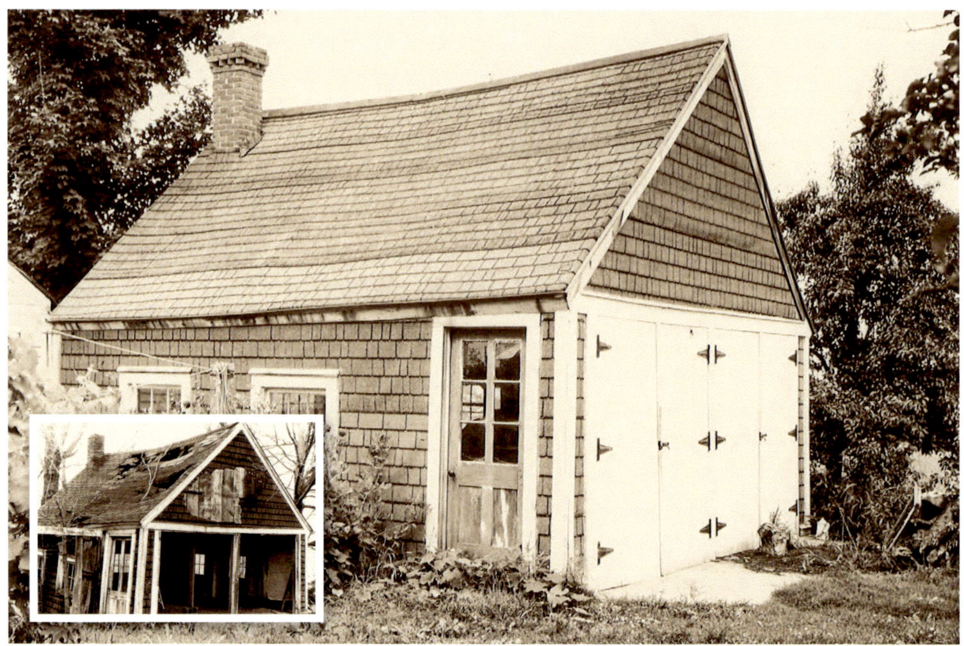

MANCHESTER: Built in 1751, the Keeney Schoolhouse, like many others, was eventually no longer needed as a school and was sold. It was used as a garden shed and later as a garage. In March 1975, the Town's Bicentennial Committee located the building and voted to restore it, in spite of its deplorable condition. The Manchester Historical Society agreed to furnish and maintain the building. Using the existing timbers as a guideline and some of the usable wood, the workers were able to reproduce the building, including the rounded ceiling. It now stands as a museum at the Cheney Homestead. (Above photograph courtesy CT State Library, State Archives, LS Mills Collection; Inset Photograph courtesy of the Manchester Historical Society)

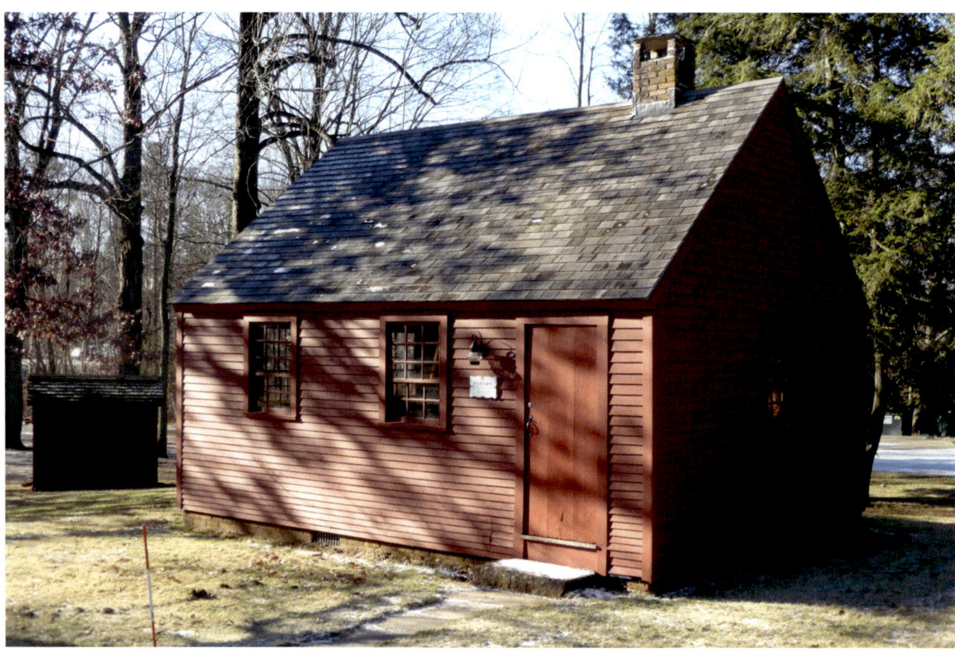

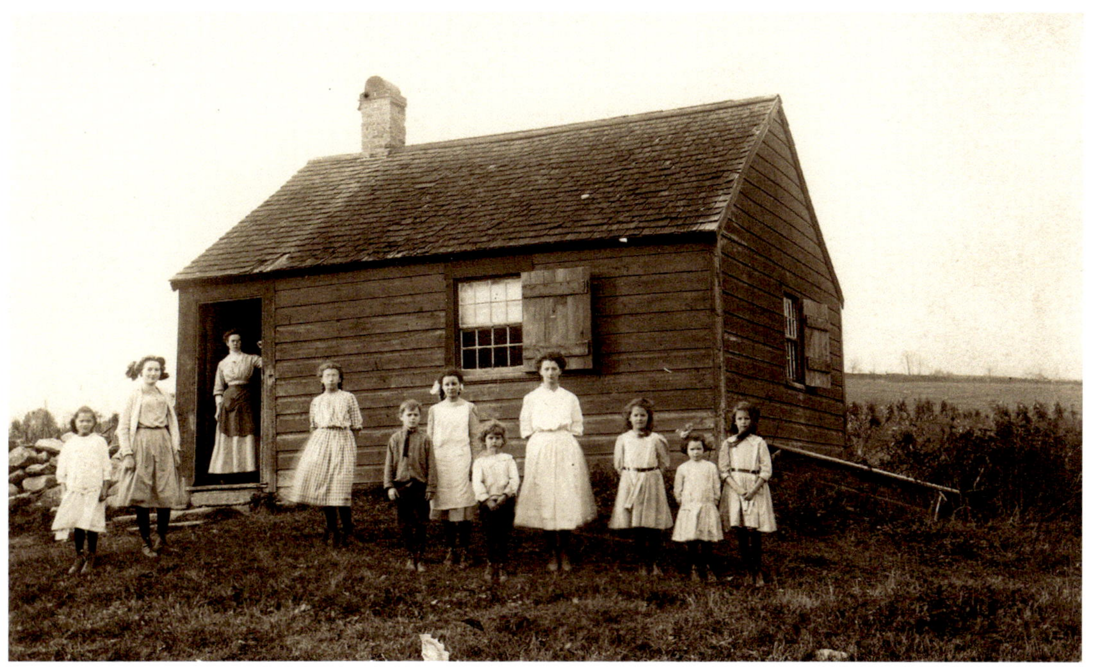

KENT: The Skiff Mountain School, built on top of a crag on a high hillside, was likely built before the Revolutionary War. The land was donated by Nathan Skiff in 1766, to provide a school for his children and others in the area, including other Skiff families. School records show that the winter session of 1845 was held for three and a half months, and each student was required to bring 20 feet of wood to heat the building. The school was used until 1914. Mrs. Pauline Skiff Gunn donated the schoolhouse to the Kent Historical Society in 1972. It has been carefully restored and one of the original four-student desks still remains. (Above photograph courtesy of Kent Historical Society)

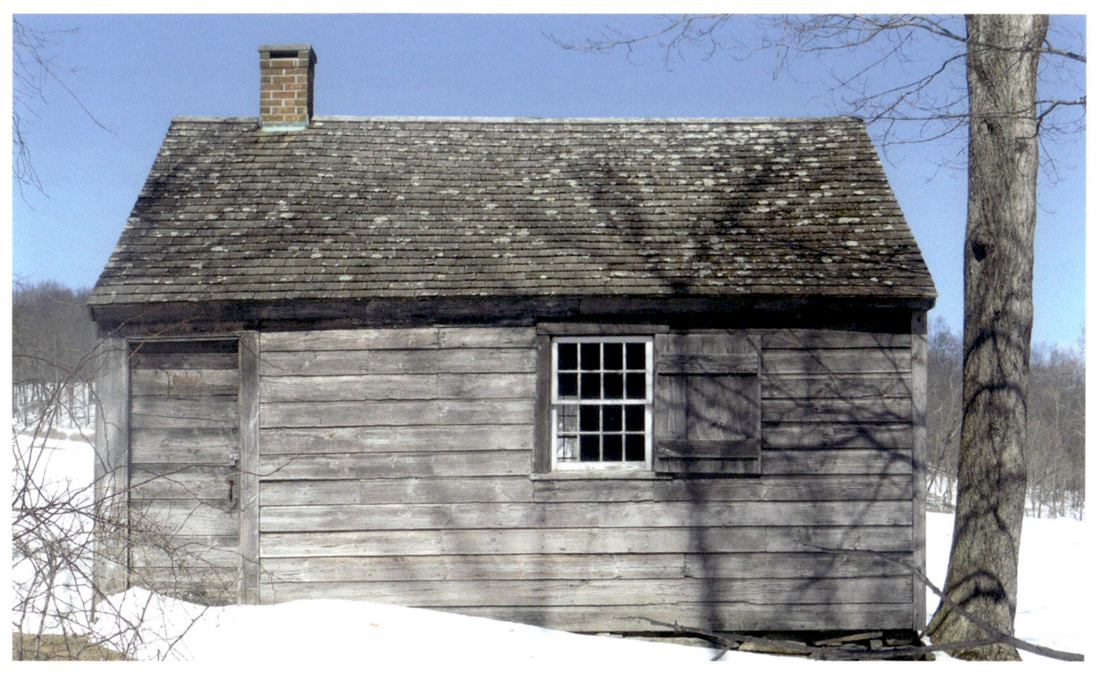

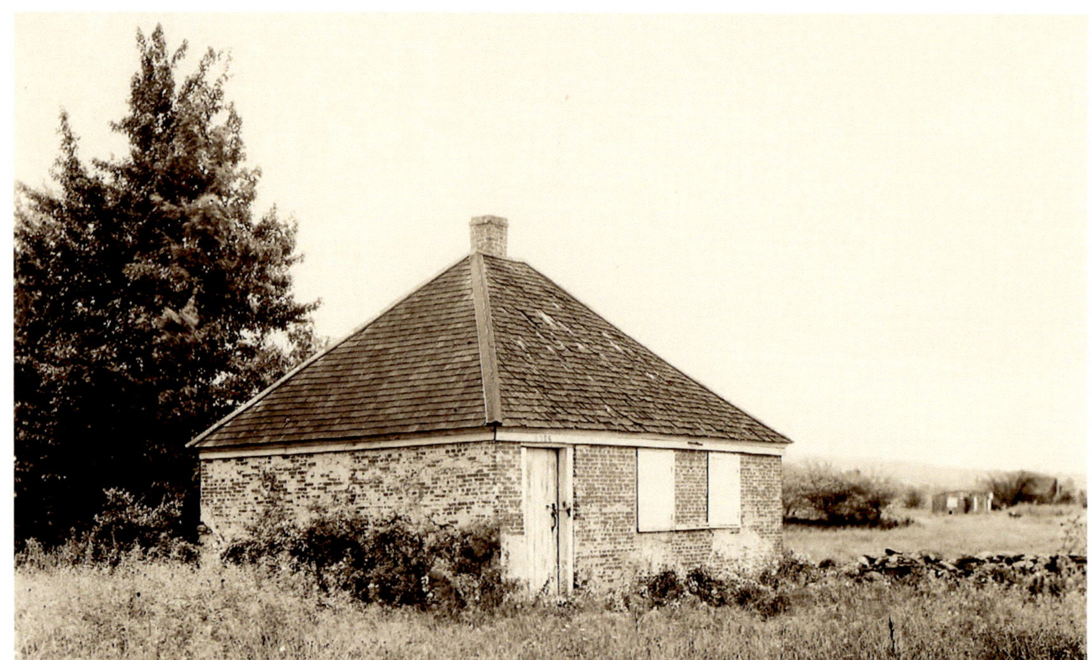

WARREN: The Brick School of Warren has been known by several names include the "Old North School," and most recently, "The Little Red Schoolhouse." The tiny schoolhouse was built in 1784 with a center chimney, set between cornfields and an apple orchard. After 140 years of continuous use, it closed in 1925. The school was purchased by Frank M. Reinhold and later given to the Warren Historical Society. Author/ Illustrator Eric Sloane lived near the schoolhouse. In his book, *The Little Red Schoolhouse*, Sloane confessed that he would sometimes go inside, sit at a desk, and think of the old days. (Above photograph Courtesy CT State Library, State Archives, LS Mills Collection)

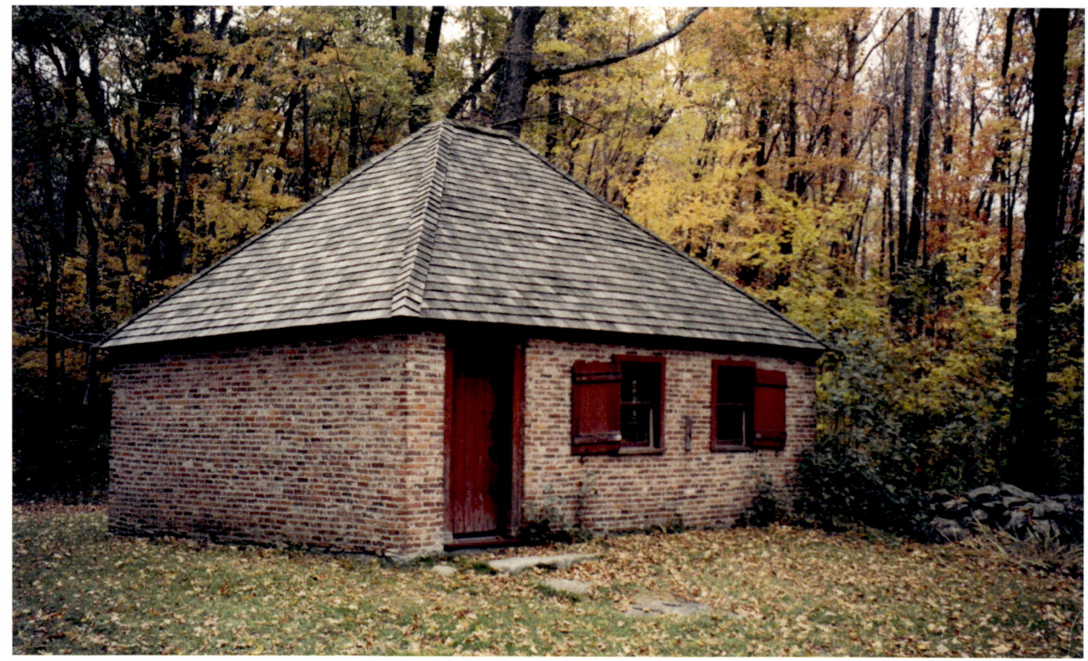

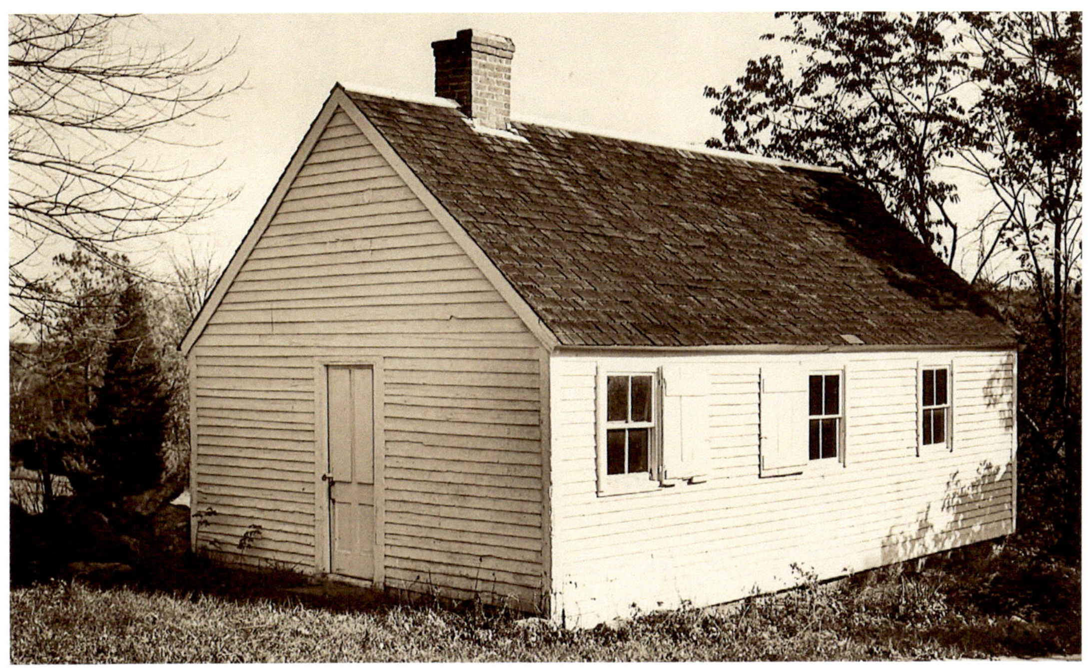

HEBRON: The Burrows Hill School is said to be the oldest schoolhouse in Hebron, constructed in the mid-1700s and possibly as early as 1730. The number of students varied over the years due to population changes and nearby factories. The historians have a list of 47 known teachers for this schoolhouse. Several renovations and restoration projects have taken place over the years. The school was closed in 1909 and the children were sent to the Center Schoolhouse. The Hebron Historical Society took over the care of the building in 1968. The building was moved 40 feet, safely away from the edge of the road in 1993. (Above photograph courtesy of Hebron Historical Society)

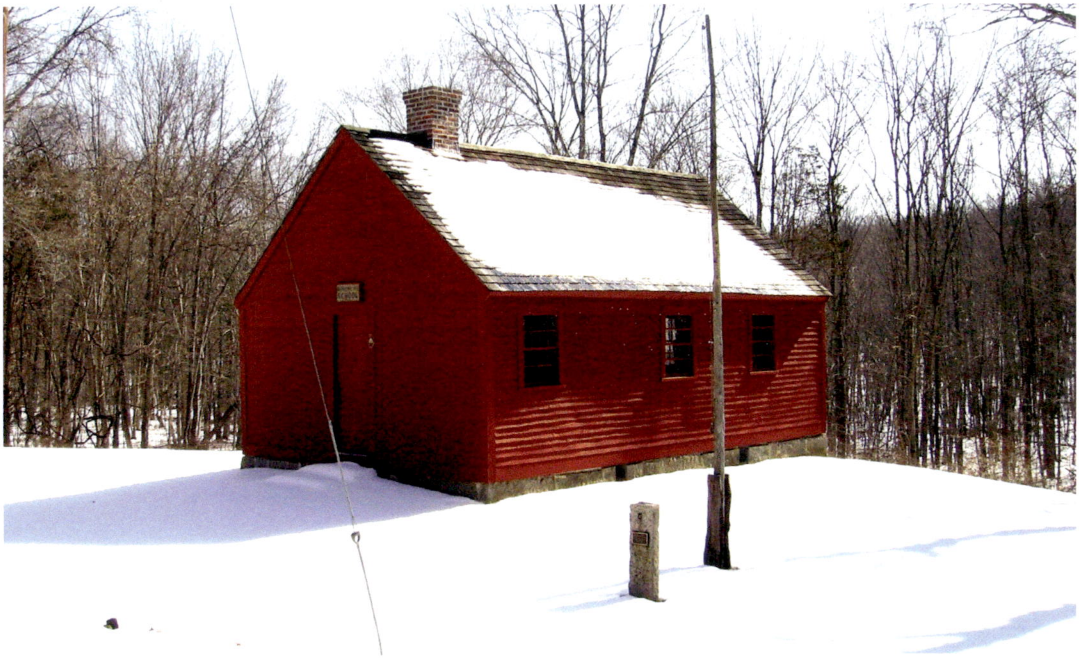

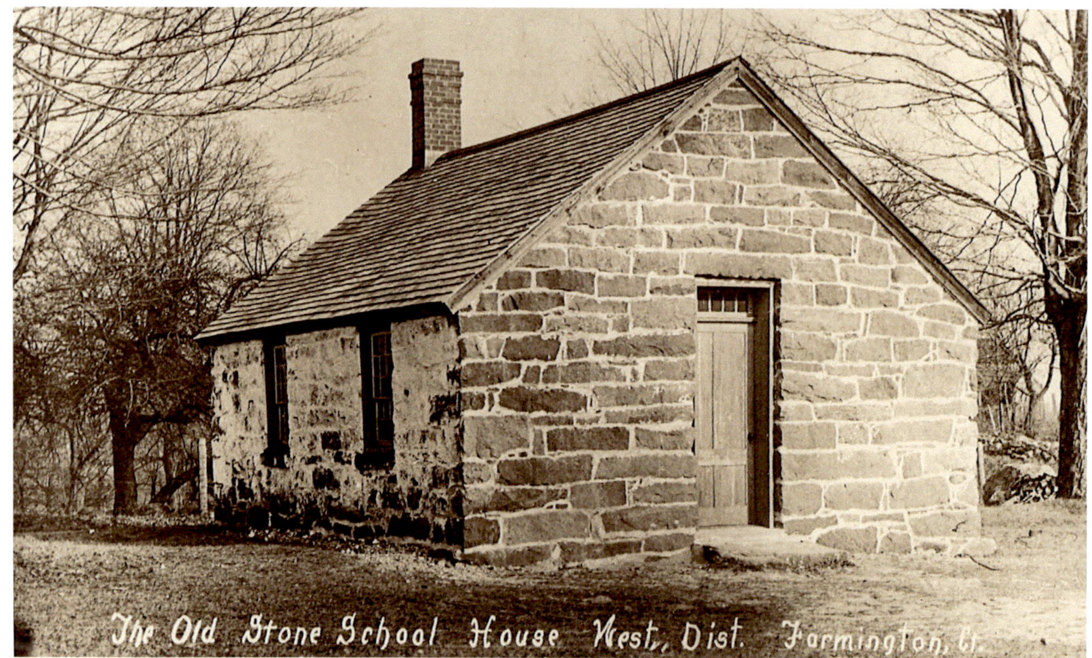

FARMINGTON: The Old West District School, commonly known as the “Old Stone Schoolhouse,” was built in 1790. The local brownstone was cut and hauled by ox-cart from a nearby quarry. When the school became overcrowded, a new one was built down the street and the doors of the Old Stone Schoolhouse were closed in 1872. The building was purchased in 1875 to be used for church services, and was called the St. Simon’s Chapel. An annex was added in 1912 to serve as a community hall, using brownstone from the original quarry. Restoration occurred in 1993 by the Farmington Historical Society. (Above photograph Courtesy CT State Library, State Archives, LS Mills Collection)

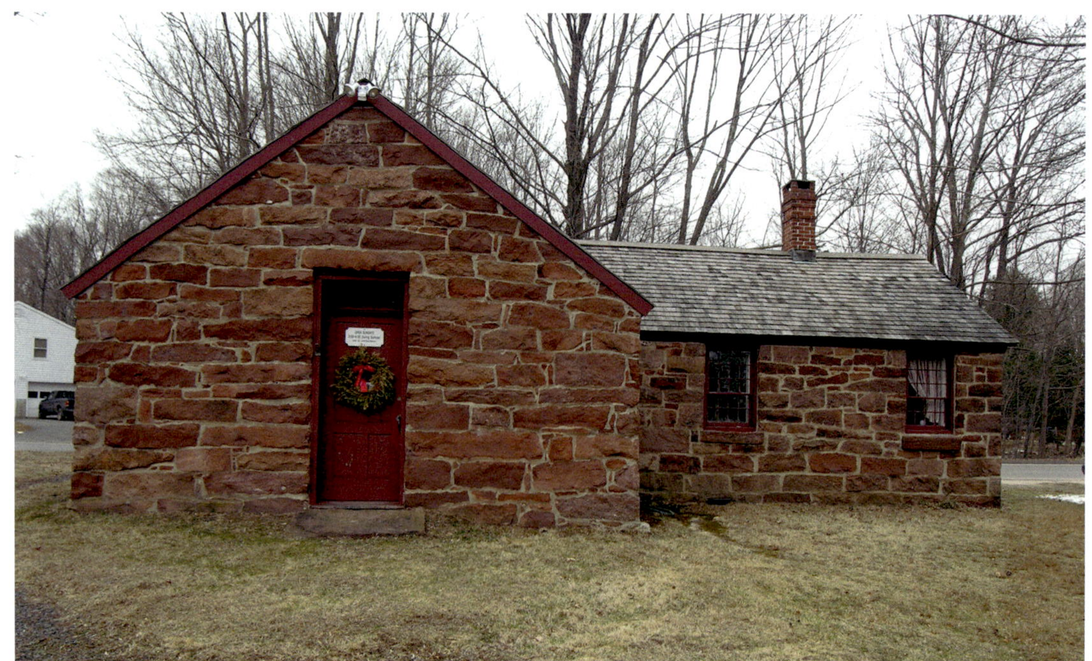

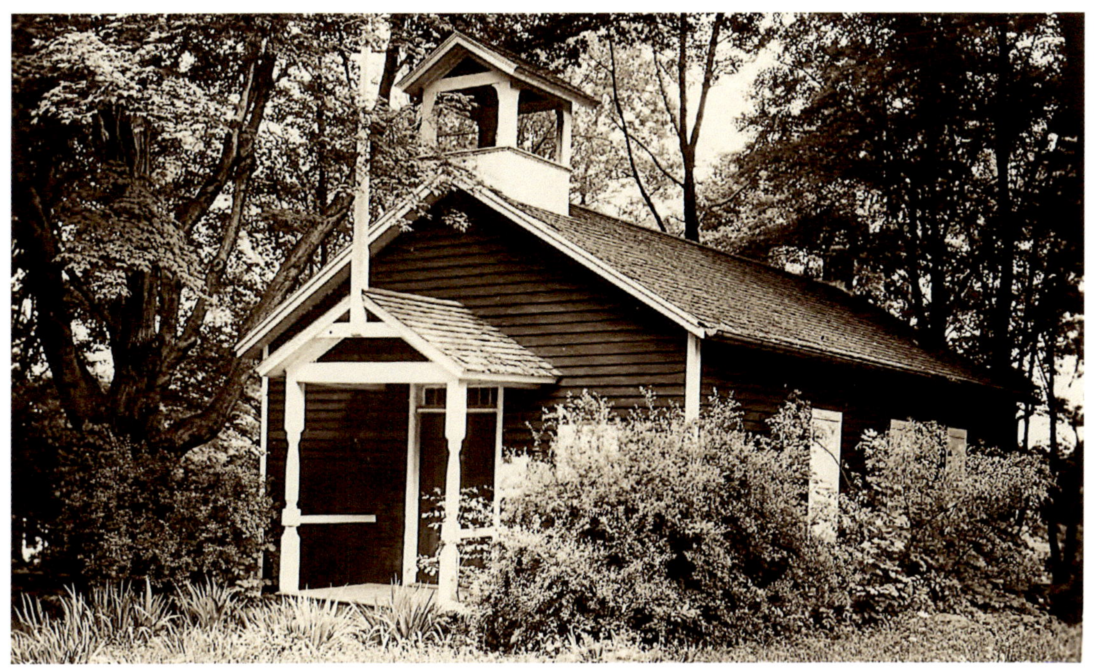

RIDGEFIELD: The first West Lane Schoolhouse was built in 1756, and the current, larger building was built a short time later. The school is nicknamed the Peter Parley School after its most famous student, Samuel Goodrich, who wrote children's books under the name of Peter Parley. He attended school there from 1799 until 1803. Being built in a triangle at the meeting of three busy roads was not always the safest place for a schoolhouse. In the early 1900s, a Model T crashed into the building. The school was used until 1915, and then it served as a library. The Ridgefield Historical Society took over the lease of the schoolhouse in 2012. (Above photograph Courtesy CT State Library, State Archives, LS Mills Collection)

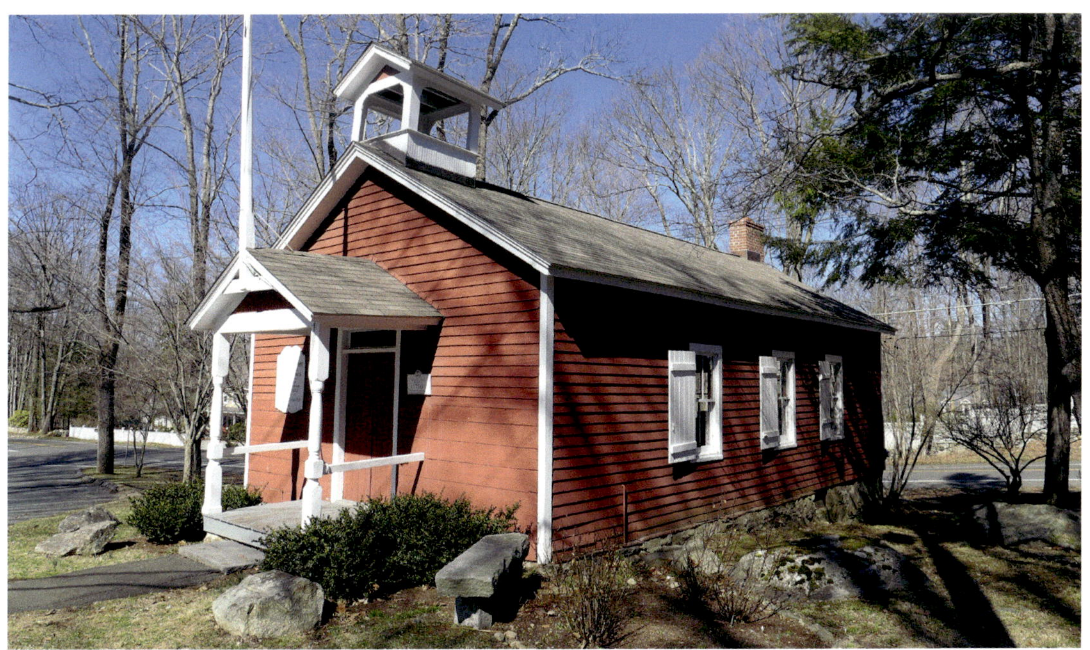

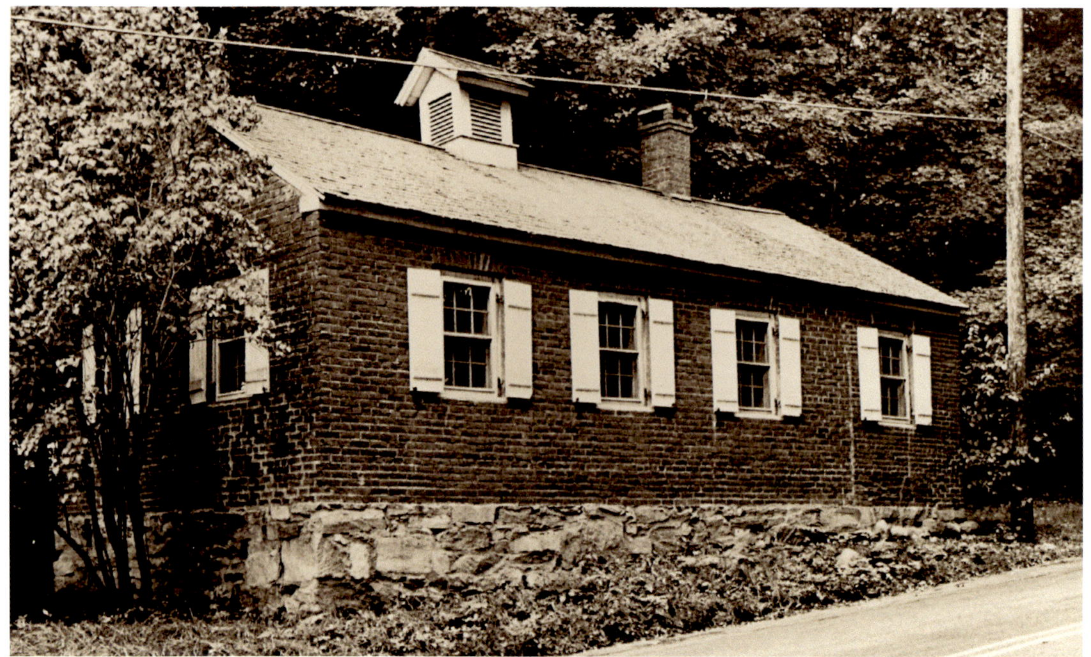

REDDING: The brick Umpawaug School was built sometime between 1790 and 1810, as one of the fourteen district schools. The school is situated on a steep road on one side, and a stream on the opposite side. Early records report, "... the little school house was built mostly on the highway." When Redding consolidated the other schoolhouses in 1929, the Umpawaug School was exempt until 1931. After sitting abandoned for a short while, the Redding Women's Civic Club restored the school. In 1964, the town purchased the building and made it into a museum. The Redding Historical Society now maintains the building. Initials from students can still be found carved into the bricks. (Above photograph courtesy of Redding Historical Society)

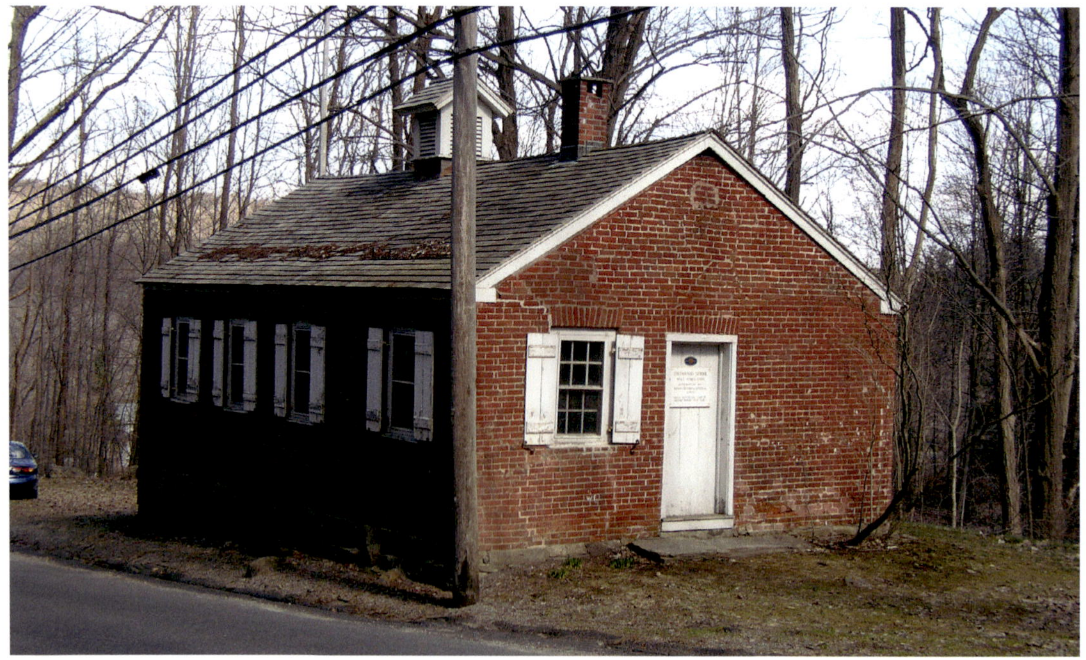

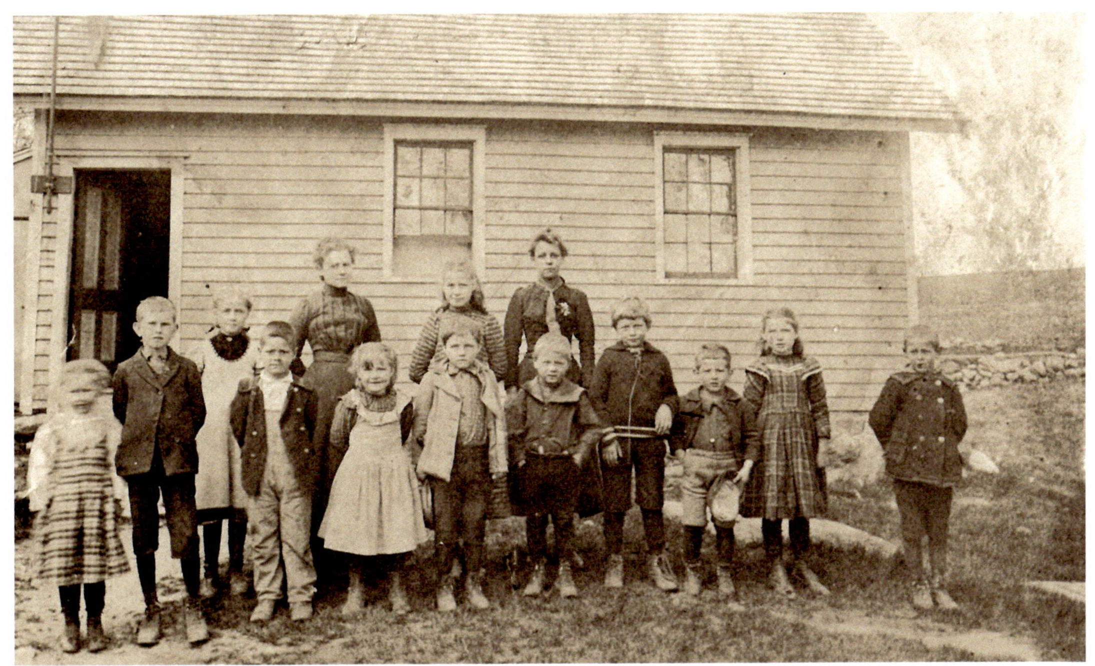

NEW CANAAN: The Rock Schoolhouse was built around 1790 on a rocky site that was not usable for anything else. Margaret Mary Corrigan, a teacher here in 1898, wrote about a December blizzard that left deep snow and six foot drifts. Margaret struggled through the snow to get to work, but she found no students at the schoolhouse. The school was closed in 1933 and moved across the street to be used as a private residence. The historical society saved the building from demolition in 1973, and moved it to the society's land. The yellow paint is based on an analysis of the old clapboards found during restoration of the school. (Above photograph courtesy of The New Canaan Historical Society)

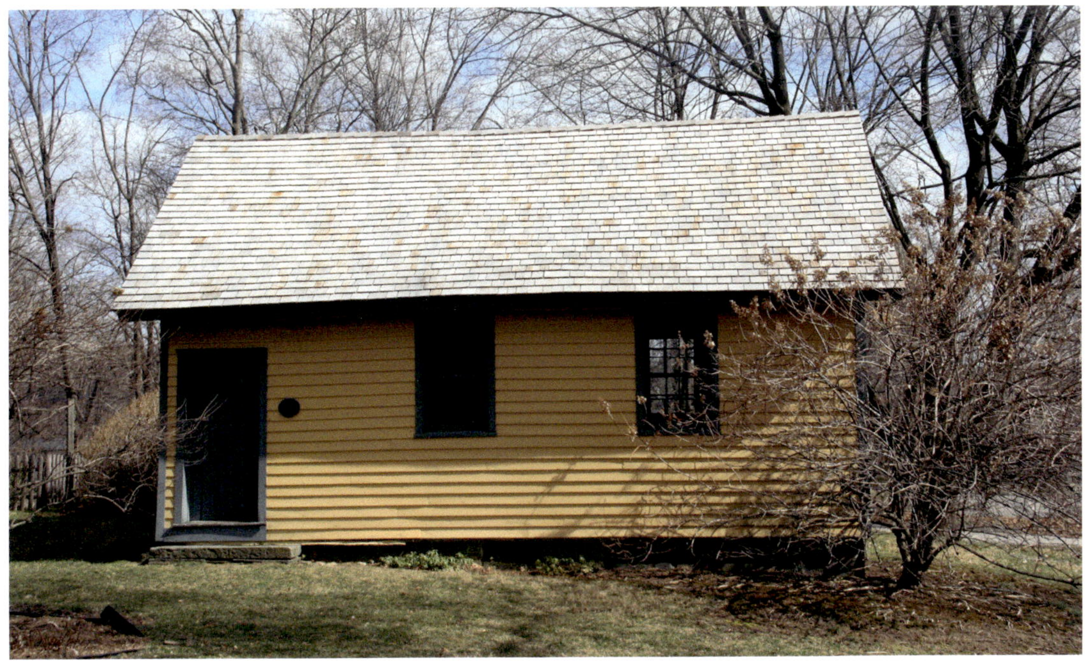

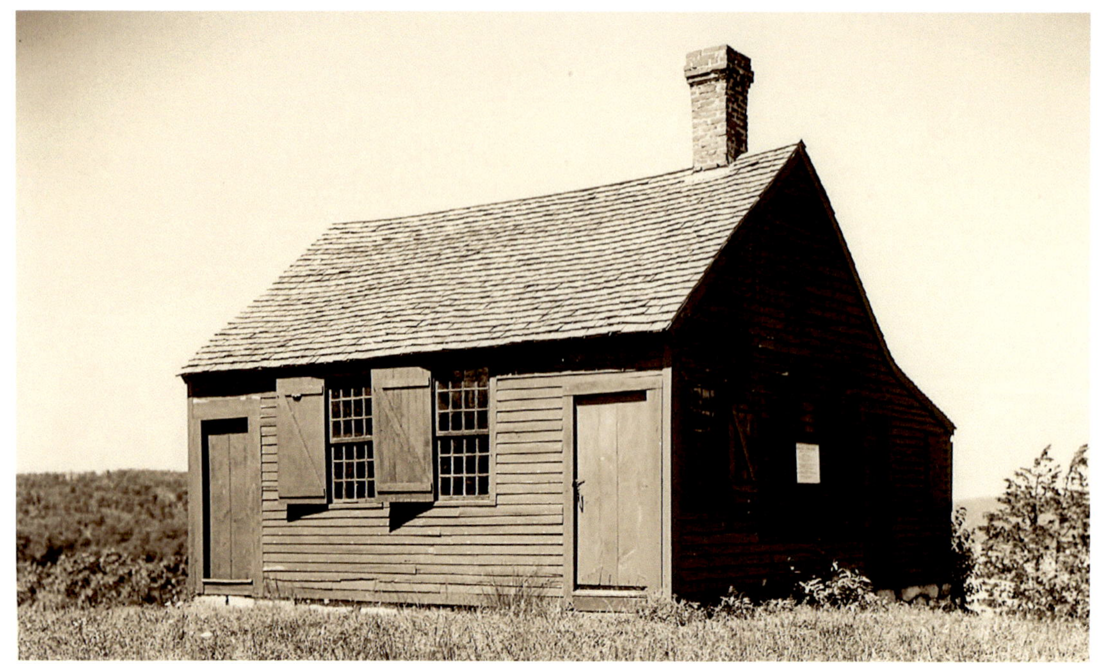

EAST HADDAM: Nathan Hale School, named after our Connecticut State Hero, began his teaching career in East Haddam for four months during the winter term of 1773-1774. The school building sat in a small triangle of land where two main roads met and was used as a schoolhouse from 1750 to 1799. The building was sold to Captain Elijah Attwood, who moved it nearby to add to his family house, where it stayed for 100 years. The family offered the building to the Sons of the American Revolution in 1899, who moved the building to the hillside, where it was restored and still stands. (Above photograph Courtesy CT State Library, State Archives, LS Mills Collection)

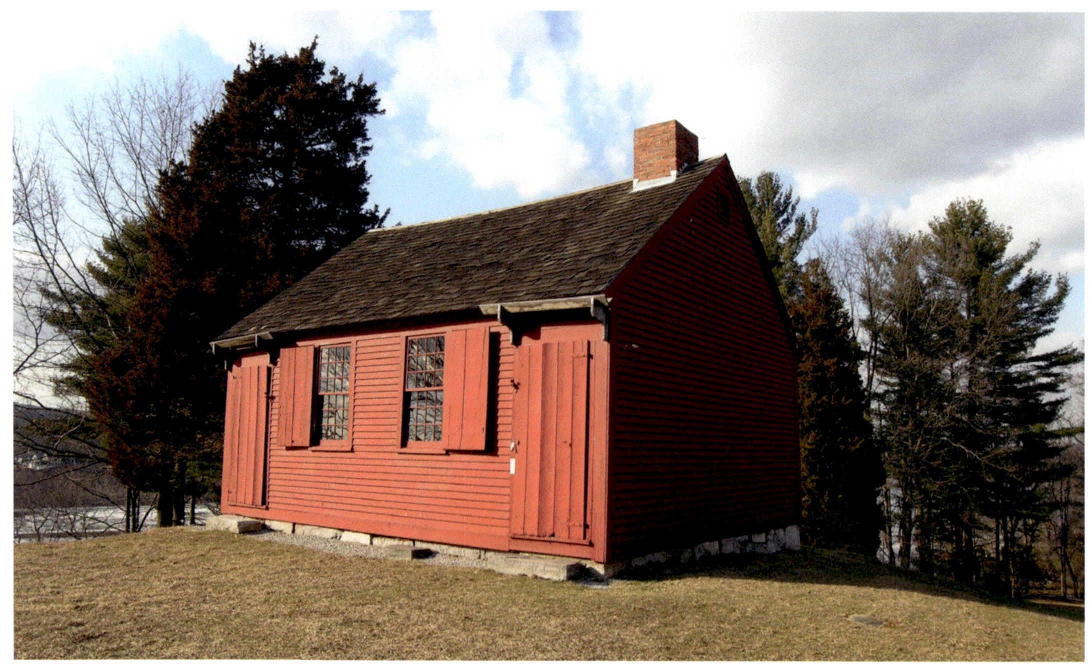

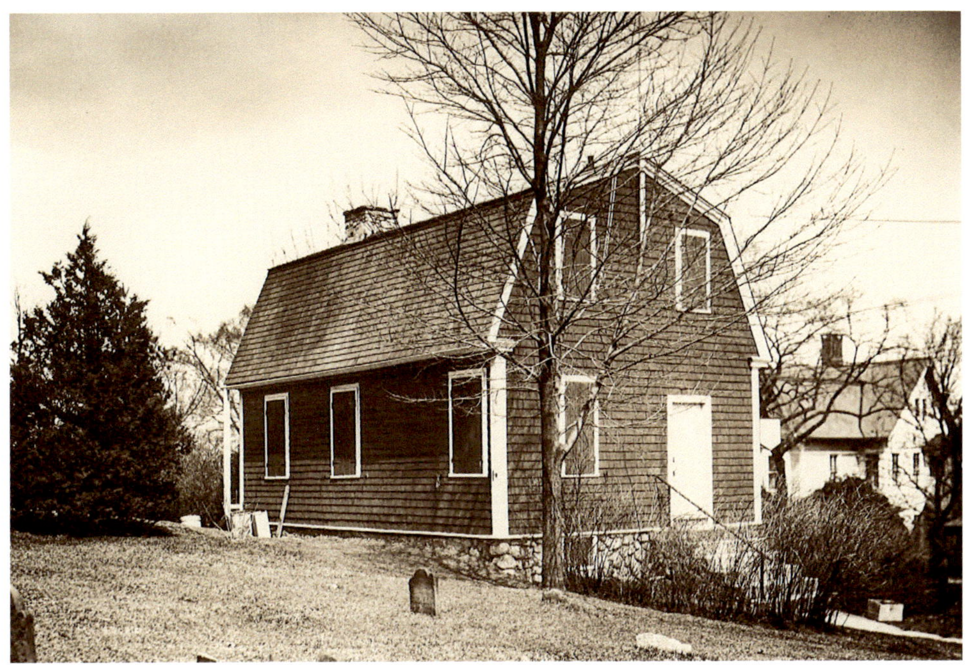

NEW LONDON: Now known as the Nathan Hale School, this was the site of Nathan Hale's second and last teaching position. The schoolhouse was built in 1773 as the Union Grammar School. In the spring of 1774, Nathan Hale arrived and taught until July 1775, when he left to become a spy during the Revolutionary War. The building was no longer needed as a school in 1833, and it served many uses through the years. In 1901, the Sons of American Revolution dedicated the building as a museum. The schoolhouse has been moved at least eight times. It finally rests in a busy plaza in the center of town. (Above photograph Courtesy CT State Library, State Archives, LS Mills Collection)

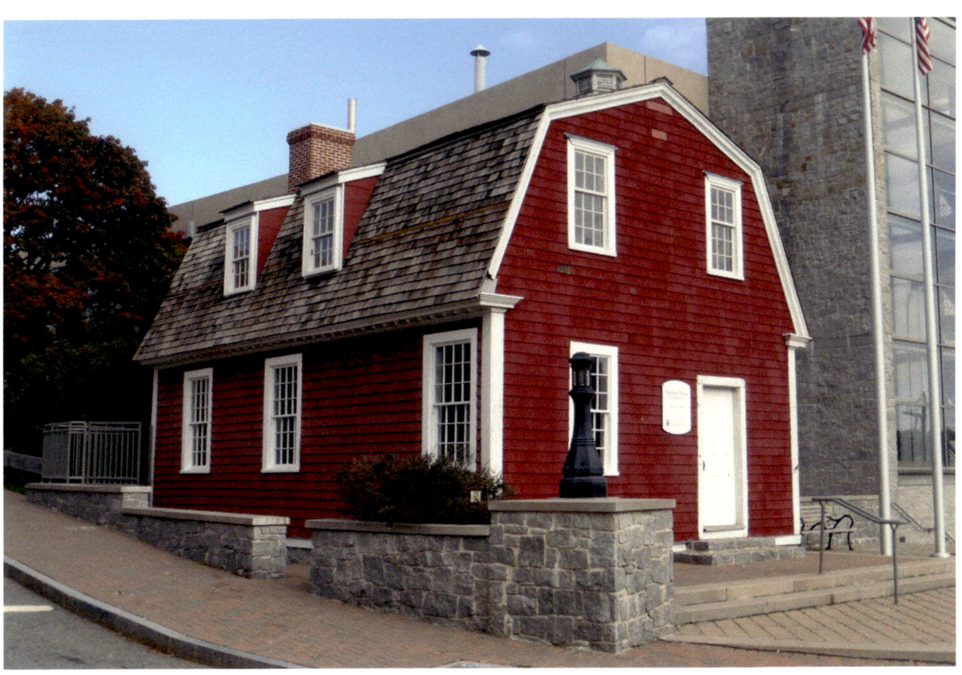

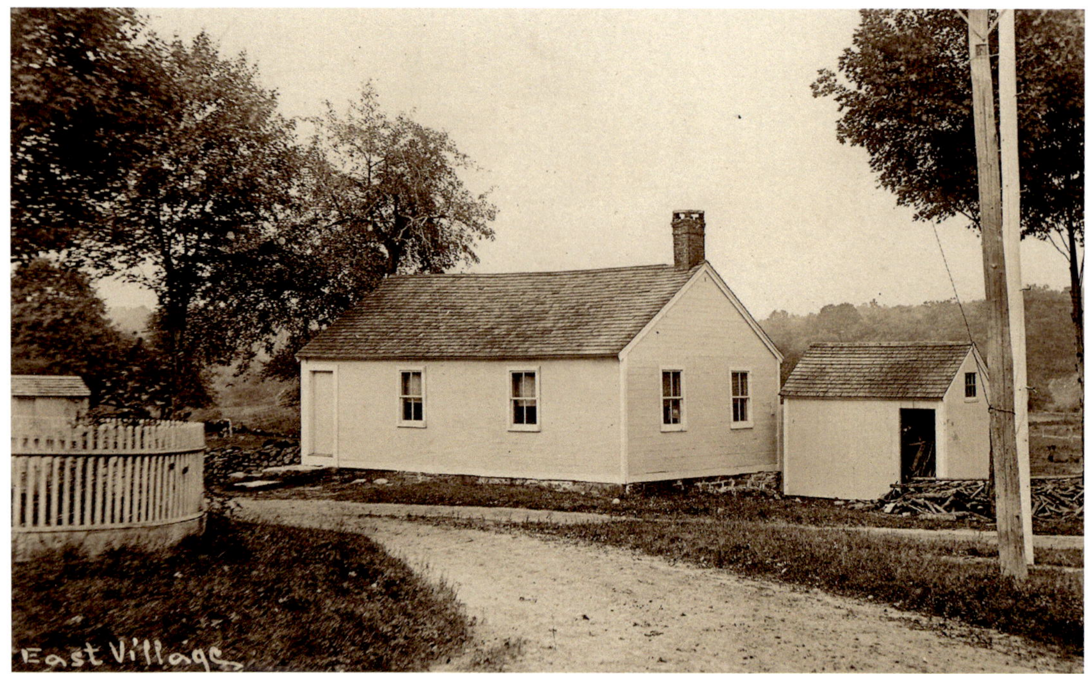

MONROE: The East Village Barn Hill Schoolhouse was built in 1790, at a time when there were ten districts schools in Monroe. It stood at the corner of East Village and Barn Hill Roads, diagonally across the street from the Methodist Church. When the town schoolhouses closed in 1935, this building was purchased by the church for $25 and moved onto the church property. The Monroe Historical Society was given the schoolhouse and in 1968, it was relocated to historical society property, and restored in 1973. (Above photograph courtesy of the Elliott Postcard Collection)

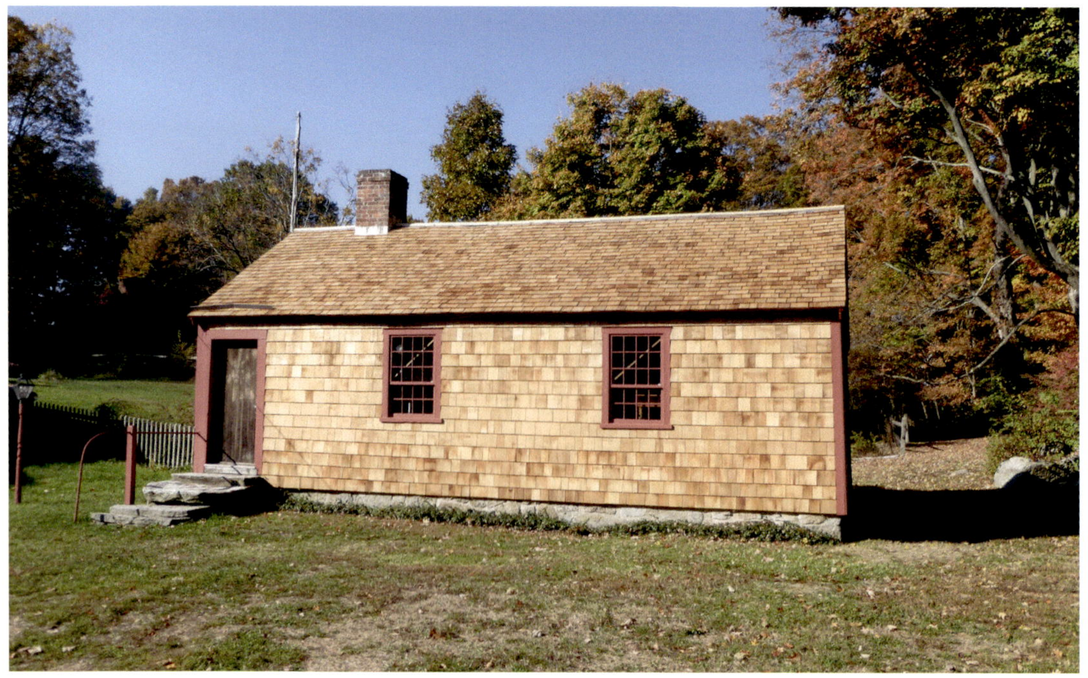

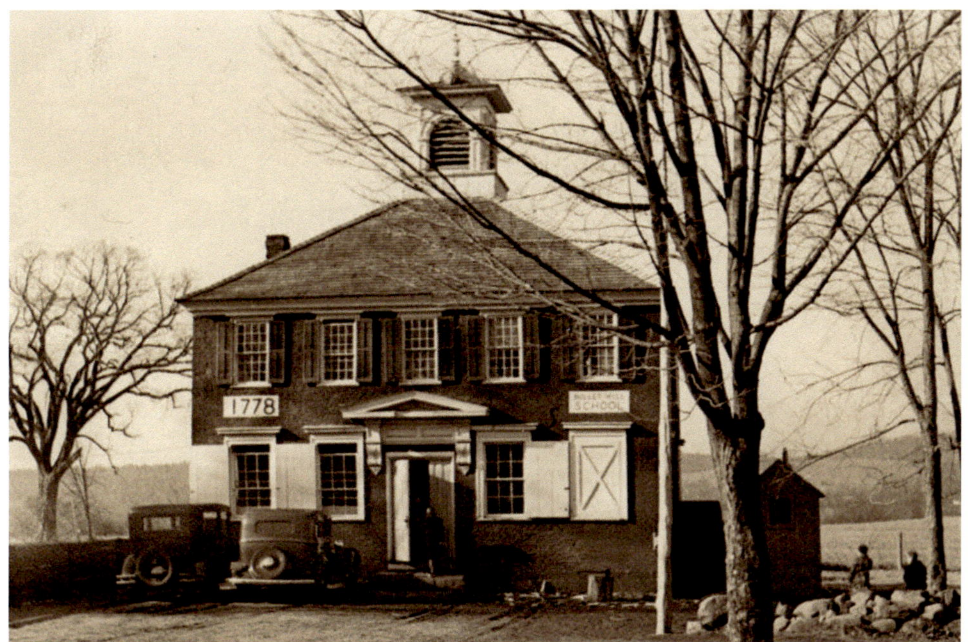

SOUTHBURY: Not all early schools were small buildings. The Brick Schoolhouse was built in the Bullet Hill district of the town sometime in the late 1700s, maybe as early as 1762. The main floor was used for school, while the upper room served many community purposes, including town and church meetings, dances, and lectures. Originally, large fireplaces existed on the north and south sides of the building. The second floor was used for schooling beginning in 1928, until the school closed in December 1941. Now owned by the town, every year each 2nd grade class in the region spends a day at the Bullet Hill School Days—A Living Museum Program. (Above photograph courtesy of WPA Architectural Survey of CT State Library Digital Collections)

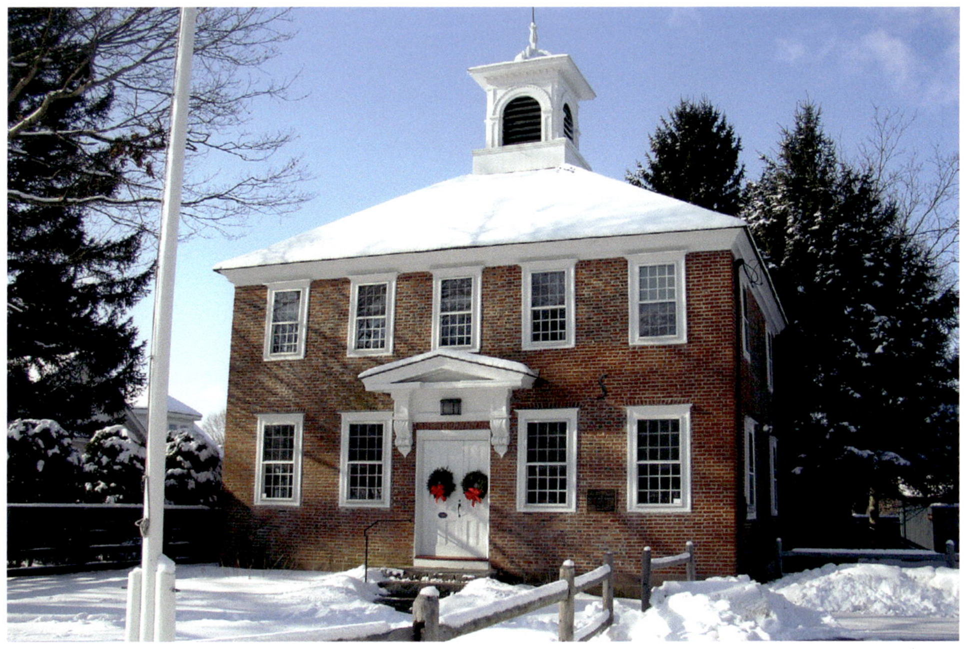

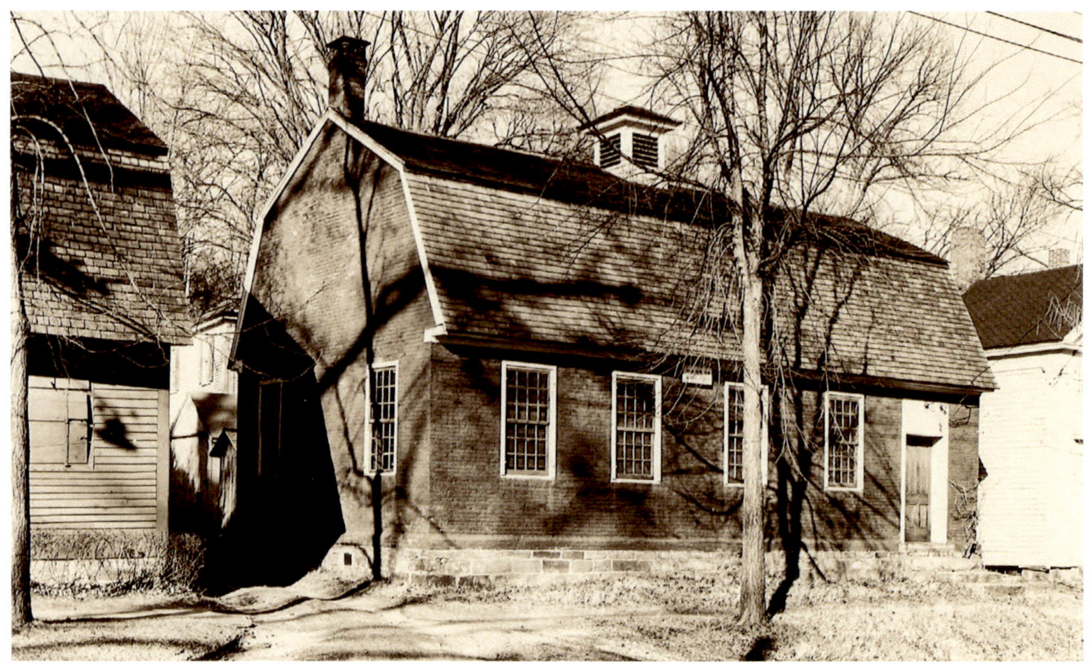

NORWICH: The Lathrop School was constructed along the Norwichtown Green in 1783, matching the clockmaker's shop next door. Dr. Daniel Lathrop, who owned and operated the first drug store in Connecticut, left funds in his will to build the free school. Through the interest on the funds, there would be sufficient money for annual improvements, as long as school was open for eleven months a year, six to eight hours a day. The school was discontinued in 1843 when the Lathrop funds ran out. The building was later used by the Noah Webster Library Association, and is now being used as the Norwich Heritage and Regional Visitors Center. (Above photograph Courtesy CT State Library, State Archives, LS Mills Collection)

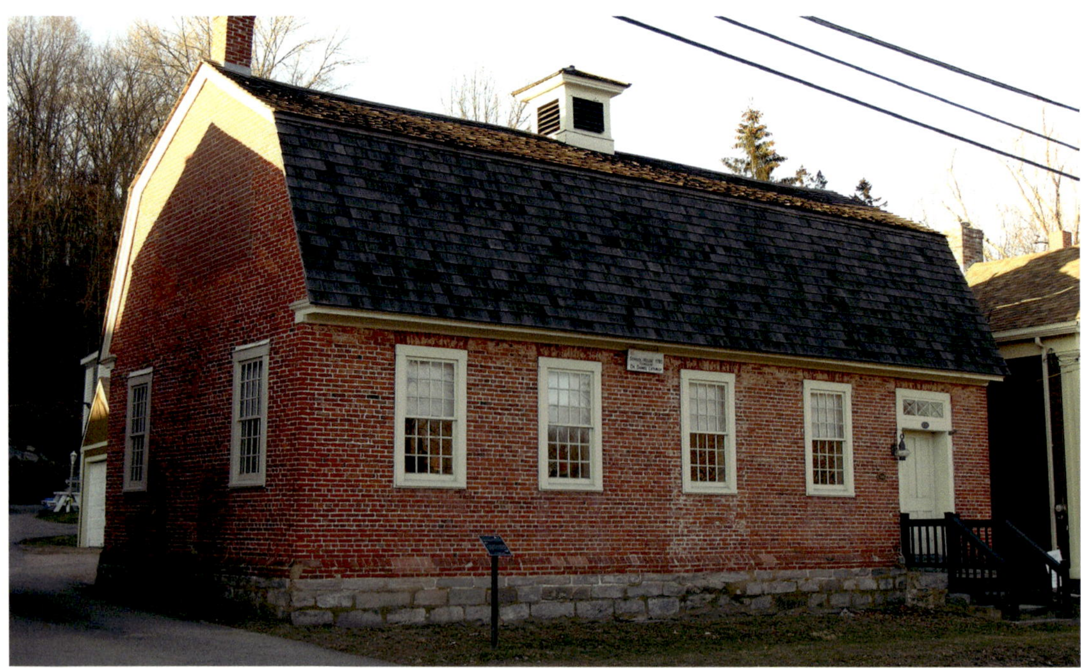

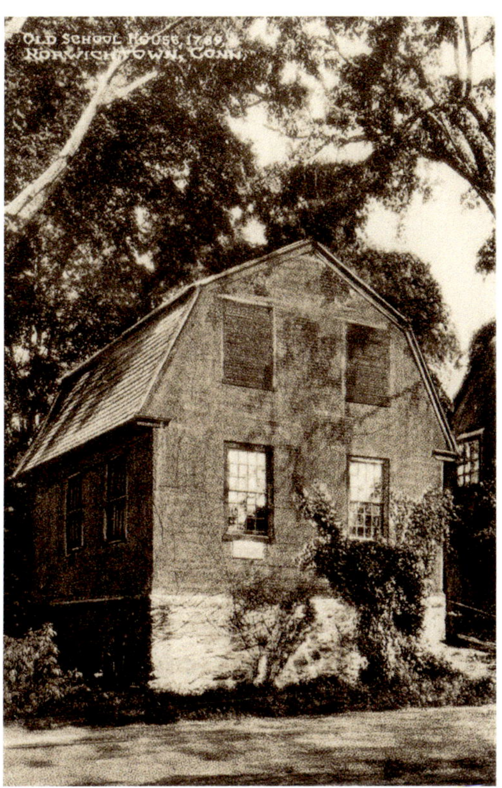

NORWICH: After the success of the nearby Lathrop School, the East District School was constructed a few years later in 1789. In addition to the daily school for the local children, a night school was added to meet the needs in this shipbuilding community by Consider Sterry. This included instruction in writing, bookkeeping in Italian, American, and English systems, and mathematics for "those gentlemen who go down to the sea in ships and occupy their business on the great water." Mr. Sterry also taught his students sea-going skills like finding the longitude and latitude at sea by observing the sun. The schoolhouse was in use until 1914. The building is currently under restoration. (Above photograph courtesy of the Elliott Postcard Collection)

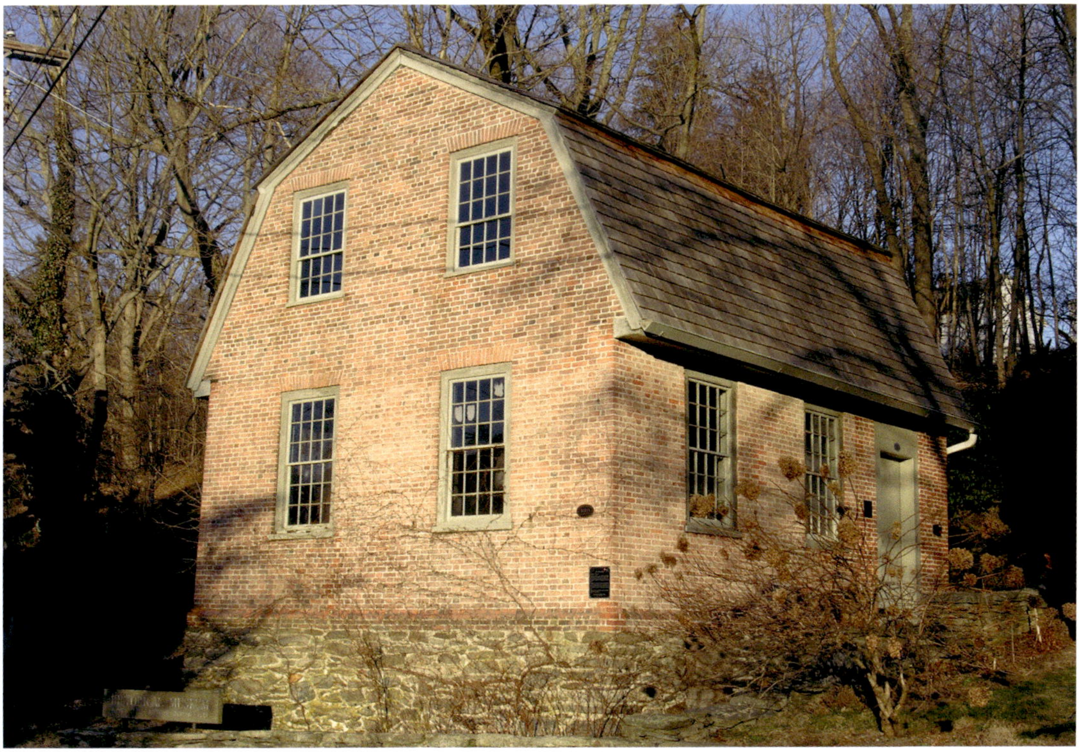

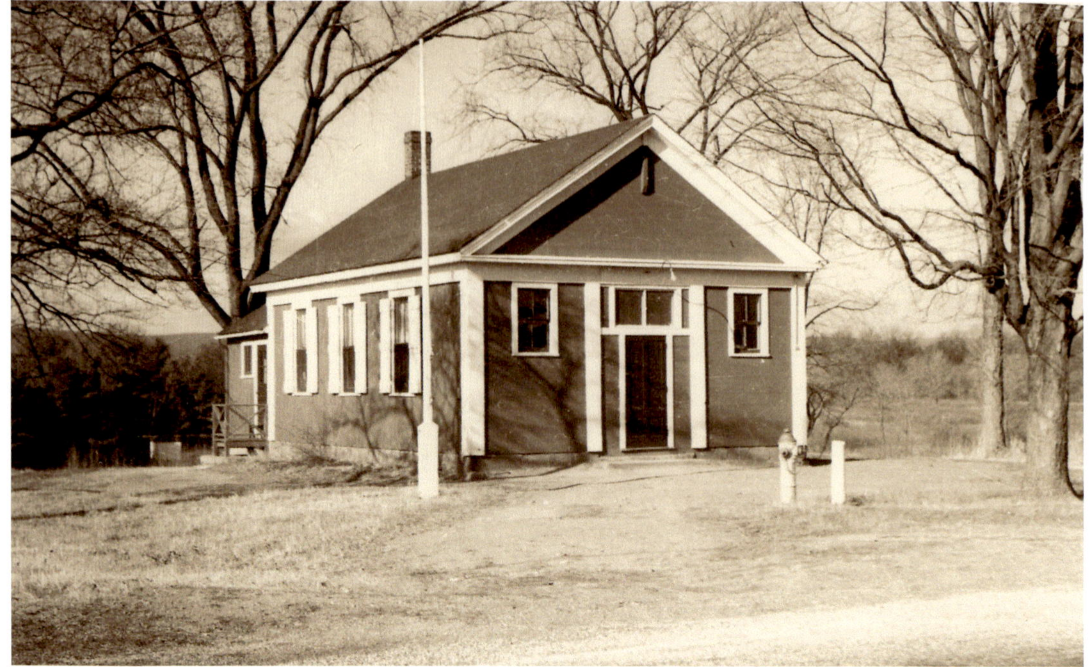

PLANTSVILLE: Now a section of Southington, the South End schoolhouse was built around 1793, replacing an earlier, smaller school that was called "The Little Brown Schoolhouse." At one time, there were shelf desks along the side of the walls. In March 1955, the children packed up their belongings and marched down to the new modern school with the same name, never to return to the one-room schoolhouse. The school was preserved by the South End Community Center and is now under the control of the Southington Historical Society. (Above photograph courtesy of the Southington Historical Society)

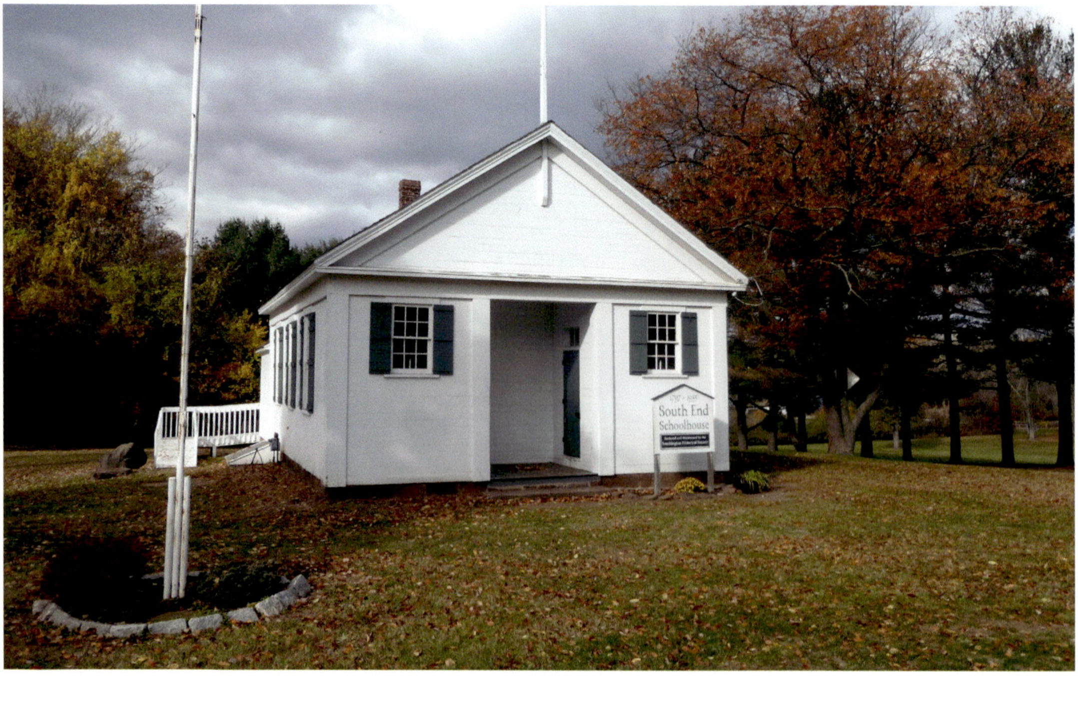

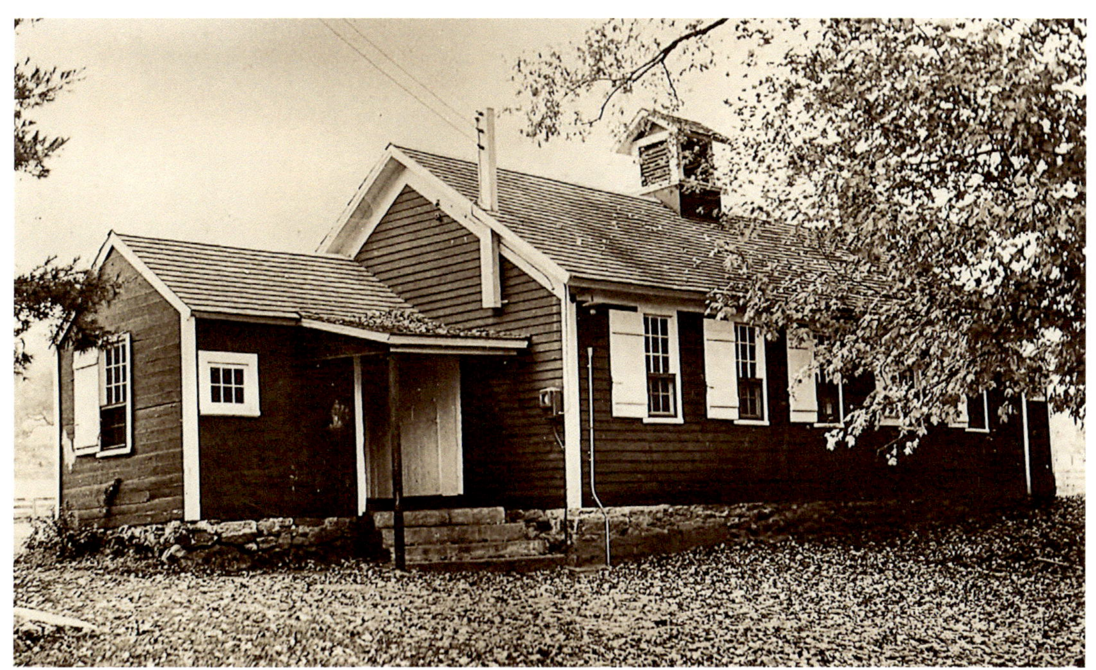

NEW MILFORD: The schoolhouse in the New Milford section of Gaylordsville was built about 1740. In 1850, the district decided that the school needed extensive repairs, but could not afford to construct a new building. Instead, they built a new foundation, moved the old schoolhouse a short distance, and made the necessary renovations. Additions were built on the north and south ends of the building in 1872. Miss Bessie Cornwell taught at the school for a total of 42 years, from 1915-1957. When the doors closed in 1967, the newspaper called it “the last one-room school house left in the state.” (Above photograph courtesy CT State Library, State Archives, LS Mills Collection)

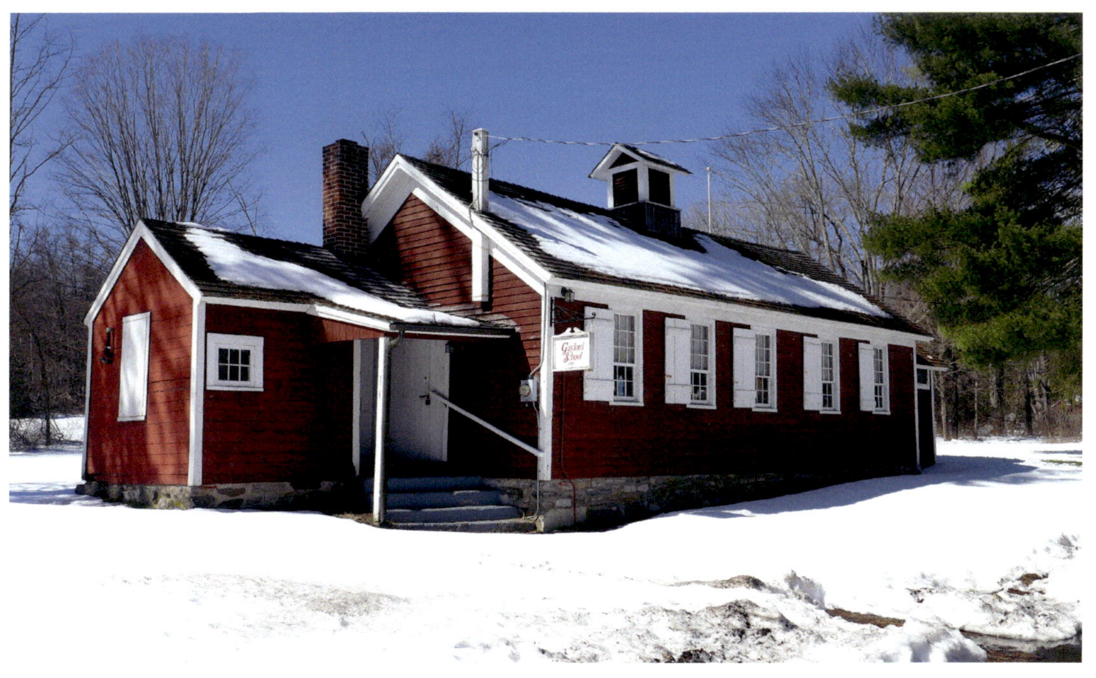

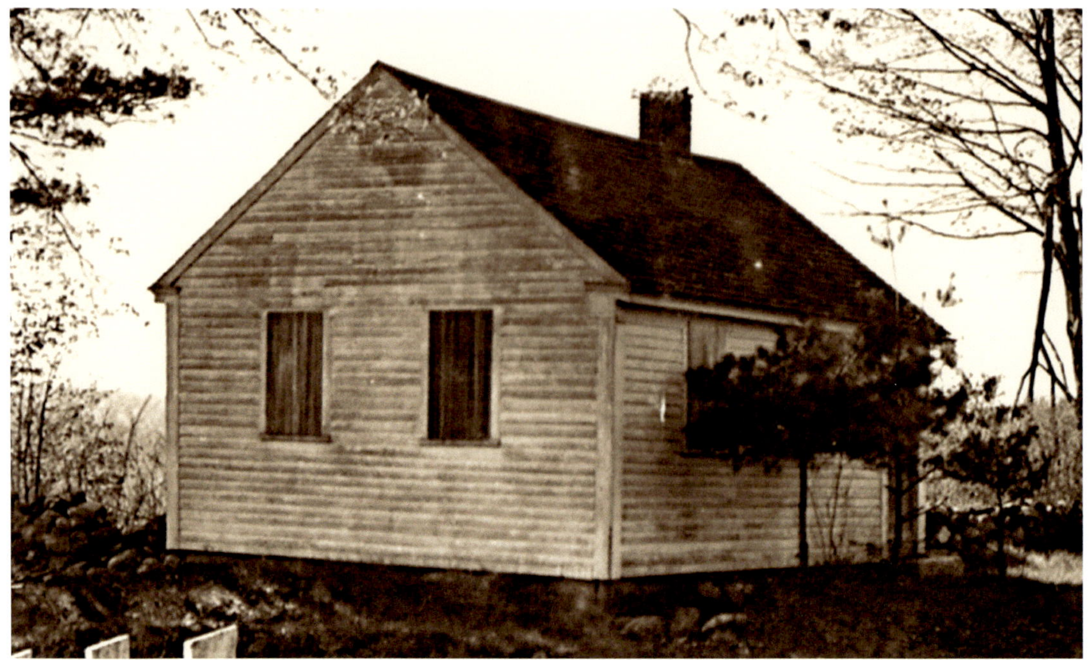

HEBRON: The Gull Schoolhouse was built around 1790 to replace a previous school that was destroyed by fire. The schoolhouse was closed in 1935 and sold in 1945. It was moved to an old field where it sat for many years. Henrietta Green, a former teacher, purchased the building and moved the old school onto her property, where she restored it. The Green family donated the schoolhouse to the town in 2000, and the next year it was moved near the downtown area on Marjorie Circle. Boy Scouts assisted with the final restoration to the outside of the building, applying fresh paint, cleaning up the yard, and repairing the stone fence. (Above photograph located in town vault, courtesy of the Hebron Town Clerk's Office)

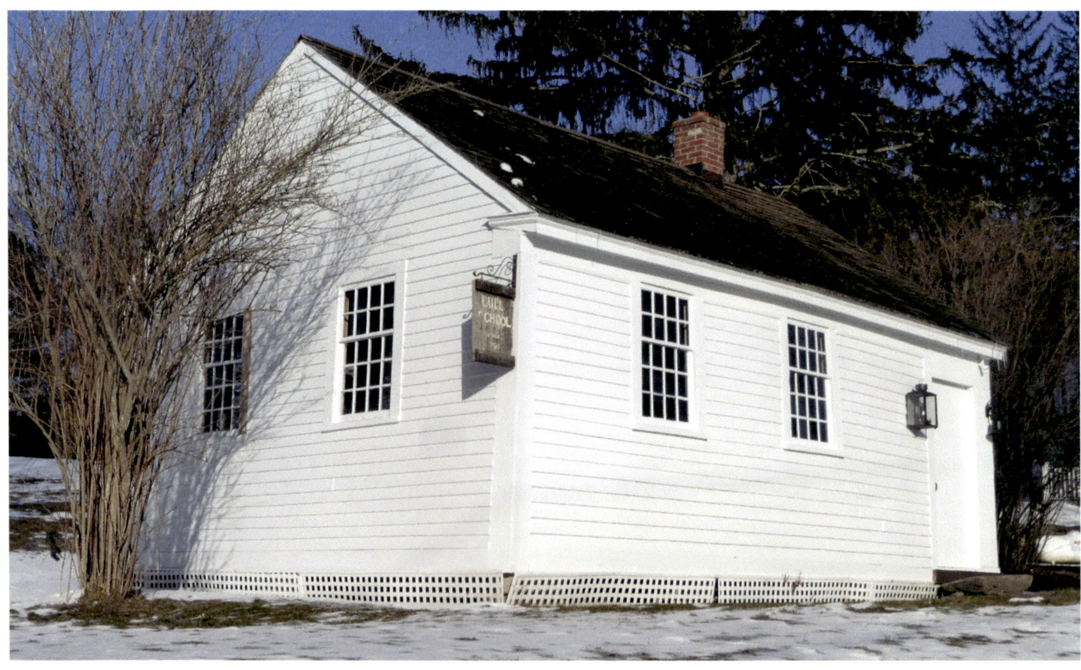

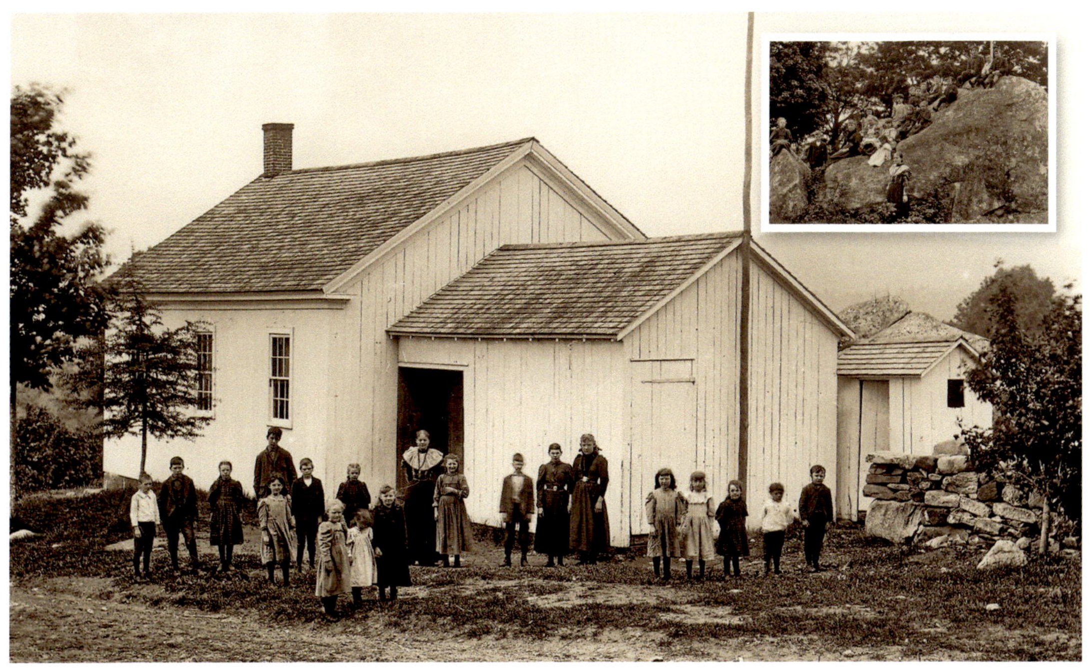

COLEBROOK: The Rock School, so named because of the giant rock located behind the building, was originally the North School District, later to become the North Middle District during redistricting. The school was built in 1799. Because of declining enrollment, the school was closed in the fall of 1911. On March 1, 1920, the town voted to sell the schoolhouse and it remained in private hands until 1970. The owners offered the school to the Colebrook Historical Society, and it was moved across the street on March 23, 1971. The photograph with the students was taken in 1985, with Lillian North as the teacher. (Above photograph and inset photograph courtesy of the Elliott postcard collection)

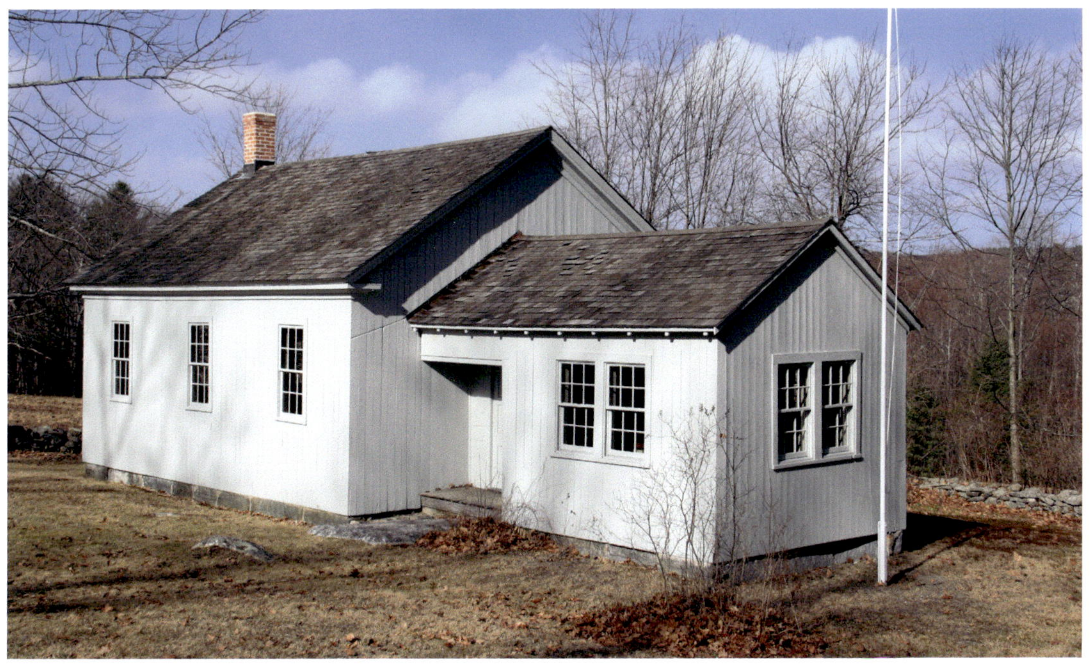

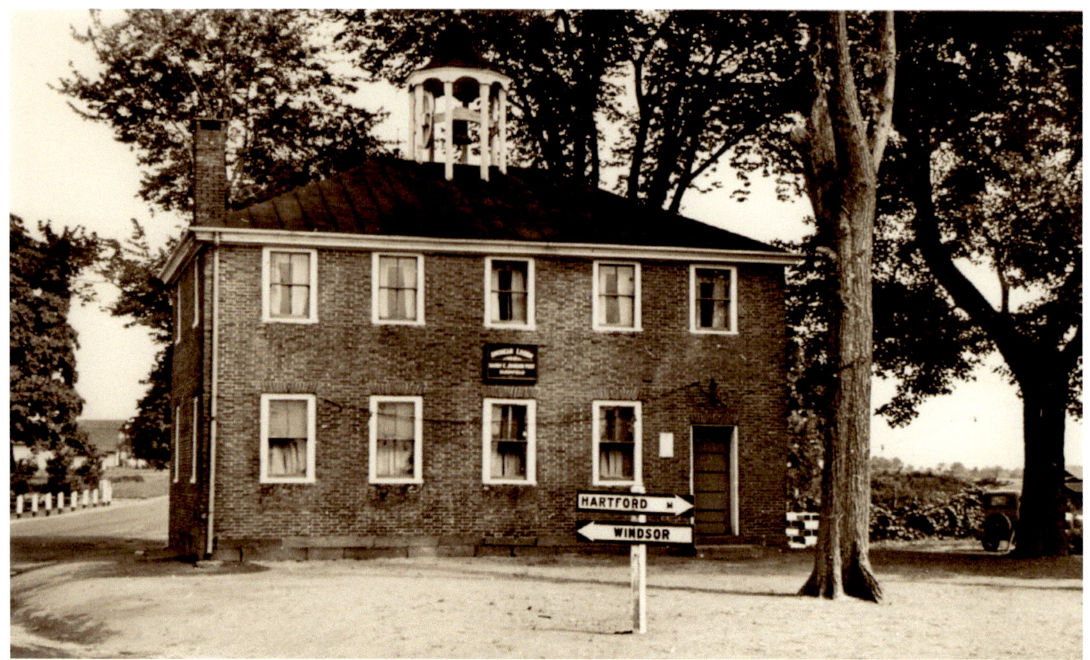

BLOOMFIELD: The Old Farm School, a 1796 two-story brick schoolhouse, is the oldest public building in Bloomfield. Originally, there was a center front door and the access to the second floor was via an outside staircase. Only the first floor with its two fire places was used as a school room at the beginning, but in 1829 the upstairs was finished and furnished with desks that still remain. An inside staircase was constructed in 1843. The school closed in 1922, and the American Legion leased the school from the town. In 1976, the building was moved 100 feet, and away from the edge of the road. The historical society now maintains the school building. (Above photograph courtesy of Wintonbury Historical Society)

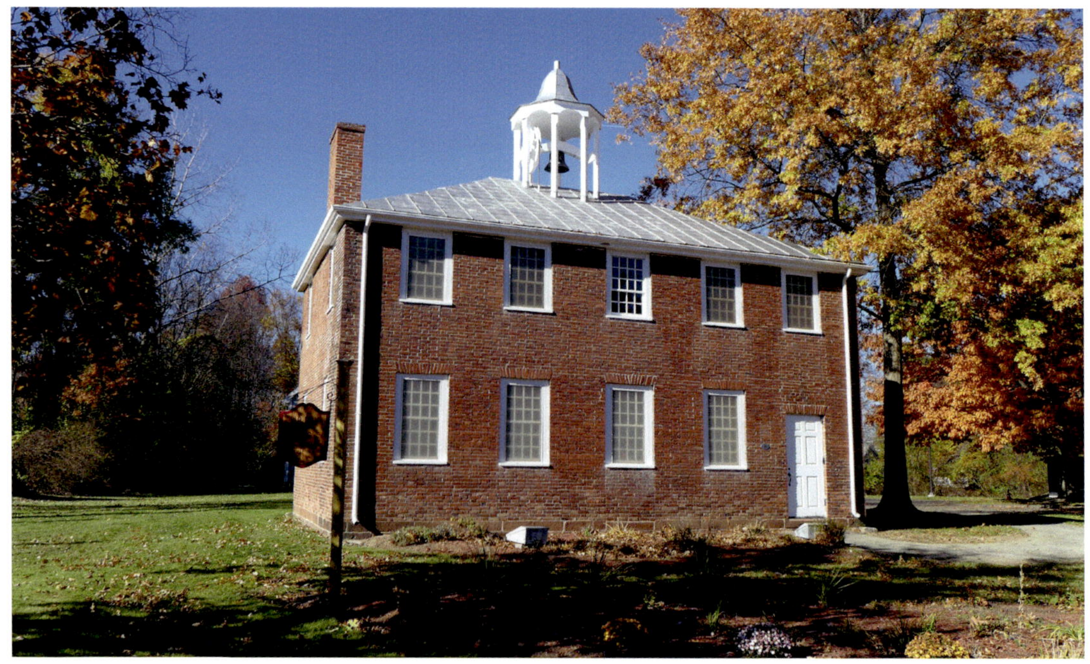

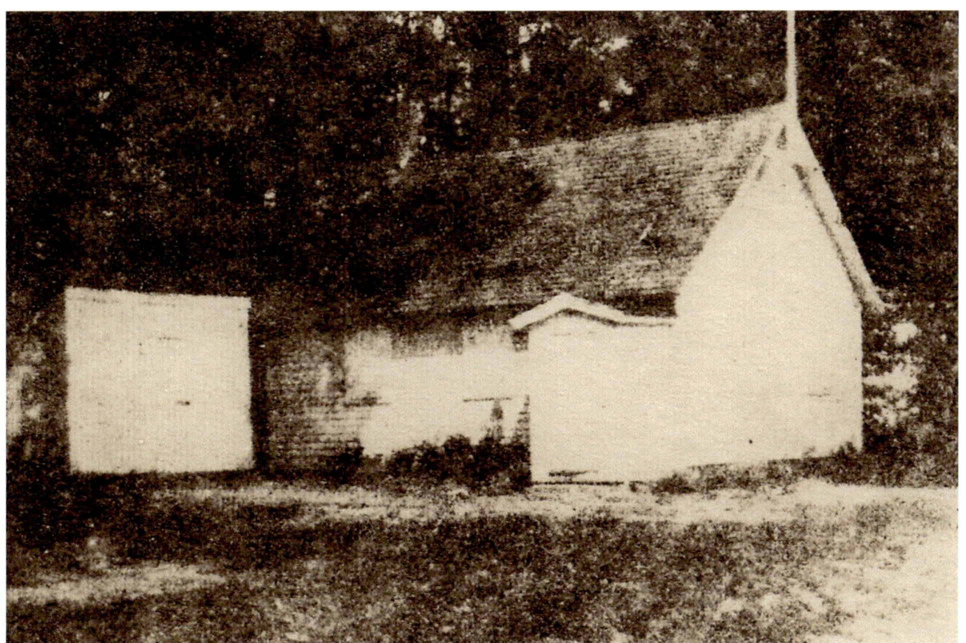

SOUTHINGTON: The first West Street Schoolhouse was built around 1750, and burned down in 1760. After a couple of years, the current structure was constructed near the same place. In 1933, the West Street School Alumni Association was started. The schoolhouse shut down on February 22, 1945, ending 183 years of continuous service. The West Street School and Community Association leased the building for 99 years and have kept the school building in good condition. Yearly picnics are held at the old schoolhouse to share memories of the old days and to introduce their families and grandchildren to life in a one-room schoolhouse. The school is now a part of the Southington Historical Society. (Above photograph courtesy of the Southington Historical Society)

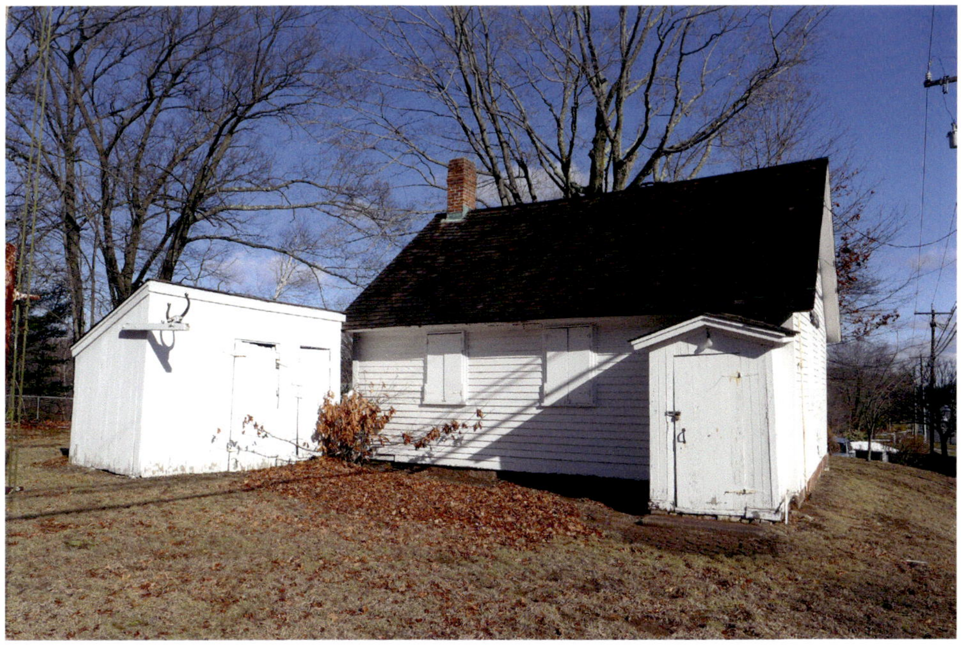

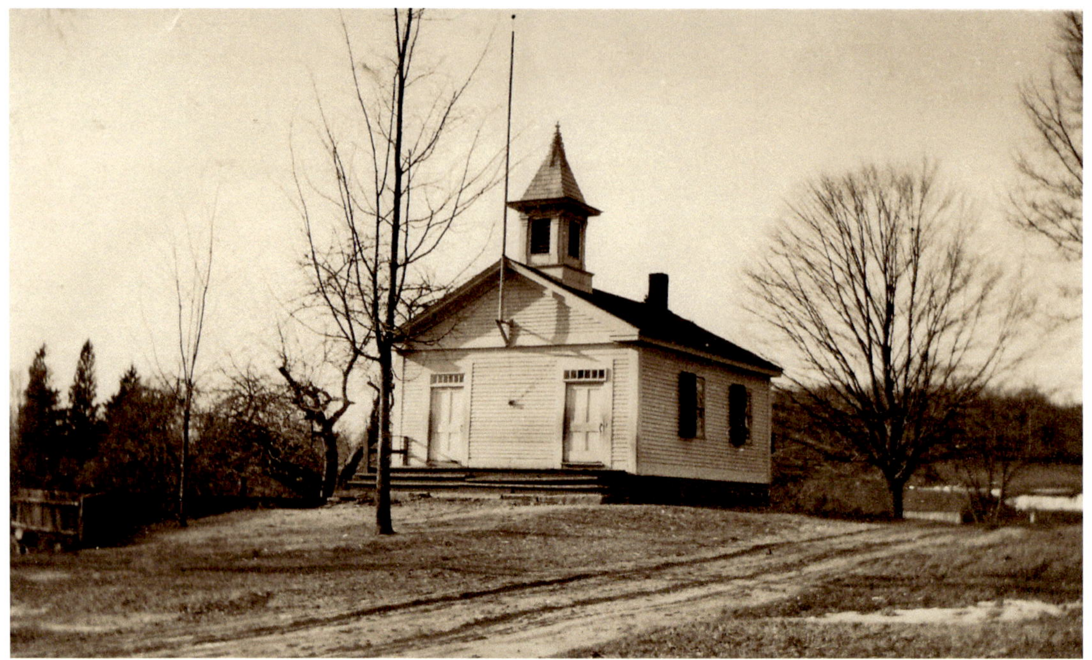

EAST HADDAM: The North School is still sitting on its original lot, were it was built in 1794 near the border of Haddam and Lyme, in an area called Hadlyme. Originally, the desks were built into the walls, with benches in front. Extensive renovations brought the schoolhouse up to the standards of 1850s schools, with two entrance doors, a modern chimney, new blackboards, and plenty of windows for lighting. A bell was added in 1865. The school closed in 1929 when the schools were consolidated into one school in East Haddam. The neighboring Congregational Church owns the schoolhouse, and the North School Society maintains it. (Above photograph courtesy of the Hadlyme North School Society)

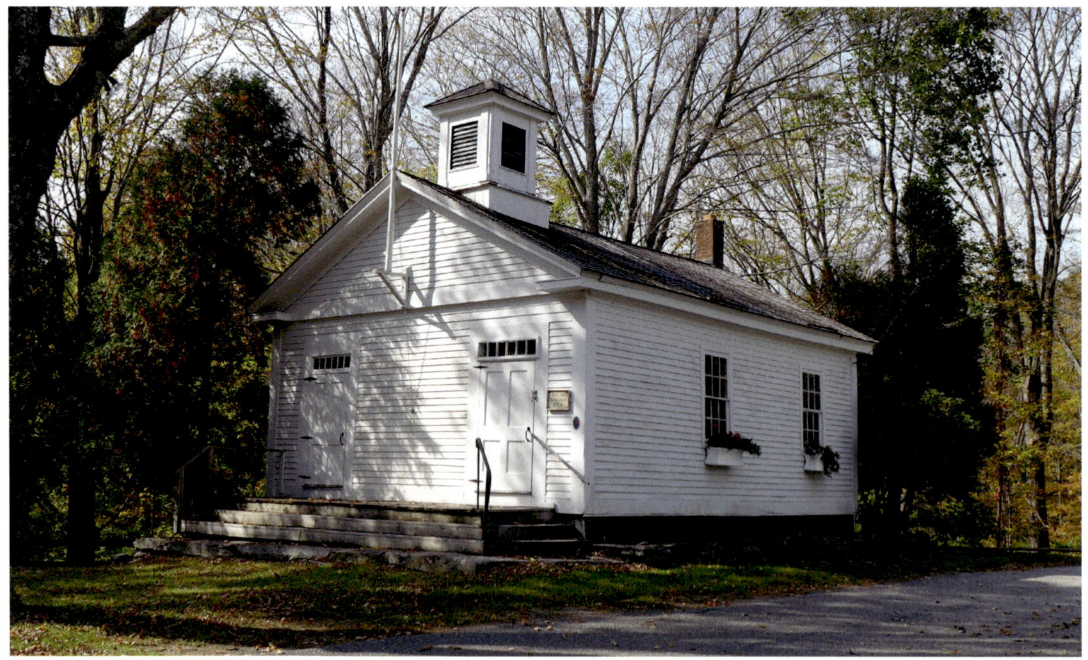

2

District Schools, 1800-1834

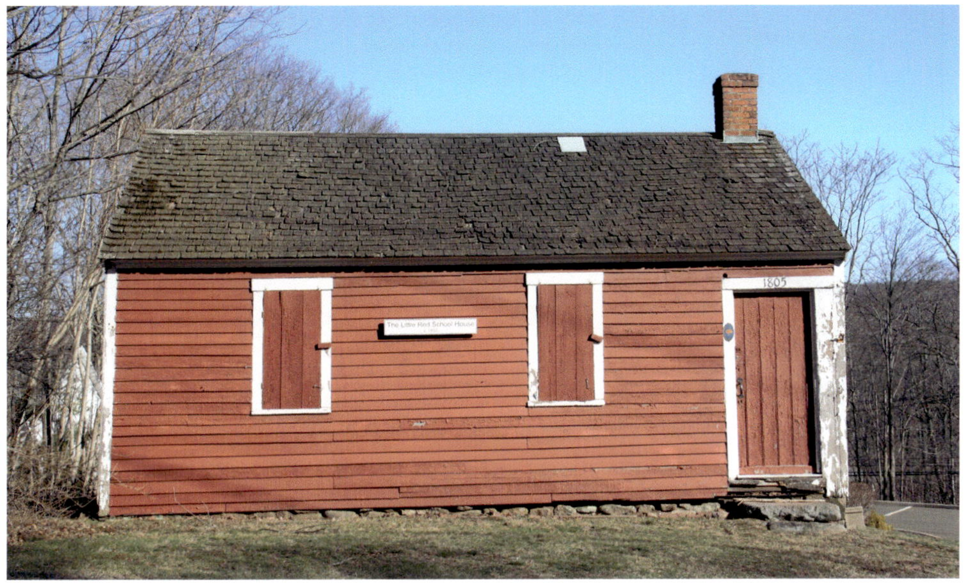

The schoolhouses between 1800 and 1834 were much the same as the earlier schools. However, they were no longer under the oversight of the church—a district committee controlled the school. Each district could set their own rules, build their own buildings, and tax the district people as they decided.

The state established a School Fund from the proceeds of the sale of the Western Reserve Lands. With money coming from the state, the districts were less likely to spend their own money on the building and upkeep of the schools, resulting in the repairs not being made in a timely manner.

The above schoolhouse is the Northford School, built in 1805 in North Branford. Like most schools of this time, the desks were sloping shelves built along three walls of the room. The children sat on simple backless benches, facing the wall. The limited lighting in the room was provided by small windows and supplemented with candles in poor weather, if candles were available.

Wood stoves became a common feature, replacing fireplaces. Staying warm in the classroom was always a struggle. One teacher wrote that it usually took two hours to completely warm a schoolhouse to the average temperature of 62 degrees. It was not uncommon for the ink in the inkwells to freeze overnight.

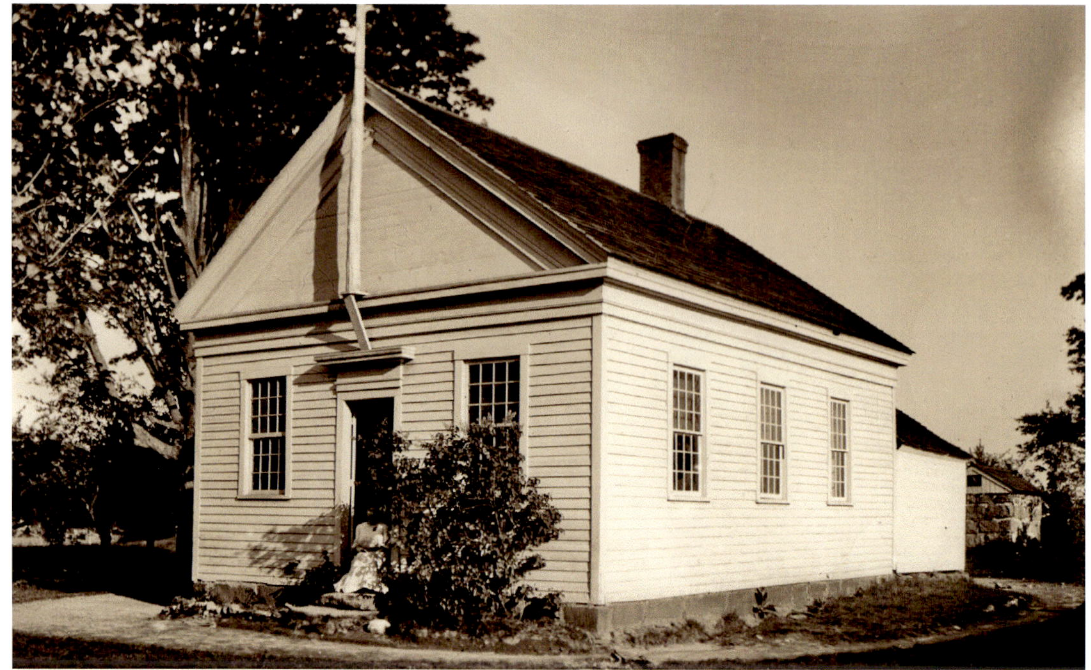

AVON: School #3, the West Avon School, was built in 1823 and was used until 1938. For many years it sat unused. When there was talk of demolishing the school to make a new library, the Avon Historical Society raised funds for the building to be moved. Even though the building is made of wood, the privy is made of large fieldstone, which you can see behind the school. For a while it served as a Living Museum, but now it is used for the historical society headquarters and storage of artifacts. (Above photograph courtesy of Marian Hunter History Room. Avon Free Public Library, Avon, CT)

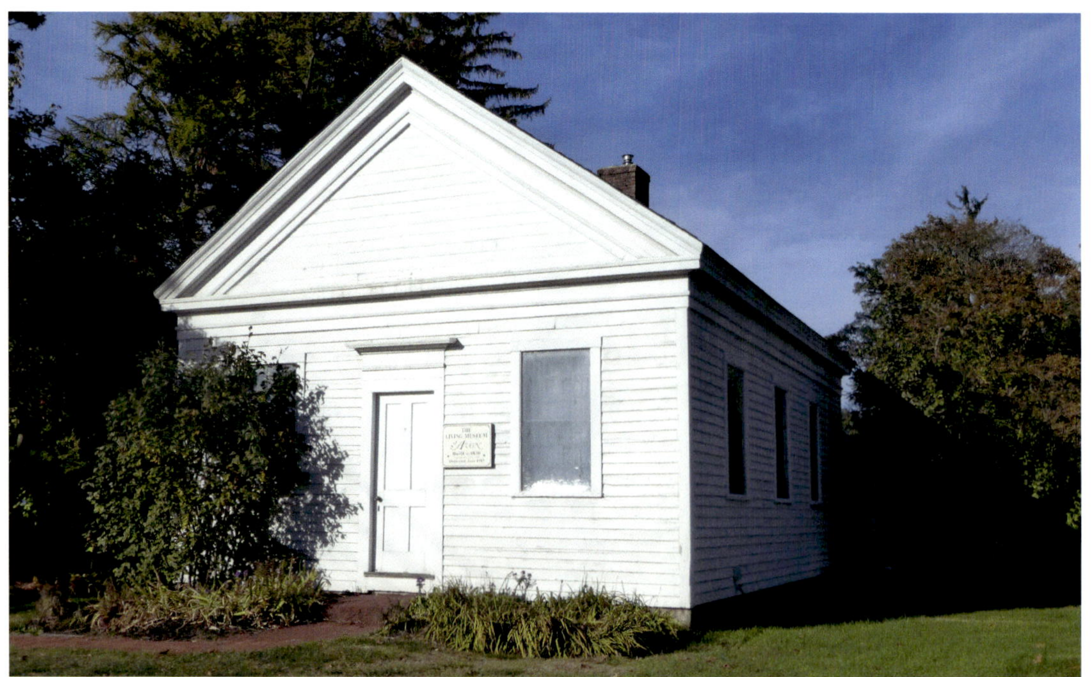

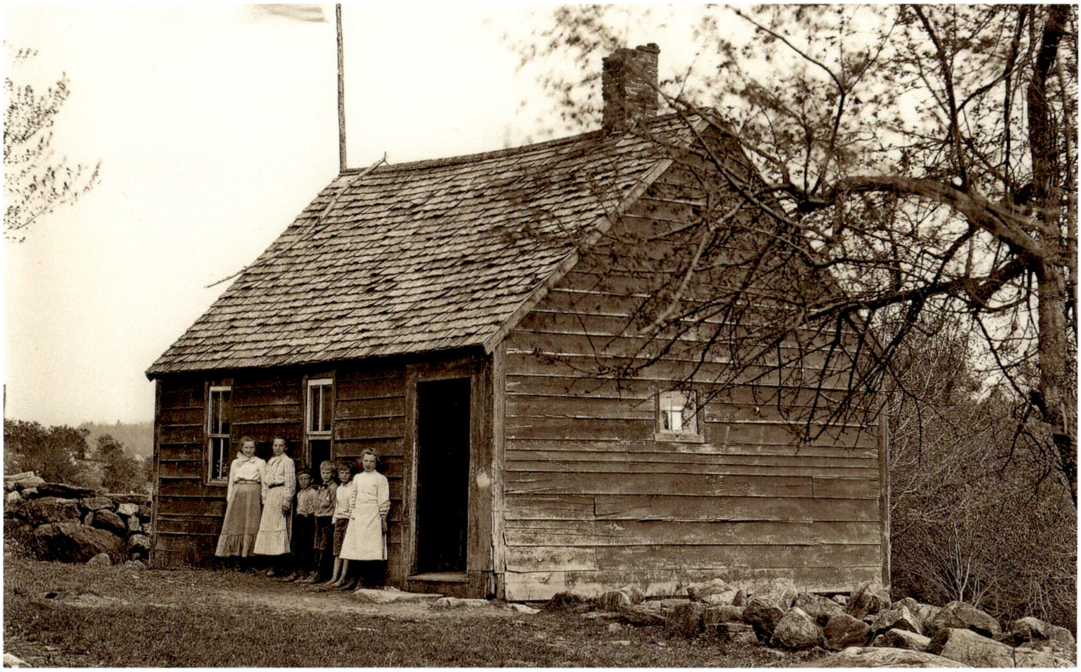

WINCHESTER: The Little Red Schoolhouse was built in 1815 to replace the "Two Chimney School," which was struck by lightning and burned to the ground. This replacement schoolhouse began with a fireplace, but they quickly installed a wood stove. Originally, shelf desks lined the wall, but they were removed to provide movable desks. The school closed in 1908. In 1916, Clifford Bristol purchased the schoolhouse where his father had taught. The property was deeded to the Little Red School House Organization in 1923, which was formed to preserve the building. (Above photograph courtesy of the Elliott Postcard Collection)

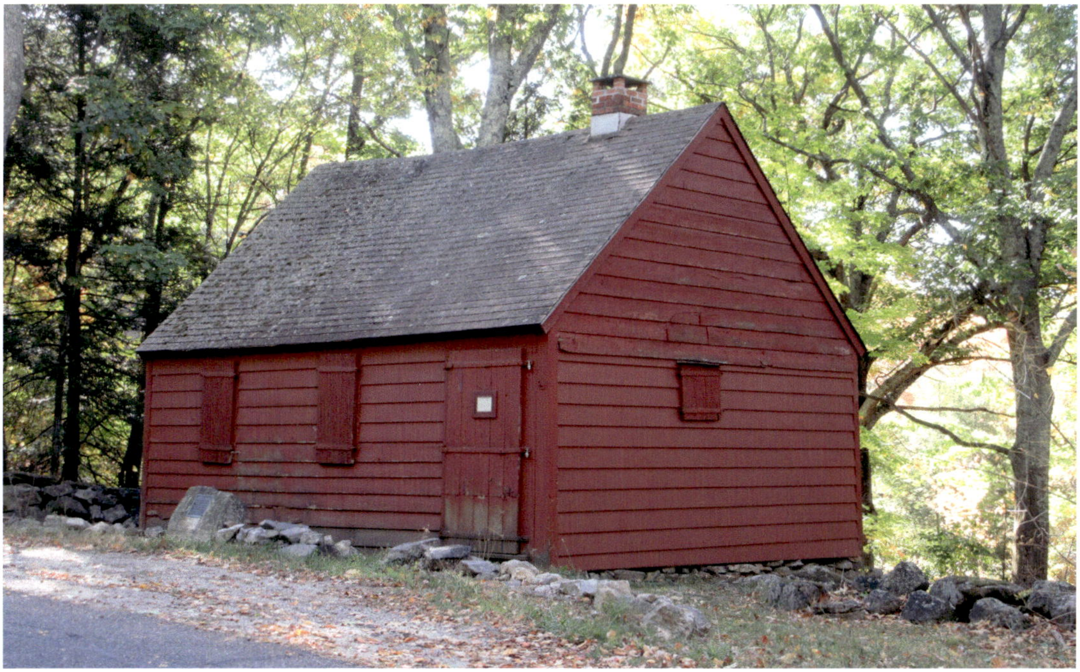

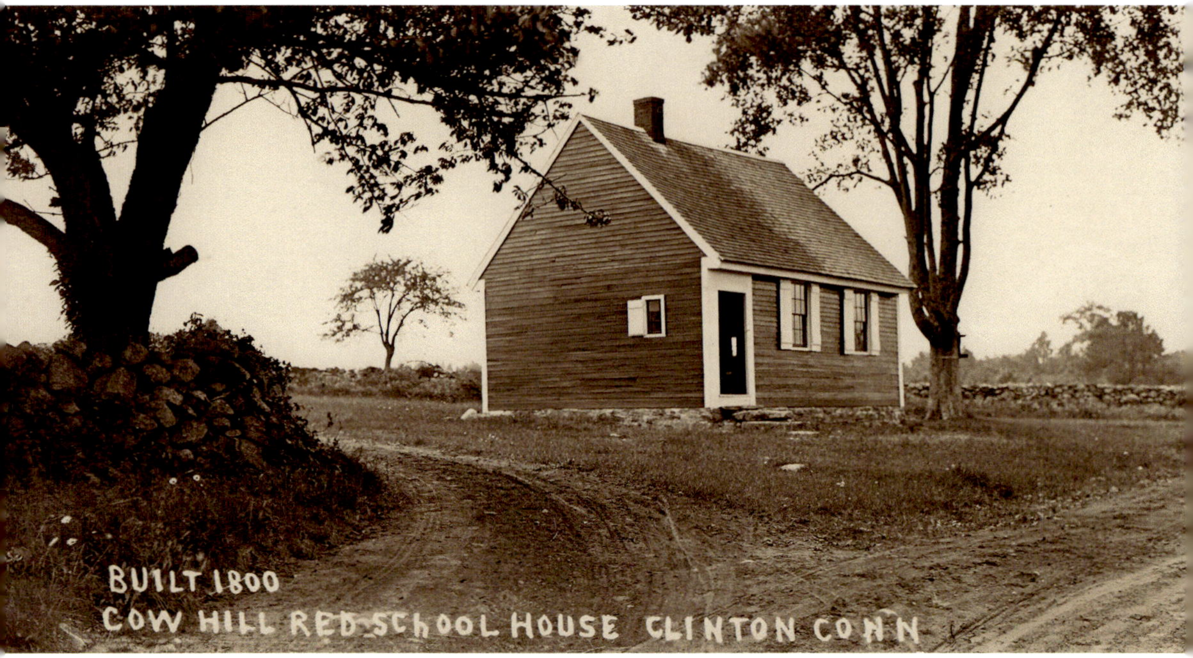

BUILT 1800
COW HILL RED SCHOOL HOUSE CLINTON CONN

CLINTON: The first schoolhouse on Cow Hill was little more than a log cabin with a large fireplace for heat. At a town meeting in 1796, the townspeople decided to build a better schoolhouse, but it wasn't until 1800 that it was completed. The area was named Cow Hill because of an early community pasture, where the cows roamed freely on the hillside. The school closed in 1894, and the alumni held a large reunion there on July 4, 1914. Renovations were made to the school in 1918 to be used as a clubhouse for the Cow Hill Red Schoolhouse Association. The town of Clinton now currently owns the building. (Above photograph courtesy of Clinton Historical Society)

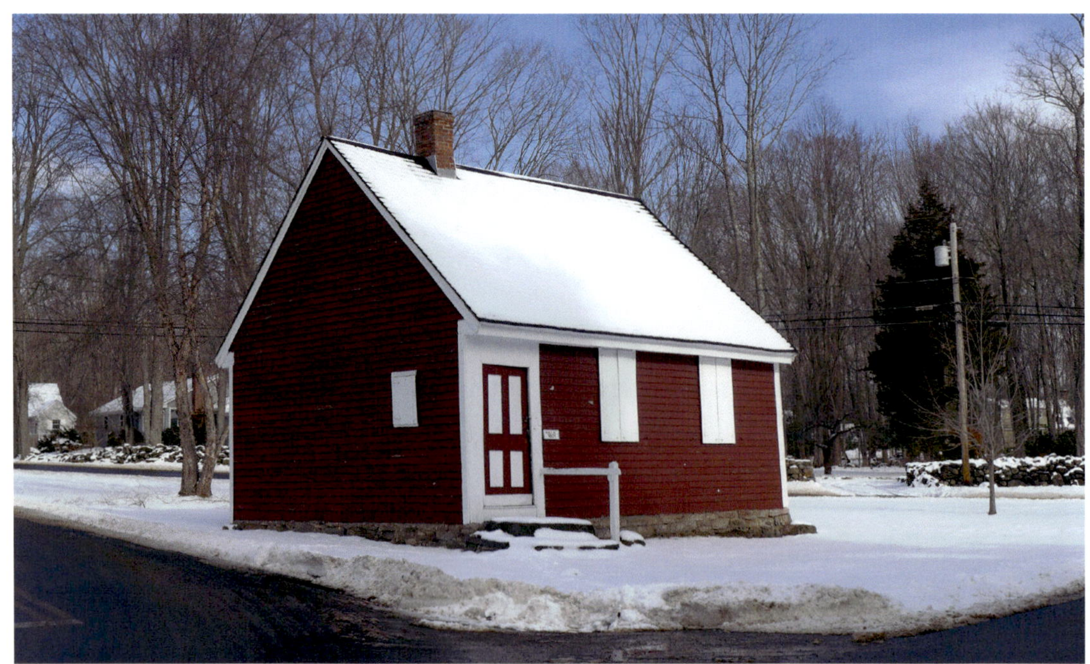

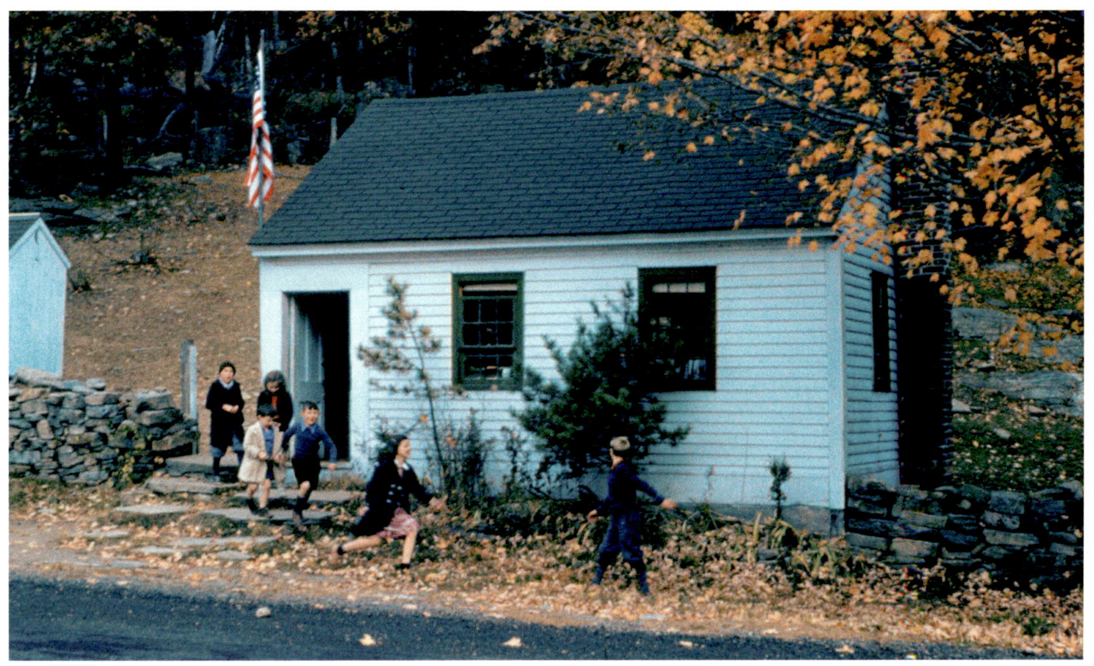

LEDYARD: The Geer family donated land for a schoolhouse in 1735 to provide education for the family and local students. The current building, made in 1813, is only 16 feet wide by 20 feet long. A school visitor reported in 1887 that the Geer Hill School had "some of the most advanced scholars in town." Used until the Ledyard schools consolidated in 1949, the schoolhouse has continued to sit in the same place with the original furnishings. The Geer family still owns the property and the school. It is maintained by the Geer Hill School Association, who have reunion meetings every two years. (Above photograph courtesy of Ledyard Historical Society, Inc., Ledyard, CT)

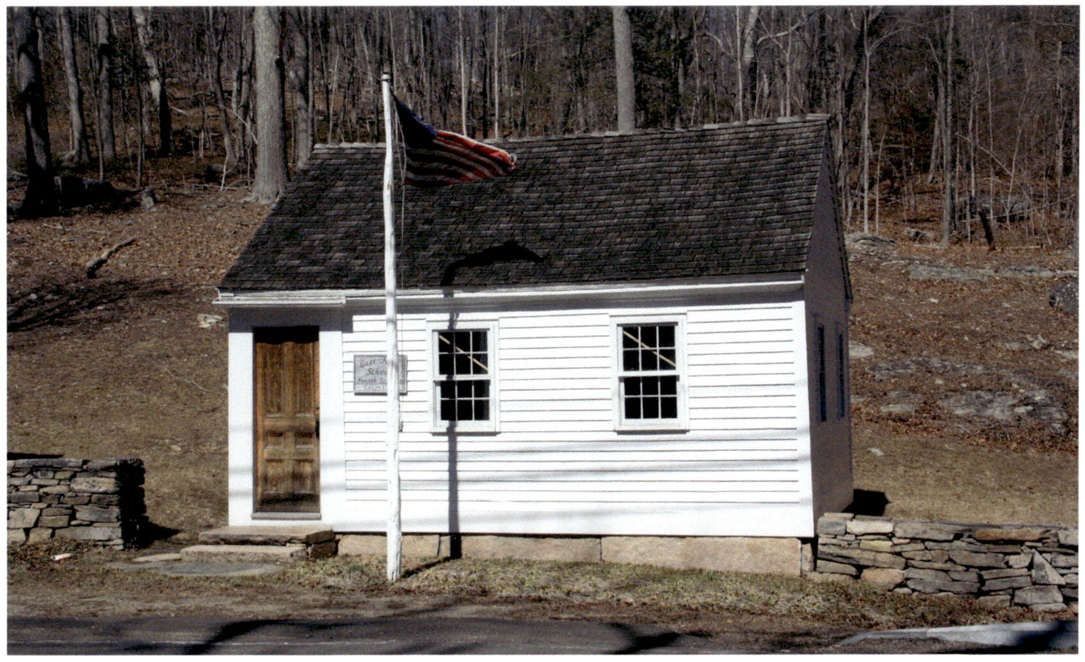

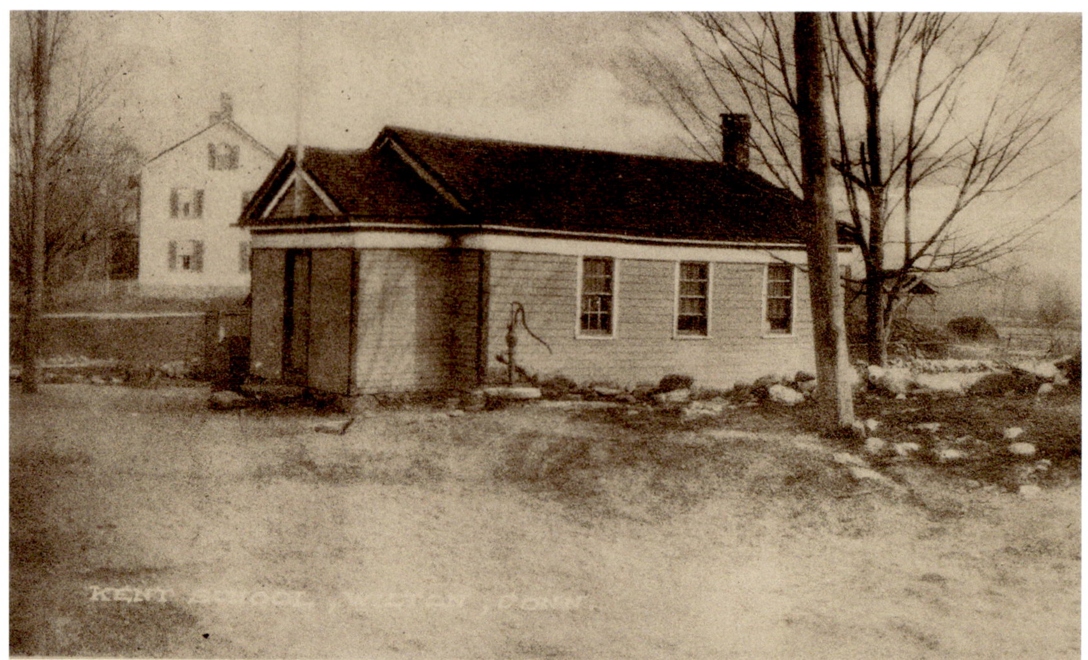

WILTON: The Kent Schoolhouse was built in 1843, as the town was renovating old schools and building new schools. The interior has a barrel ceiling, which helped circulate the warmth from the wood stove. The school closed in the spring of 1929. For a while it was used by the YMCA for classes and by the Wilton Athletic Club for their headquarters. It was moved in 1971 to Lamberts Corners with other repurposed historical buildings, including the David Lambert House, circa 1724, a 1790 general store, the 1889 Hurlbutt Street Post office, and an 1852 railroad station. The schoolhouse is used as a commercial building, administrated by the Wilton Historical Society. (Above photograph courtesy of the Elliott Postcard Collection)

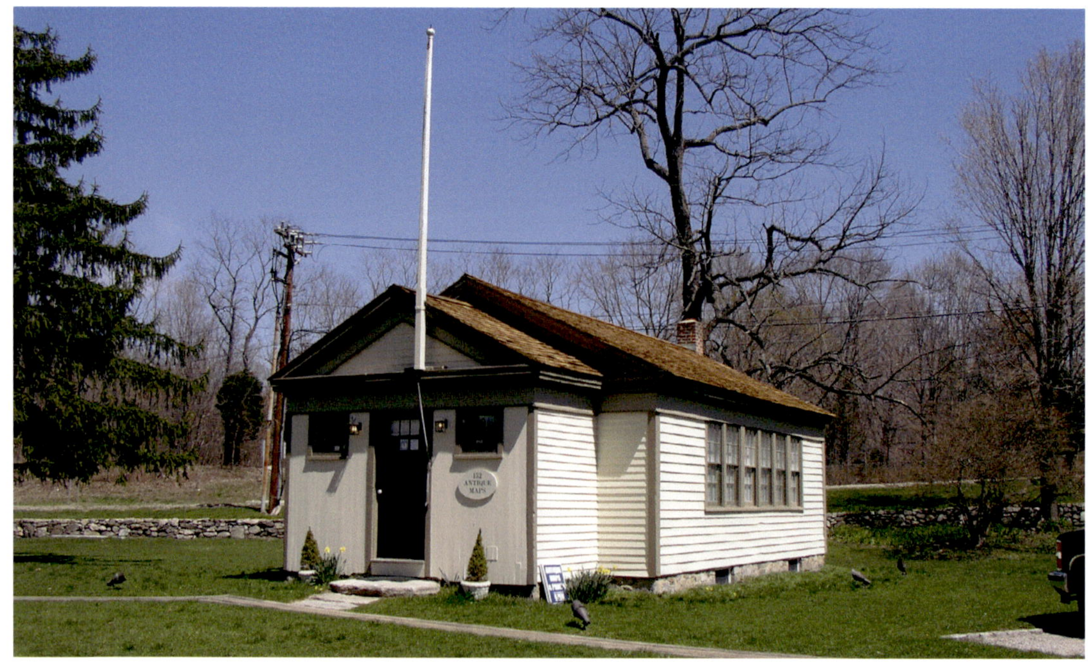

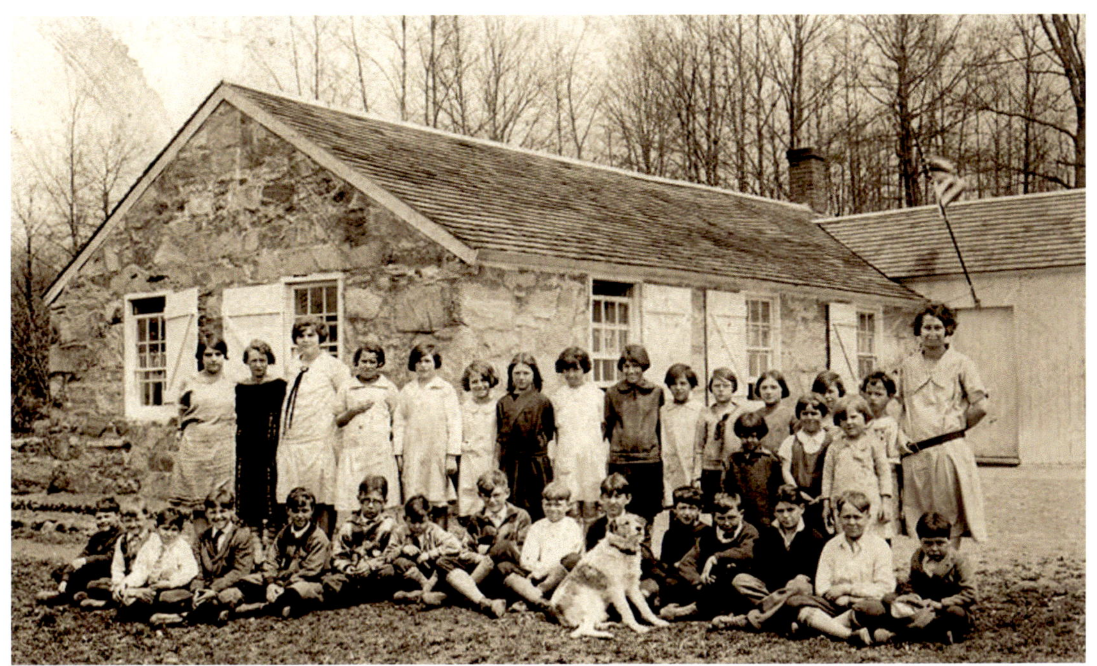

WOLCOTT: The Woodtick Schoolhouse, now known as the Old Stone Schoolhouse, was built from local stone from the Wakelee quarry in 1821, to replace a wooden schoolhouse that burned. Due to increasing population, the building was extended in 1898. The town voted to replace the old schoolhouse with a two-room brick building in 1930. The stone school was used continuously for 109 years before being sold in 1930 to Miss Emily Morris, whose grandfather taught there in 1829. The school came out of retirement and was used again in the 1942 school year. Miss Morris gave the school to the Wolcott Historical Society in 1962. The class photo is from 1929. (Historical photograph courtesy of the Wolcott Historical Society)

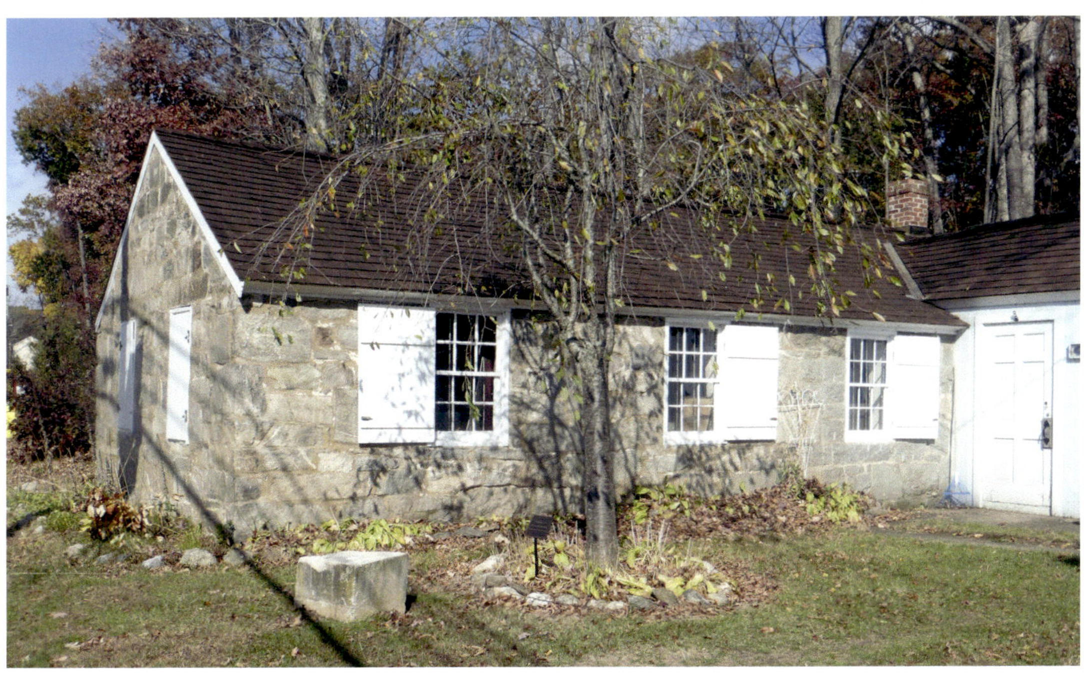

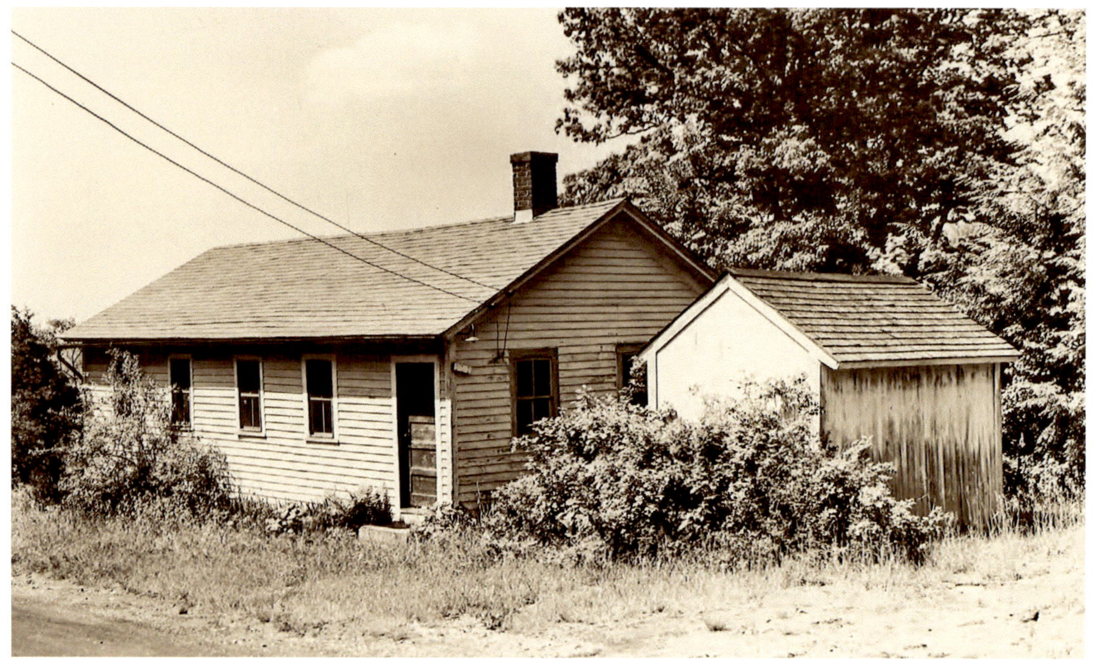

CANTON: East Hill School was a remote school set on the side of a hill, with the road on one side and a sharp incline above a brook over the other. It was built in 1832, and in addition to the school day, became the community center where local social activities were held. In 1923, water was supplied to the building and a furnace was added. The school was closed in 1942 when all the students were sent to the consolidated school, the Cherry Brook School. An original outhouse is still standing. The building is now used by the Collinsville Boy Scout Troop 77. (Above photograph courtesy of CT State Library, State Archives, LS Mills Collection)

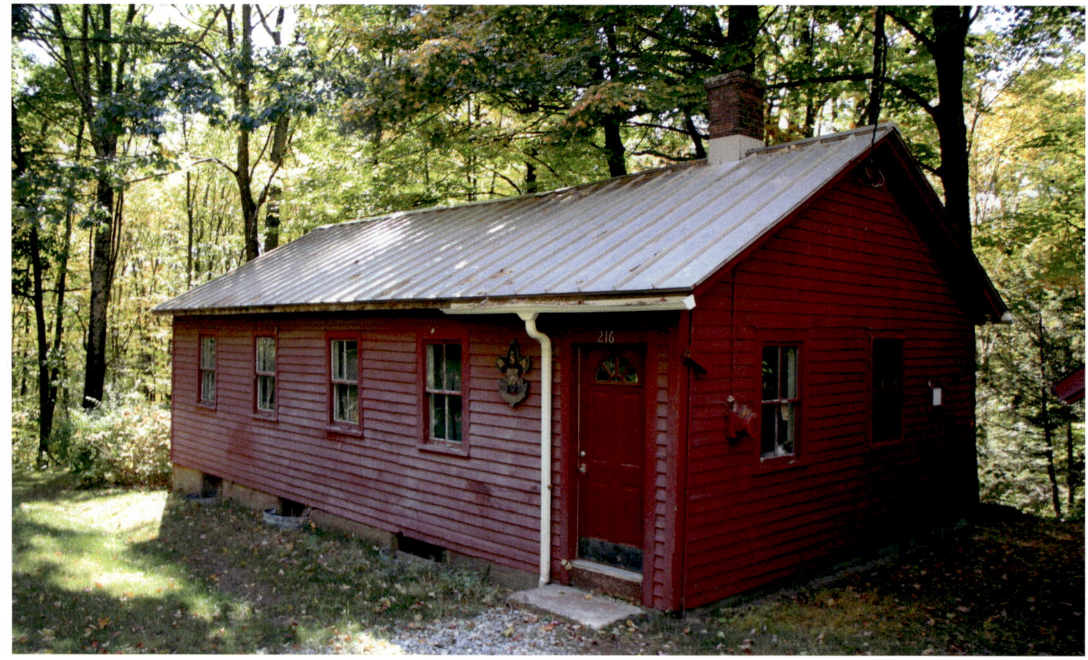

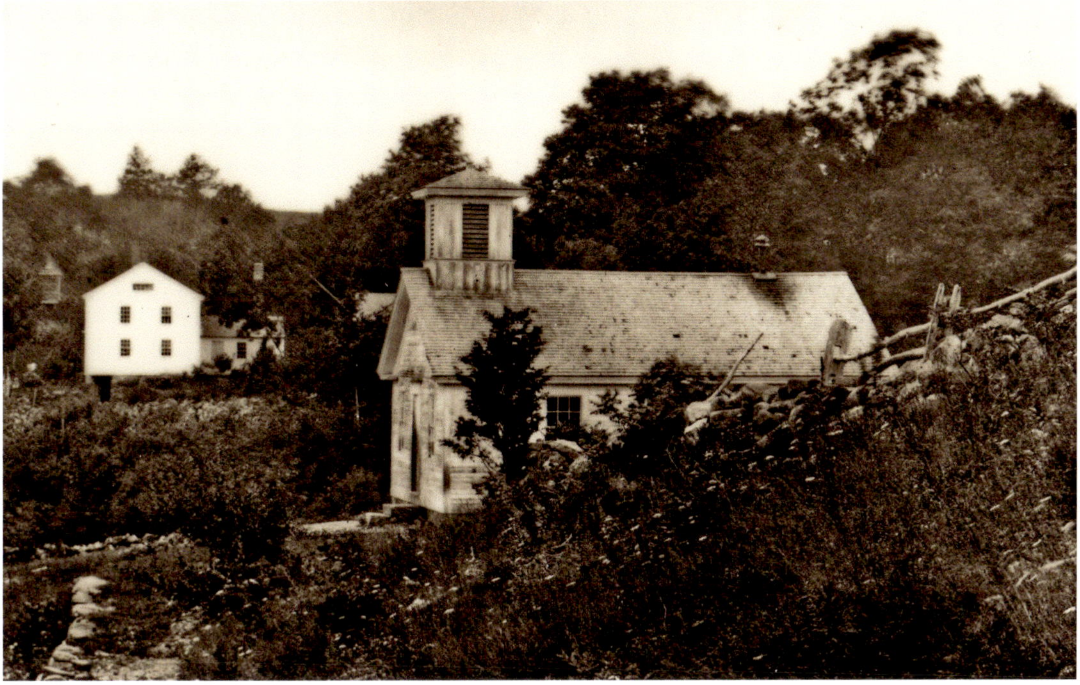

HADDAM: The Haddam Neck Schoolhouse was built in 1822. The school, complete with cupola, nestled on the hillside. When it was built, the school boosted of a library of 50 volumes, modern desks, and a wood stove. In 1873, the Congregational Church was constructed across the street. The school was moved to the church property in 1916, and continued to be used for the next nine years. The old schoolhouse is now used as the church's parish house. (Above photograph courtesy of Haddam Historical Society, Haddam, CT)

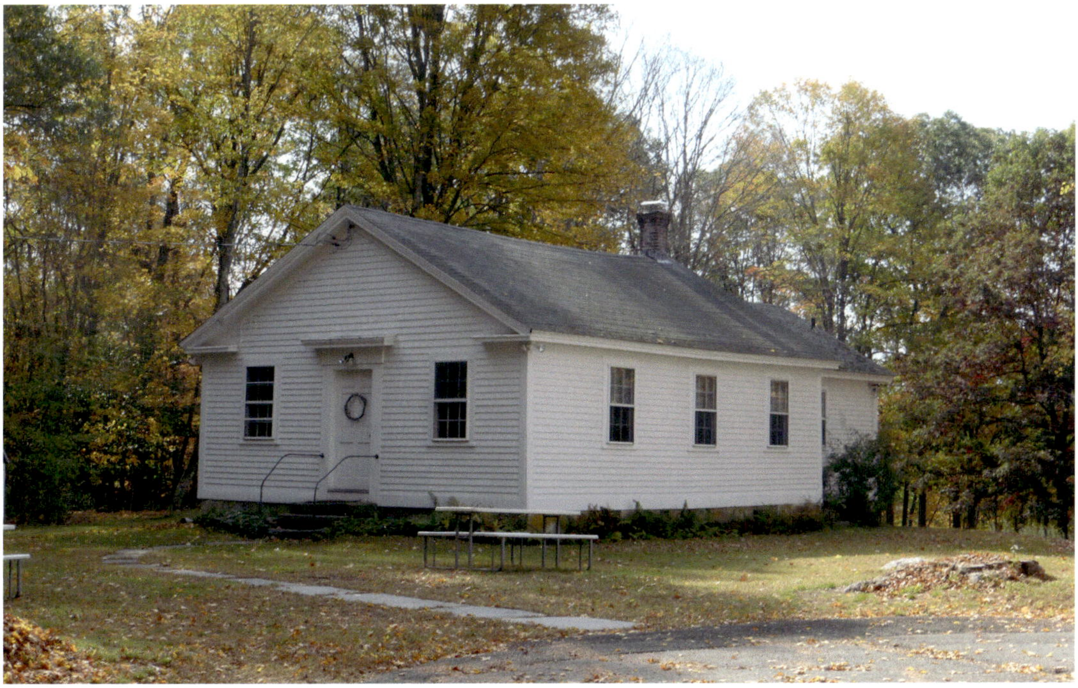

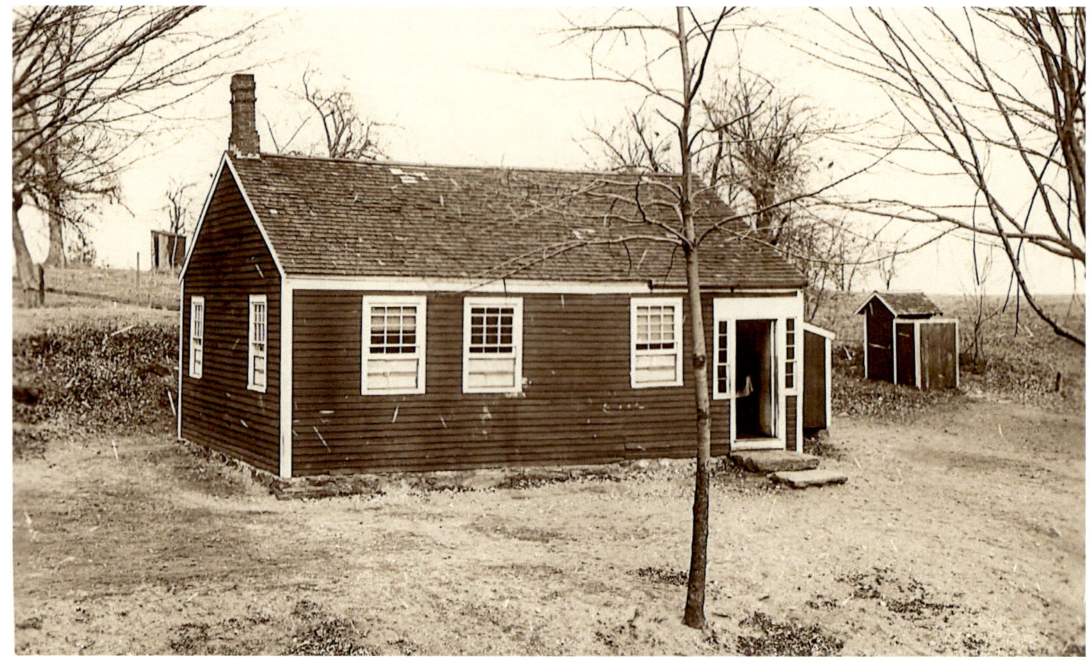

BURLINGTON: The Center Schoolhouse still stands where it was built in 1806 near the town center. Electricity was added to the building in 1924. The district schools were consolidated into one brand new six-classroom building and all the town's students began attending there in 1948. After the schoolhouse sat vacant for a few years, the Burlington Library moved in and stayed until 1969. The Bicentennial Commission ran a store out of the old school in 1976. The building underwent renovations, which were completed in 1988. As an Eagle Scout Project in 1999, the schoolhouse had a facelift, with a new paint job. (Above photograph courtesy of CT State Library, State Archives, LS Mills Collection)

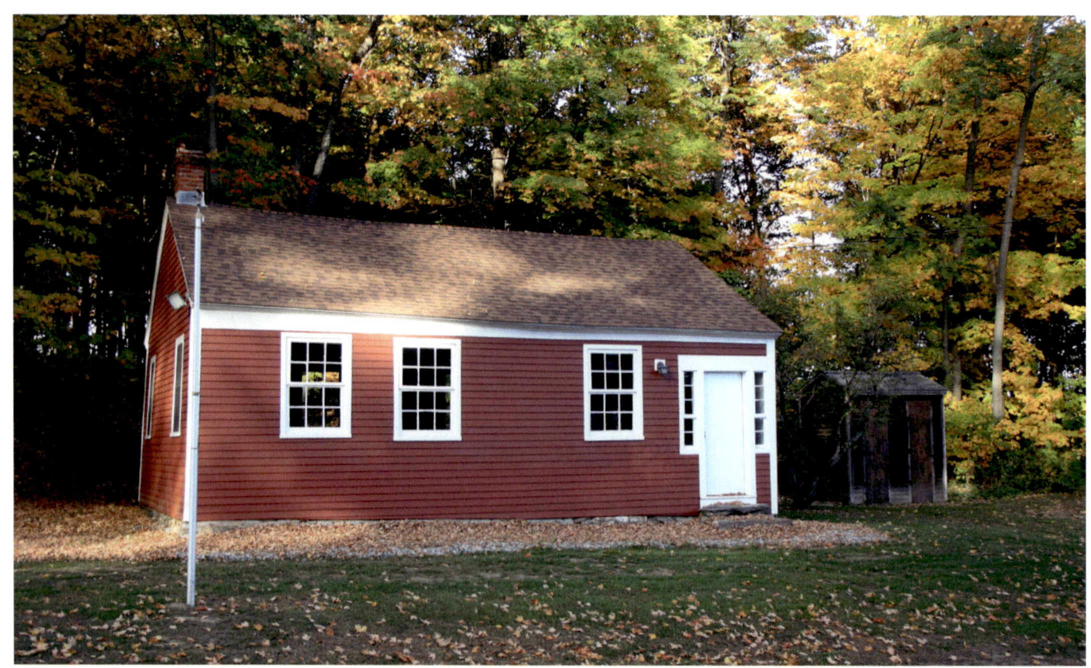

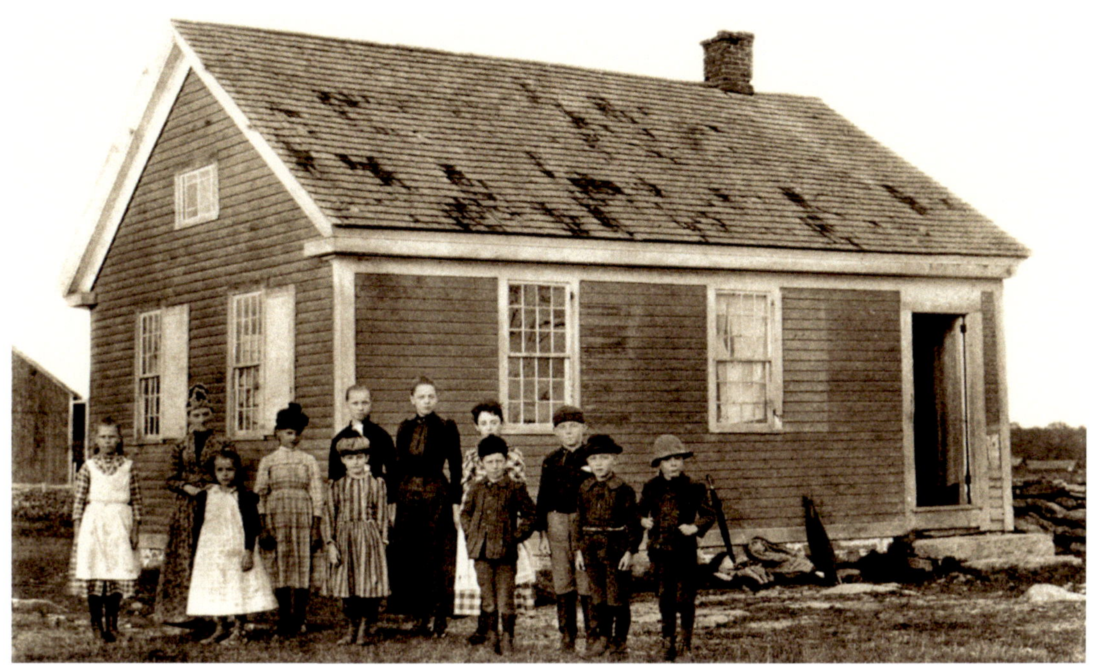

KILLINGWORTH: The Union District School was built in 1800, and is the earliest schoolhouse still standing in town. It is locally known as the "Little Green Schoolhouse" and may have always been painted green. One student of note was Titus Coan, who attended the school as a student and later returned as the teacher. He was an early missionary to Hilo, Hawaii, from 1834 to 1882. After some renovations in 1849, the school continued to be used until 1948, when all the town's small schoolhouses were closed. In 1980, the Killingworth Historical Society purchased the building. The school was restored, along with the outhouse, which is also painted green. (Above photograph courtesy of Killingworth Historical Society)

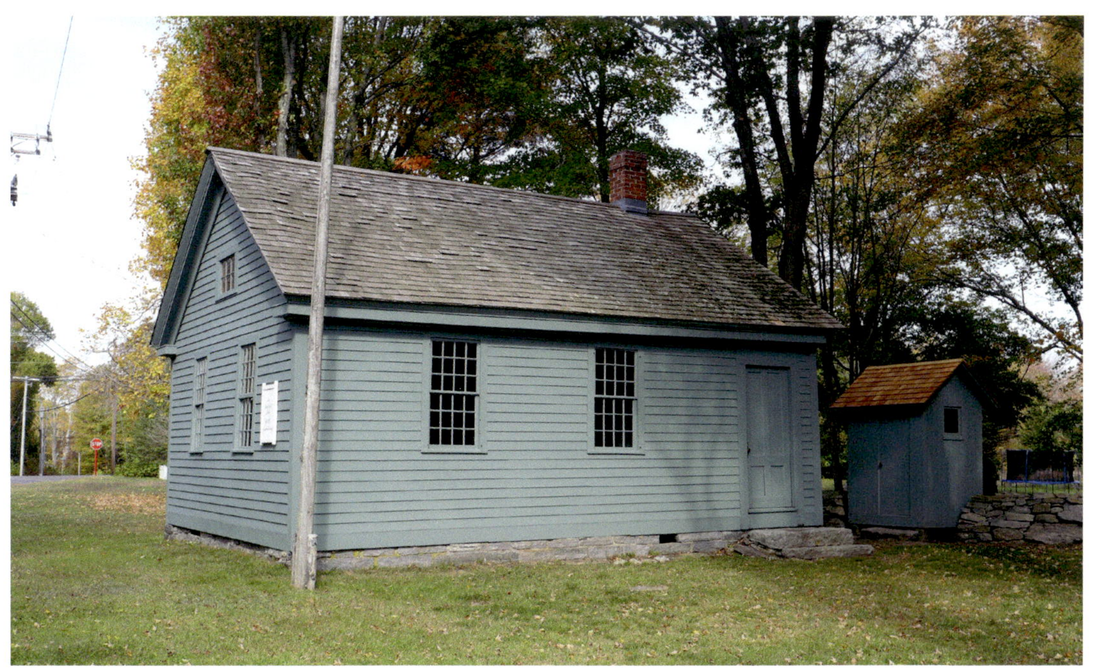

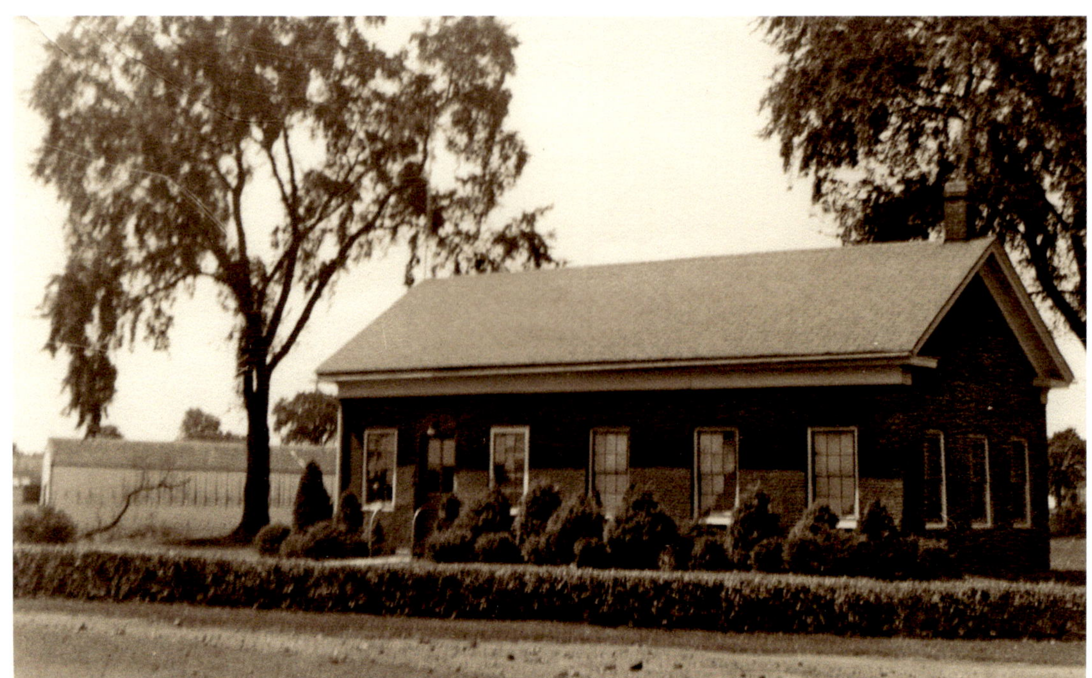

ENFIELD: Once set on the edge of a tobacco farm, the brick Wallop Schoolhouse was built in 1800, after the 1754 school burned down. The school was used continuously until 1947, when the teacher became ill and the students were sent to other schools. A fire severely damaged the building in 1959, and the Enfield Historical Society came in to repair and renovate the building. The building is restored and used as a schoolhouse museum. In the old photograph, you can see a tobacco barn in the background. The schoolhouse is now surrounded by a modern neighborhood. (Above photograph courtesy of Enfield Historical Society)

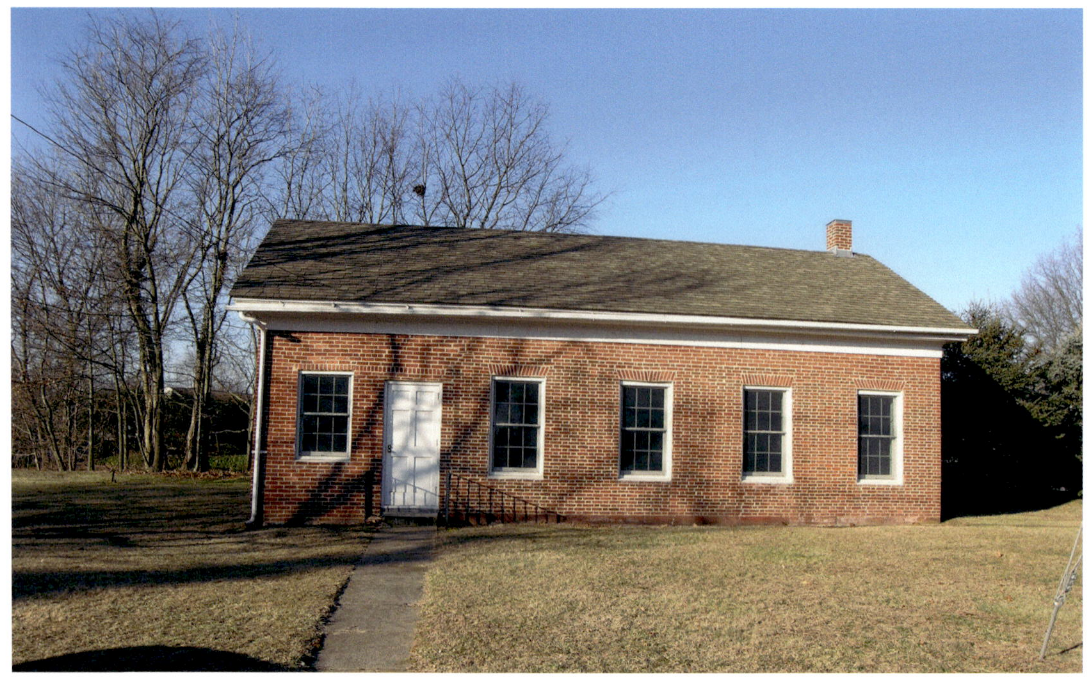

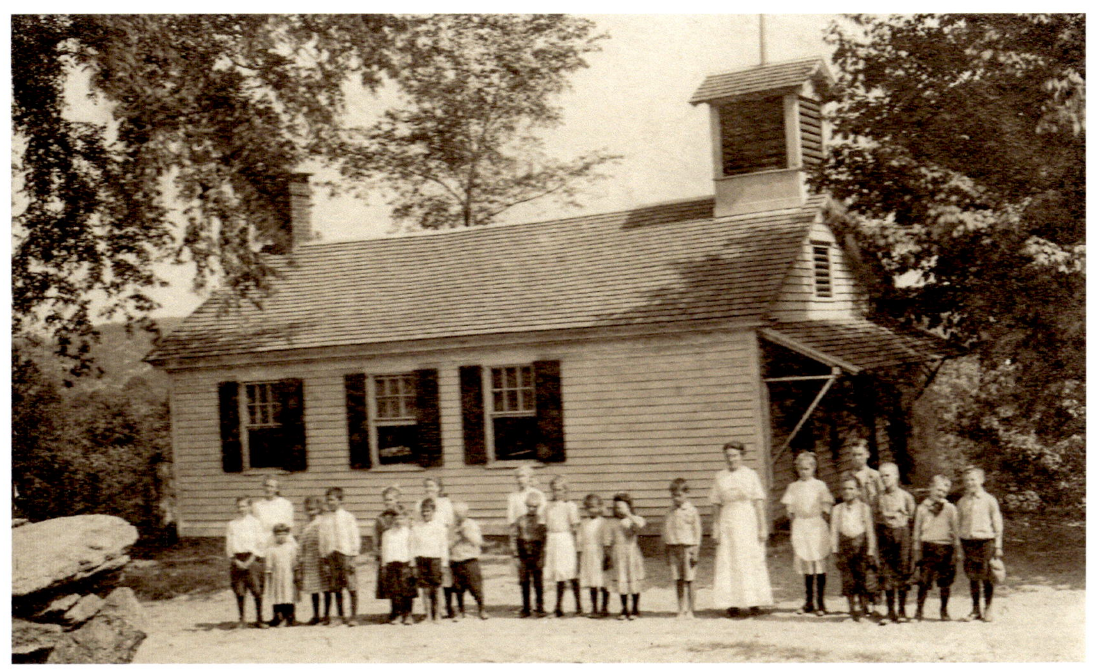

BETHANY: Center District School was built in 1834, on Amity Road, a main road in town. Due to the constant traffic, the schoolhouse was moved in 1931 a short distance east, to a safer location away from the road. The one-room schoolhouses were closed and the students were sent to the Community School in 1934. The schoolhouse was eventually moved to a permanent location on the Community School grounds, near the school entrance. Bethany began restoration on the old schoolhouse in time for the United States Bicentennial celebrations in 1976. A Center Schoolhouse Committee was formed in 1982 to oversee the Old Center Schoolhouse. (Above photograph courtesy of Bethany Historical Society)

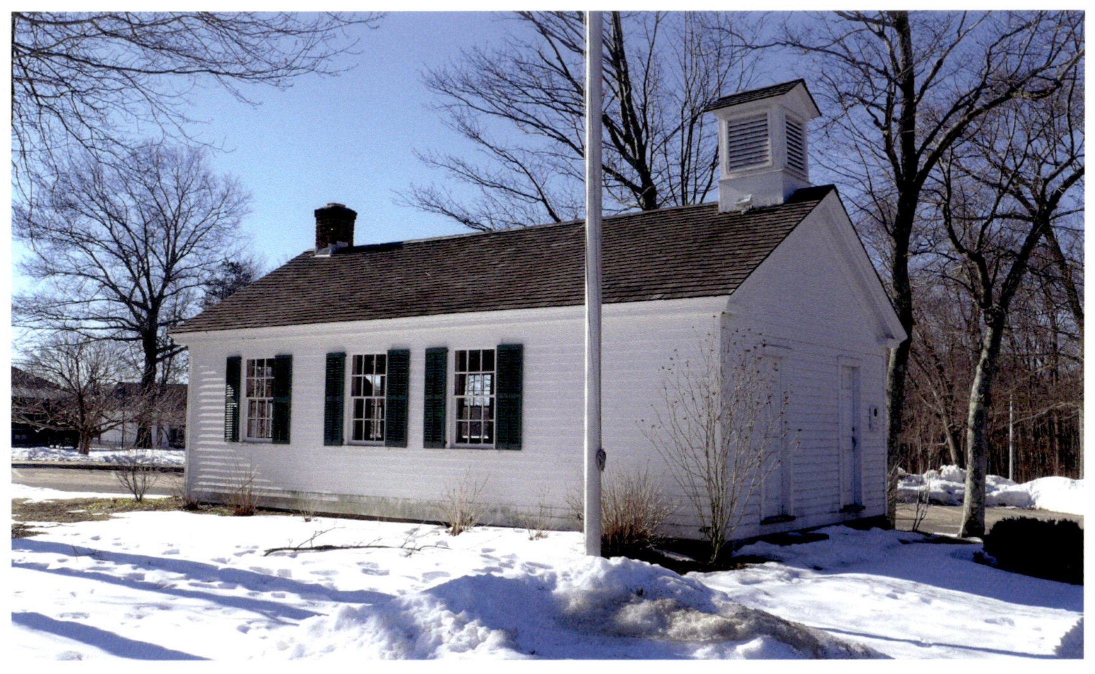

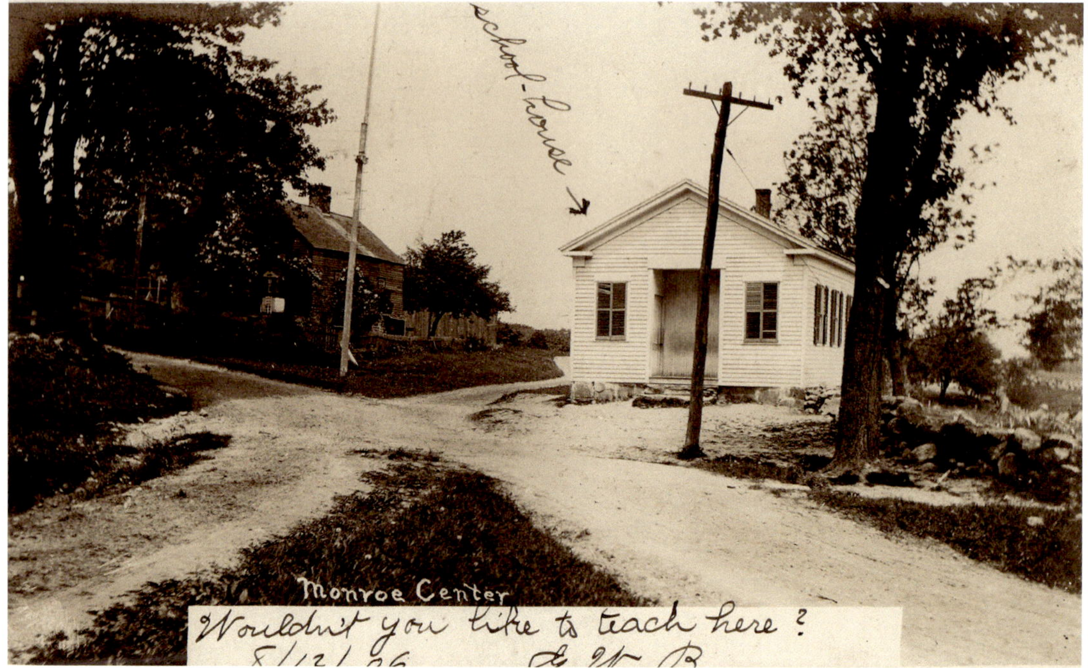

MONROE: The Monroe Center School, the 10th district school, was built in 1830, on a triangle-shaped lot at the corner of Wheeler Road and Tannery Road. The schoolhouse was closed in 1935 and auctioned off. The Congregational Church purchased the school and moved it next to the church. Already sitting on their property was a slightly larger building, Beardsley Hall, which was used for Sunday School. The two buildings were placed back to back to be used as meeting and educational rooms. (Above photograph courtesy of the Elliott postcard collection)

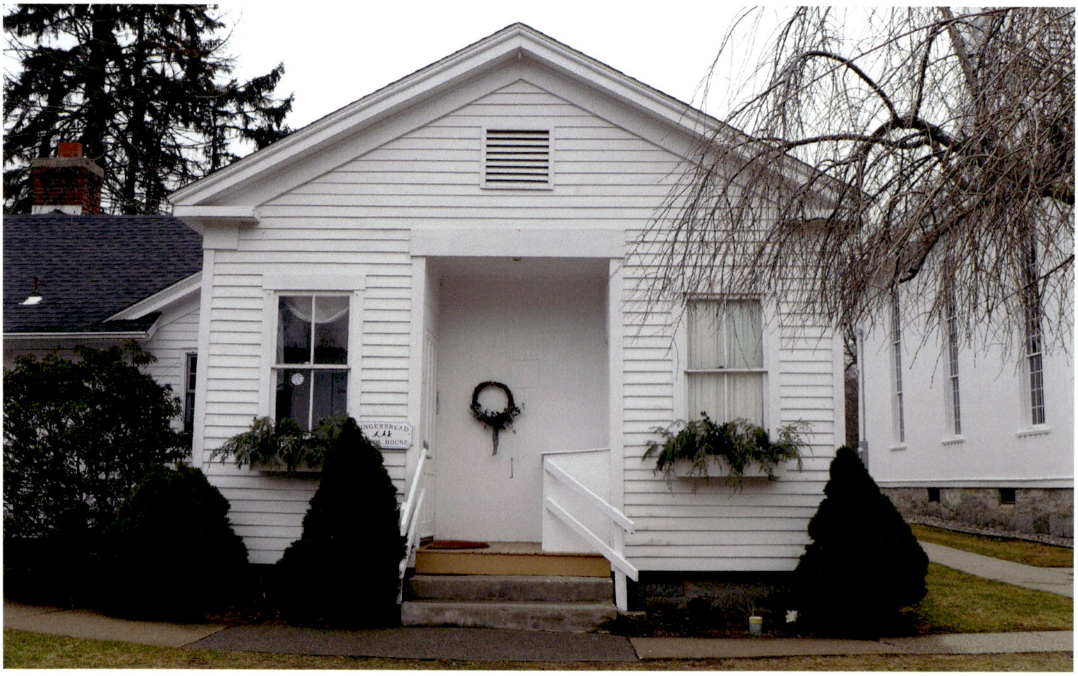

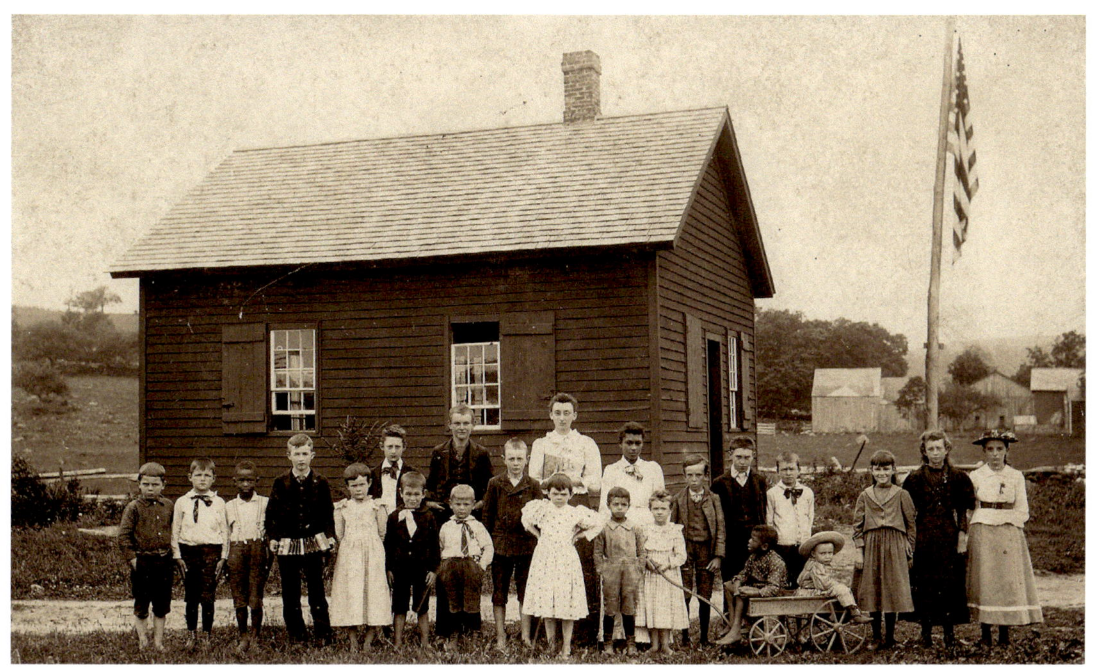

NORFOLK: The North Middle School, now known as the Little Red Schoolhouse, was one of the town's eleven district schools. According to the sign on the building, the "stake set" was in 1827, a common 19th century term to signify that the location was agreed upon, acceptable, and official. The town schools were consolidated in 1922, and all the one-room schools were closed. In 1961, the schoolhouse was restored. The old photograph was taken by Marie Hartig Kendall about 1890, at the time when there were very few women photographers. Her specialty was the architecture, landscape, and people of rural Norfolk. (Above photograph courtesy of Norfolk Historical Society)

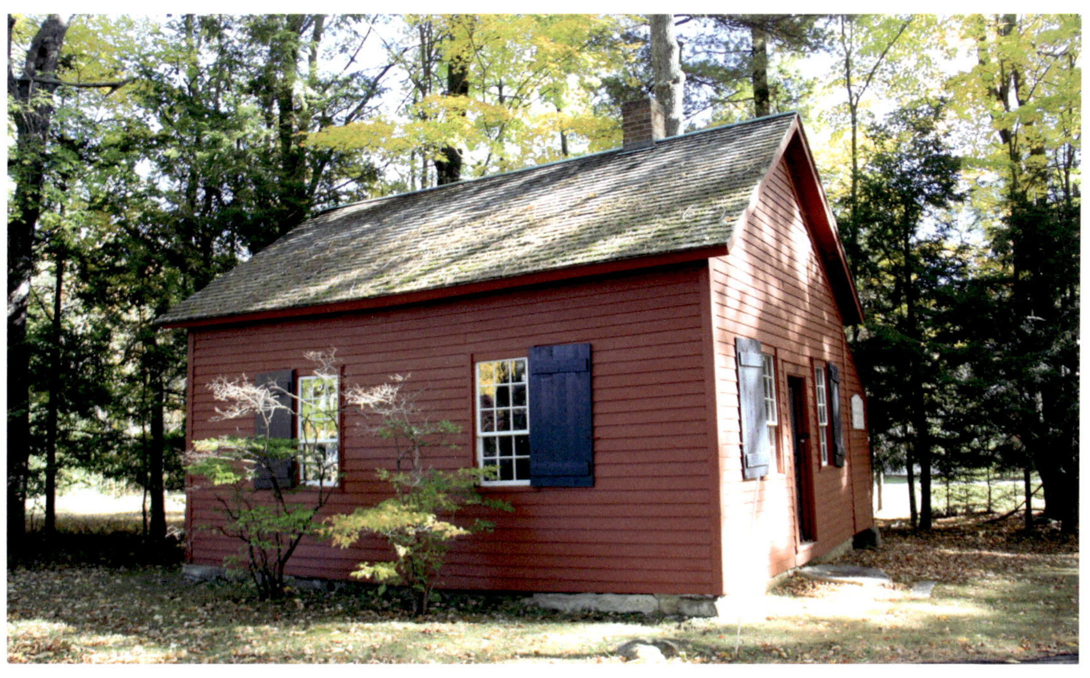

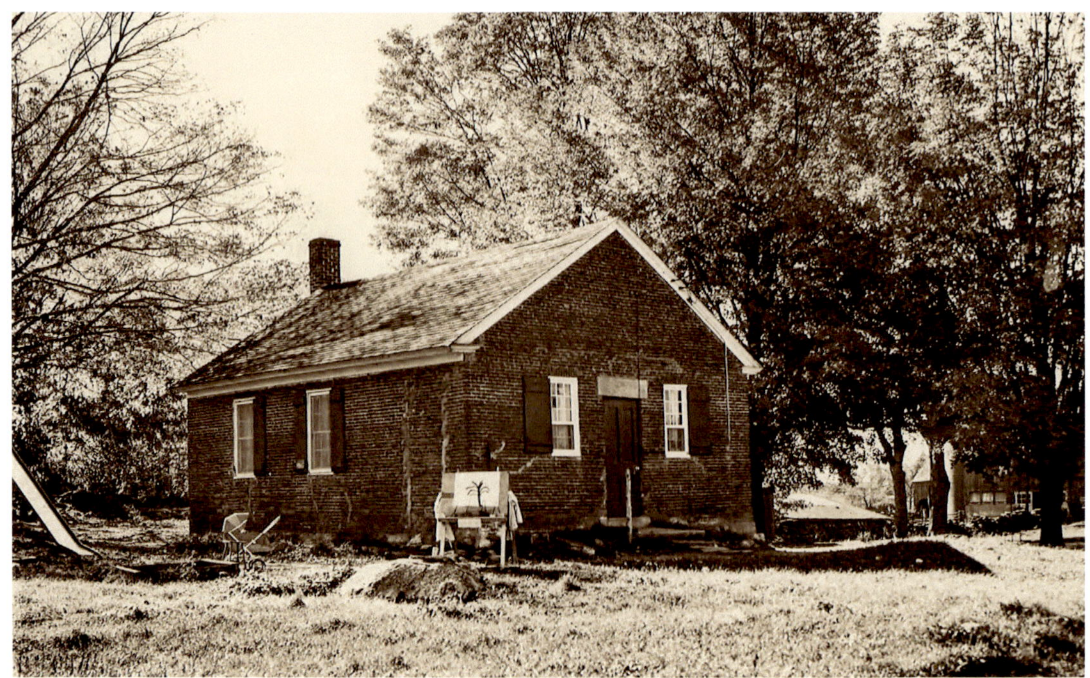

COVENTRY: The brick for the school was made from local clay about 1825, near the area where an earlier wooden school once sat and burned down. In 1849, the district voted to put in blackboards and a year later to purchase desks. A library was added in the northwest corner of the building for the use of the students. The schoolhouse was used into the 1950s. The building fell into disrepair and was finally purchased and restored. The Coventry Historical Society received the donation of the school in 1967, and still maintains the building. (Above photograph courtesy of CT State Library, State Archives, LS Mills Collection)

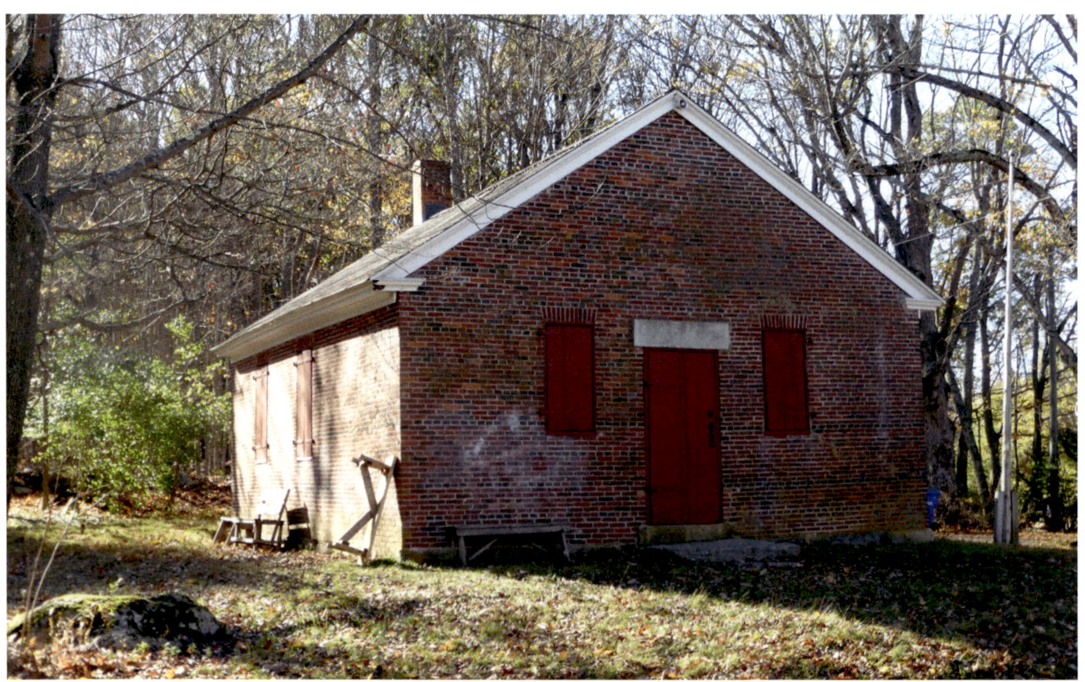

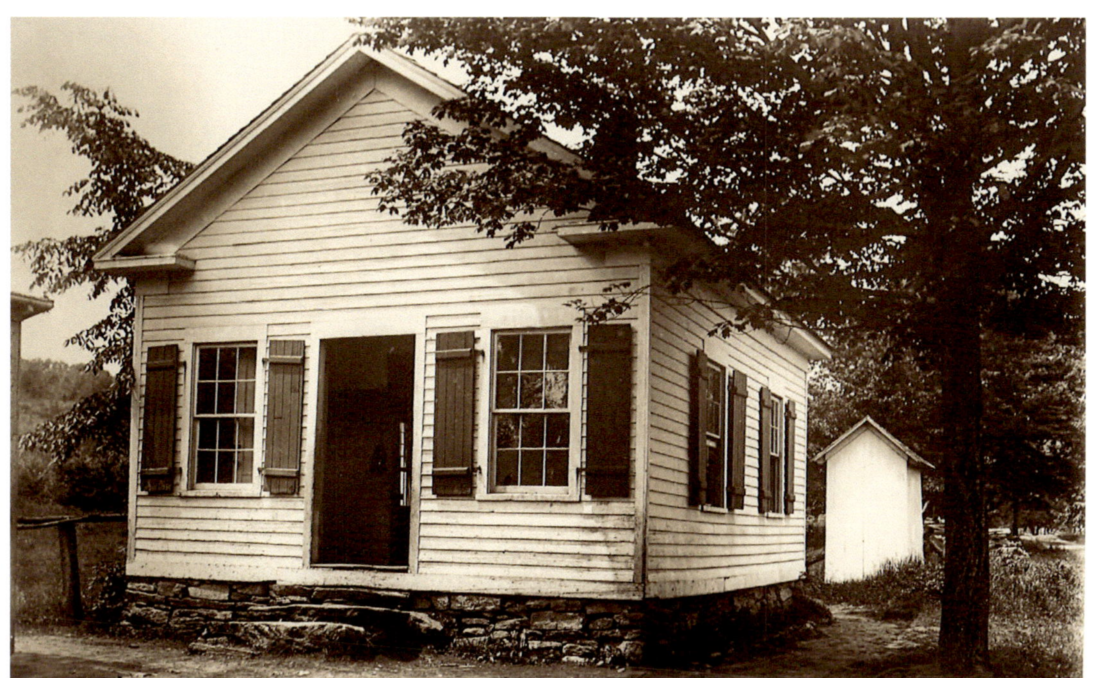

BEACON FALLS: Records exist as early as 1799 concerning this school district. In 1821, the schoolhouse was built by the town of Oxford. As this tiny school sat in one place, at the corner of Rimmon and Pinesbridge Roads, the town lines changed around it. One 1859 notice of the district meeting for this school lists all three towns of Oxford, Bethany, and Beacon Falls. The Rimmon School remained open until Laurel Ledge Elementary was built in the 1950s and all the little schoolhouses were closed. The school is privately owned and not open to the public. (Above photograph courtesy of CT State Library, State Archives, LS Mills Collection)

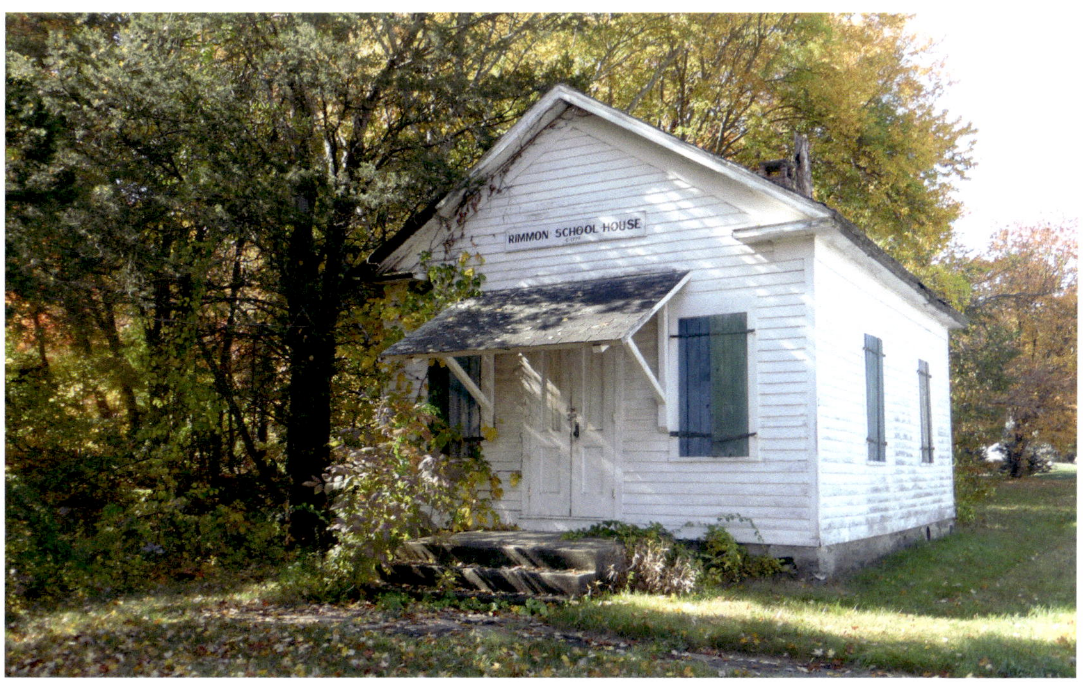

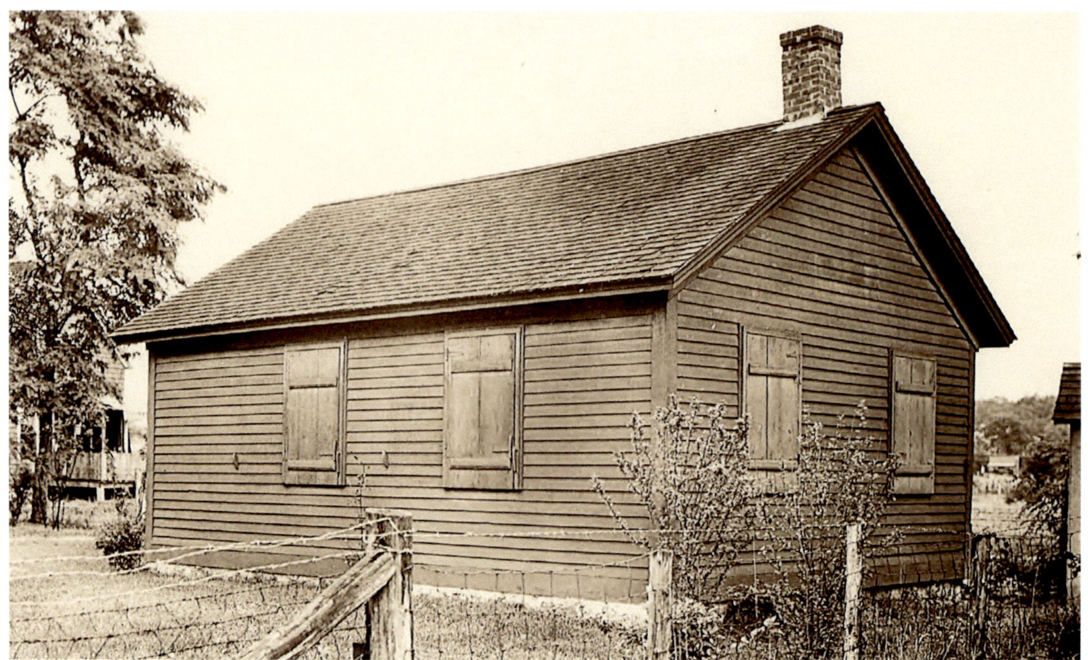

EAST LYME: The New Boston School was founded in 1734 as the first district school between Boston and New York, by order of Governor Joseph Talcott who wrote to Thomas Lee to "set aside land to establish a school." The current building was from 1805 and once sat on a slight rise 500 yards away from the current location. The school closed in 1922. In 1926, the East Lyme Historical Society purchased the building and moved it to the grounds of the Thomas Lee House. It was used a summer residence for 25 years, and saw other uses until 1973, when it was restored as a schoolhouse. (Above photograph courtesy of CT State Library, State Archives, LS Mills Collection)

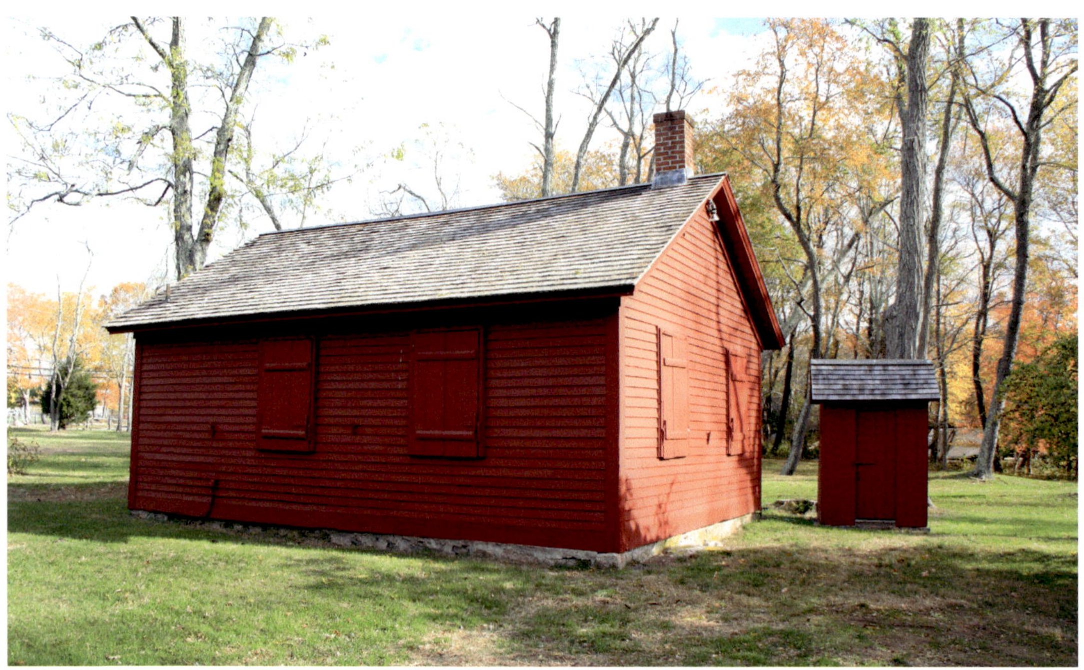

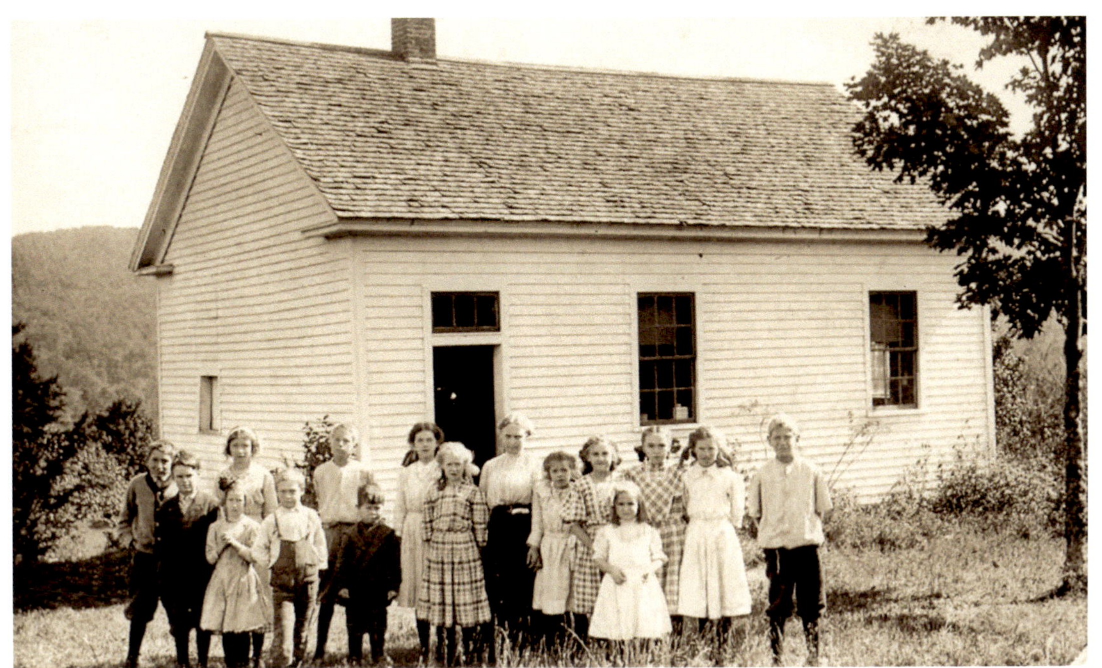

BARKHAMSTED: The Center School was built in 1821, and a second floor was added in 1824. The main floor was used as a district school while the upper floor held a select school for a while and was later used for public purposes like dances and prayer meetings. By 1870, extensive repairs were needed on the first floor and the town decided to simply lower the upper floor to ground level. The repairs were complete in January 1878. The schoolhouse was used until 1937, when the students were sent to Pleasant Valley School. After being used for storage for 40 years, the Barkhamsted Historical Society moved the schoolhouse in 1980. (Above photograph from Elliott Postcard Collection)

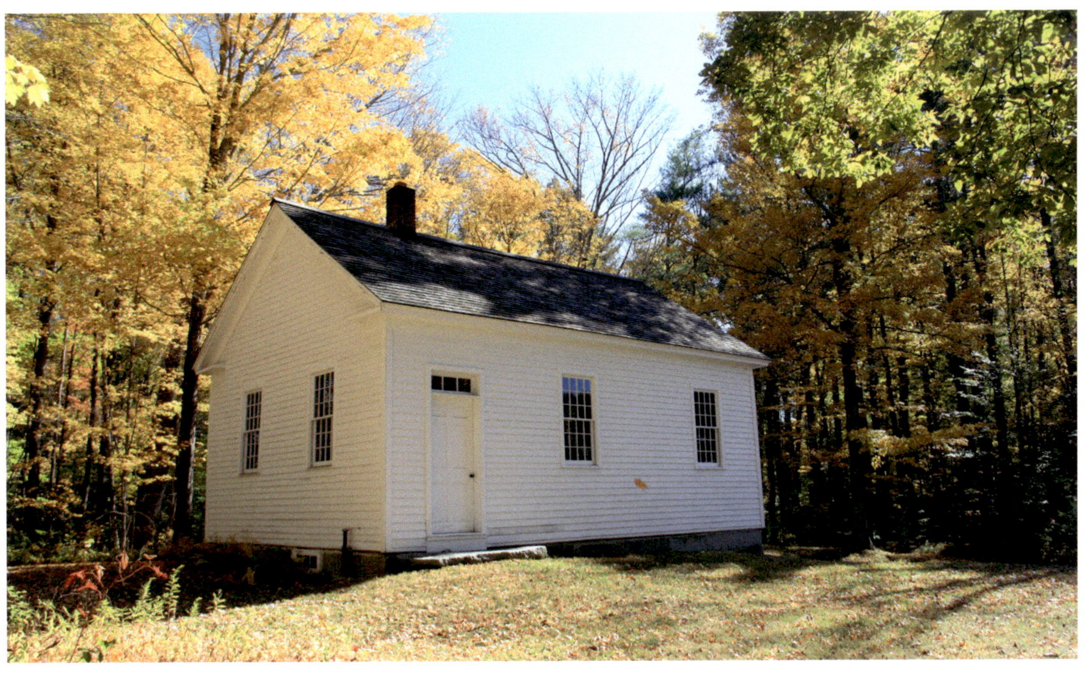

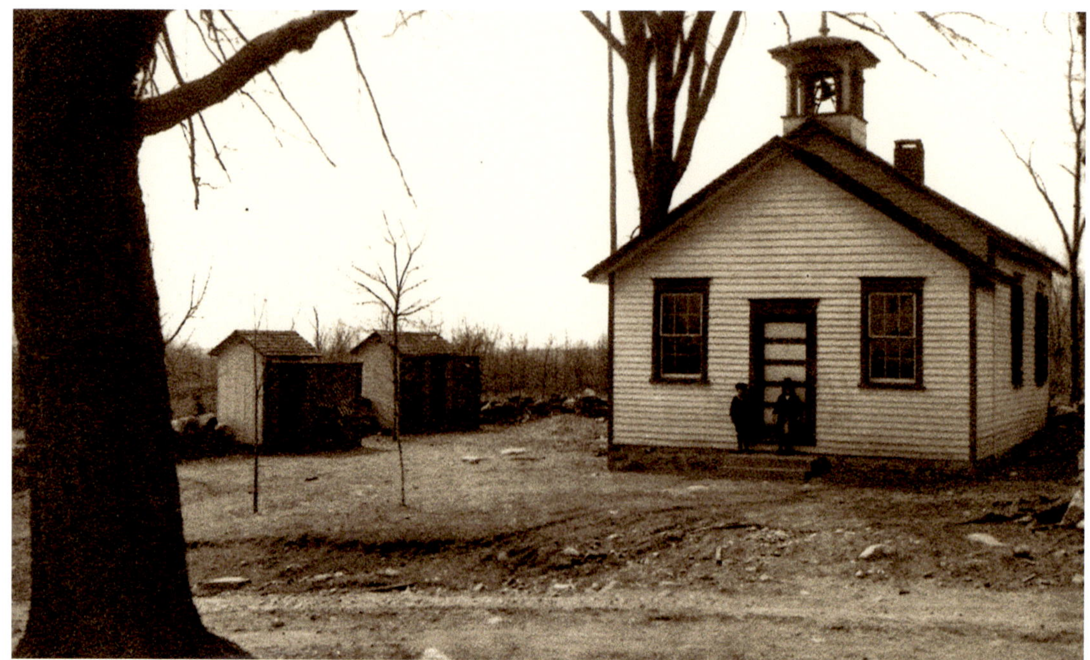

WILTON: In 1833, land was deeded for new school at "Hurlbutt's Hole." The schoolhouse was built the next year in one day through careful planning and the hard work of the district men. The schoolhouse was first moved to a lot on Hurlbutt Street in 1876, and expanded by about six feet. Electricity was added in 1929, and through the kindness of local residents who donated a radio, the community gathered around to listen to the inauguration of Herbert Hoover. The school closed in 1935, and moved again 10 feet north, removing the front vestibule to make it appear as the original building in 1834. (Above photograph courtesy of Wilton Historical Society)

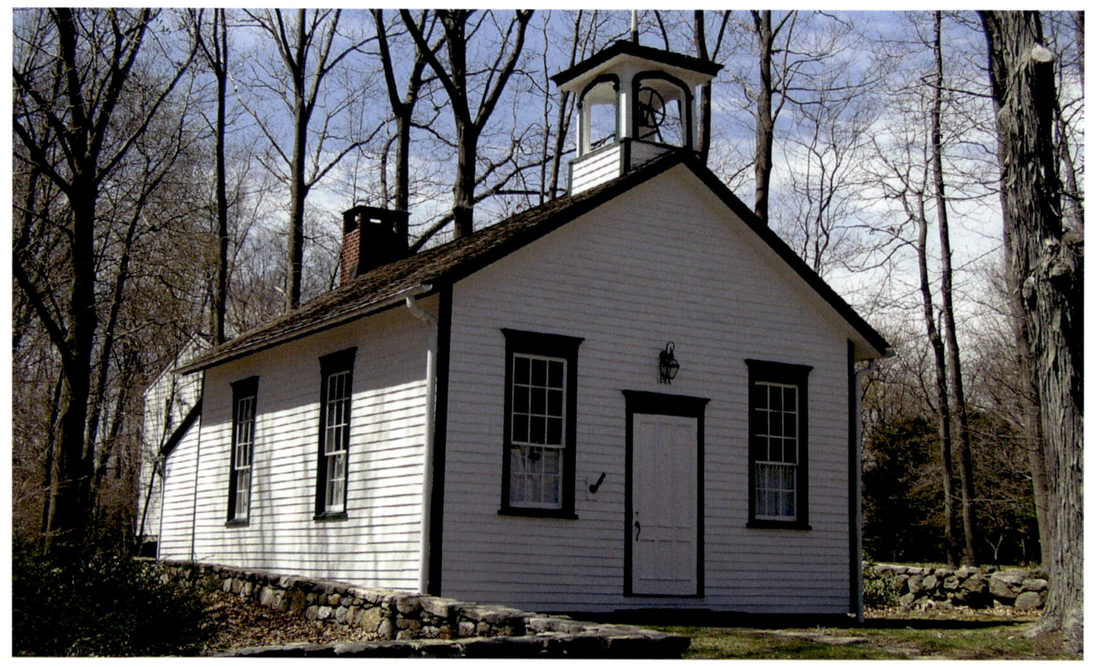

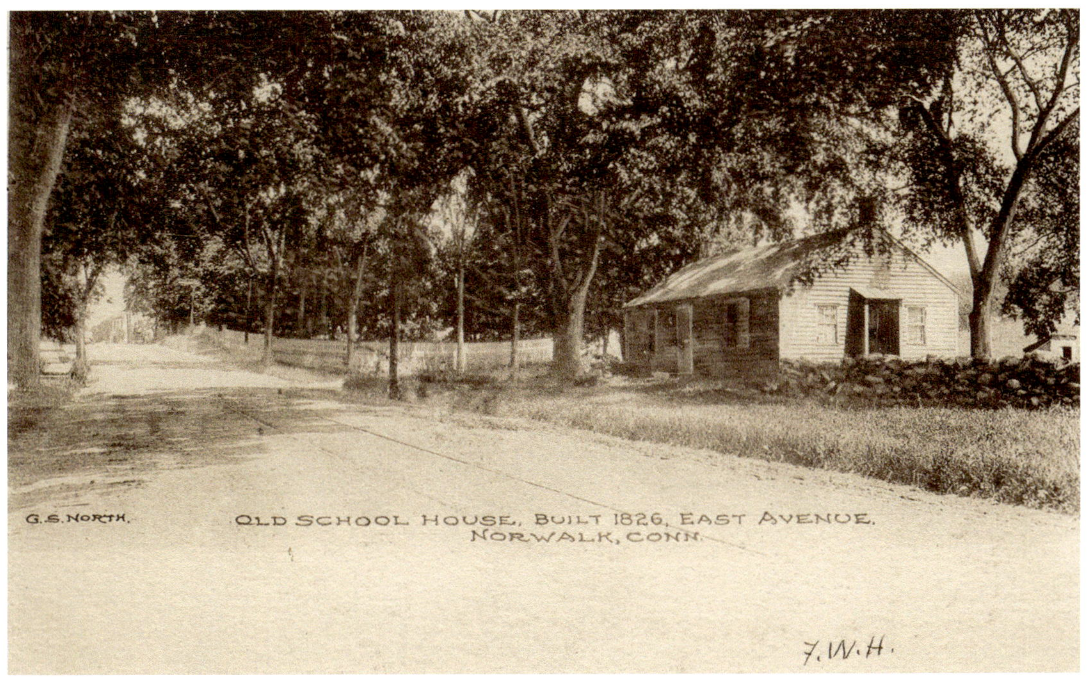

NORWALK: This East Avenue Schoolhouse, also known as the Center District Schoolhouse, and the Downtown School, was built in 1826 near the location of an earlier schoolhouse that was burned down by the British during the Revolutionary War. It served as a school into the 1870s. In 1971 it was moved to the Norwalk Historical Society property on Mill Hill, where it still stands. The local teachers started the Little Red Schoolhouse program in the 1970s for their students to learn more about the schoolhouse and Norwalk history. (Above photograph courtesy of the Elliott Postcard Collection)

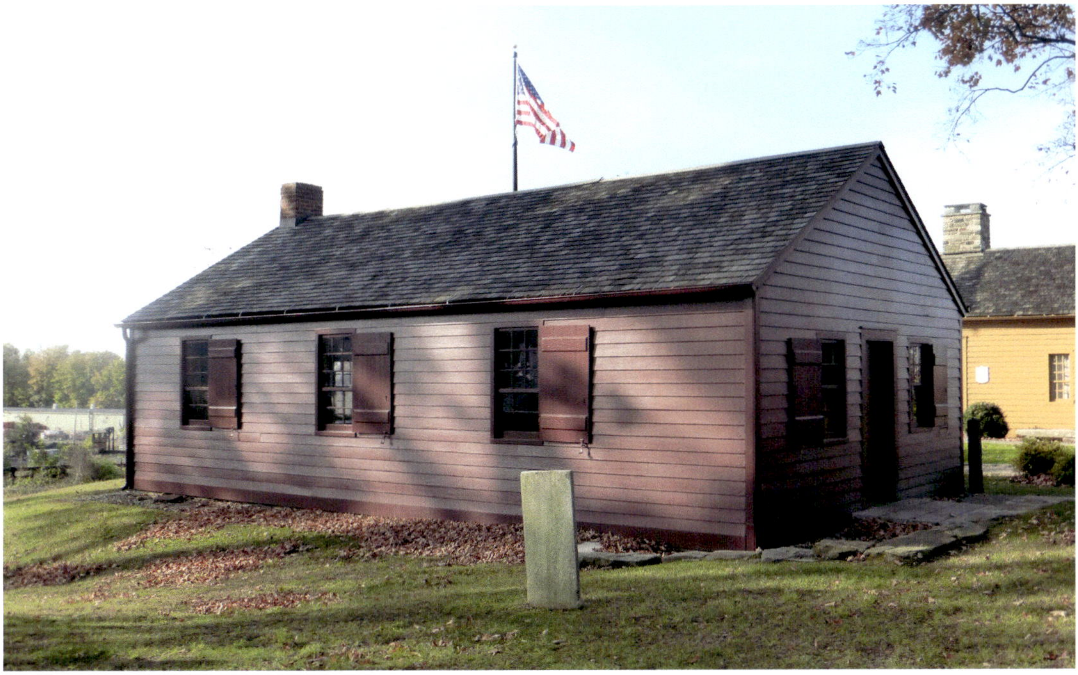

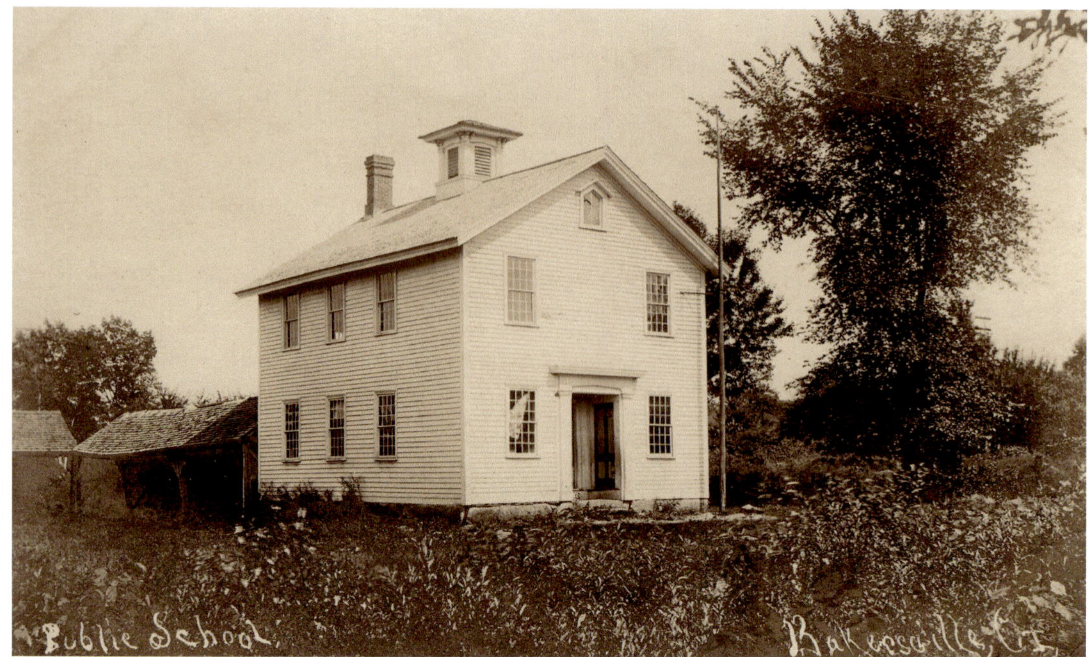

NEW HARTFORD: Bakerville School started in 1824 by subscription by a group of people who wanted the best education for their children. The horse sheds for the adjacent church were attached to the back of the schoolhouse. The sheds were moved after the children discovered they could climb out a schoolroom window and sit on top of the shed. For a while school was held in the upper room and meetings and social events were on the first floor. Eventually, both floors were classrooms. The school was closed when the Barkhamsted Consolidated School opened in 1942. Barkerville Public Library started using the building in 1951 and can still be found there today. (Above photograph courtesy of the Elliott Postcard Collection)

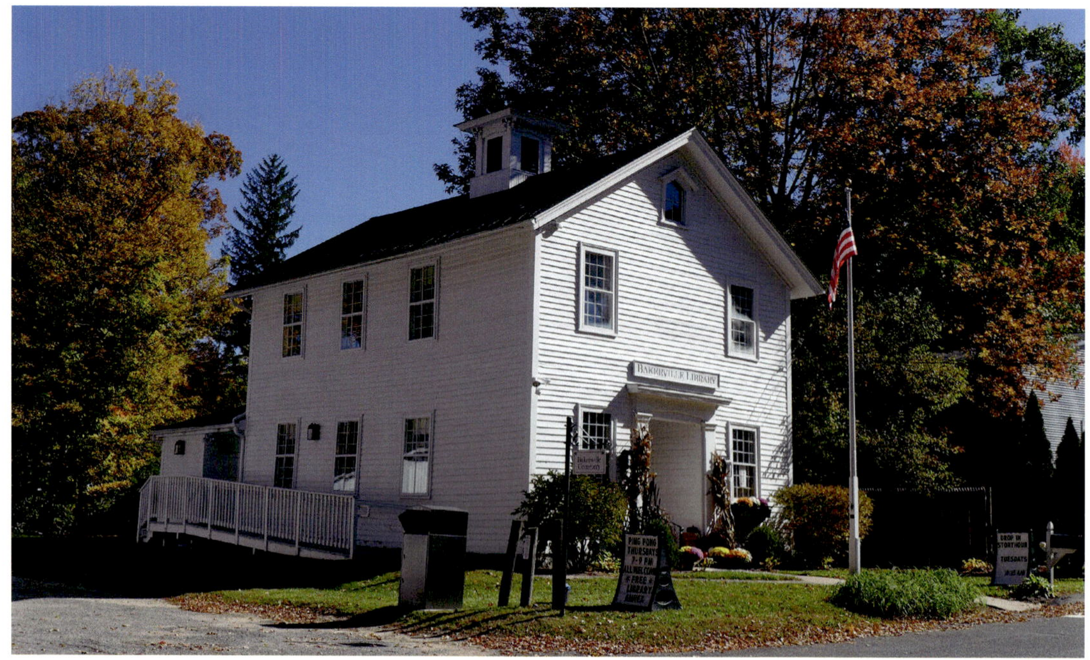

3

TIMES OF CHANGE, 1835-1860

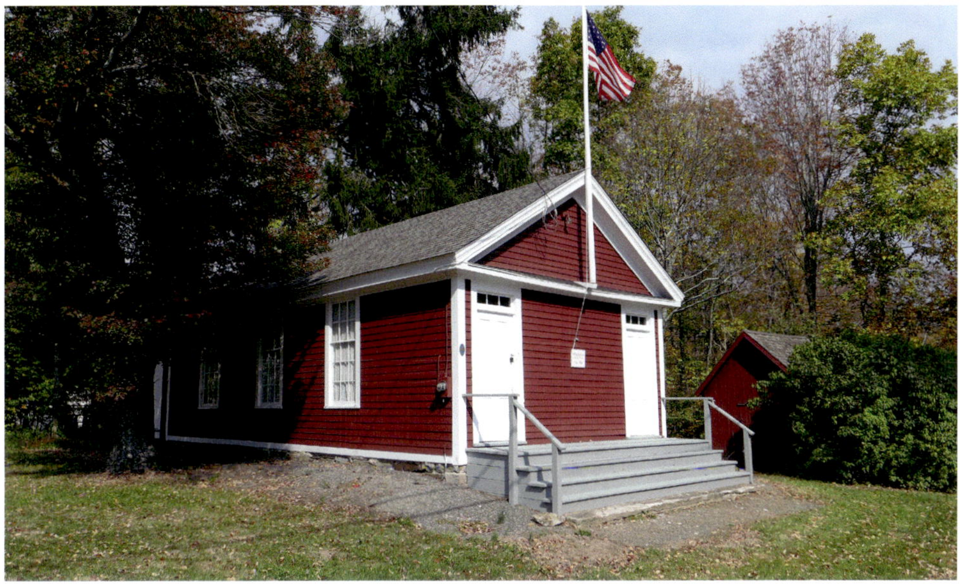

An educator, Henry Barnard, collected information around Connecticut about the condition of schoolhouses and published a scathing report of schoolhouses in the state. He pointed out that many of the schoolhouses were little more than barns, with poor ventilation and lighting. Barnard advocated the use of two entrance doors and individual desks, as well as classroom tools like maps, globes, standardized textbooks, and library books.

Due to the new awareness of schoolhouse conditions, many districts followed Barnard's advice and called out their carpenters to renovate their schools or build new ones.

Millington Green School was built in 1854 across from a triangular town green where the Meeting House once sat. This 10th district schoolhouse of East Haddam replaced an earlier schoolhouse that stood on the opposite side of the green. The school was used until 1936. Concerned citizens restored the schoolhouse in 2005.

As more factories were built in Connecticut, children were needed to help in some of the smaller, dirtier tasks. The families needed the money that the children brought in and there was no time for schooling. Fortunately, Connecticut lawmakers agreed that the child labor force needed to be educated. Many factories built their own factory schools; the children were allowed to leave the factory a few hours a day to work on their studies.

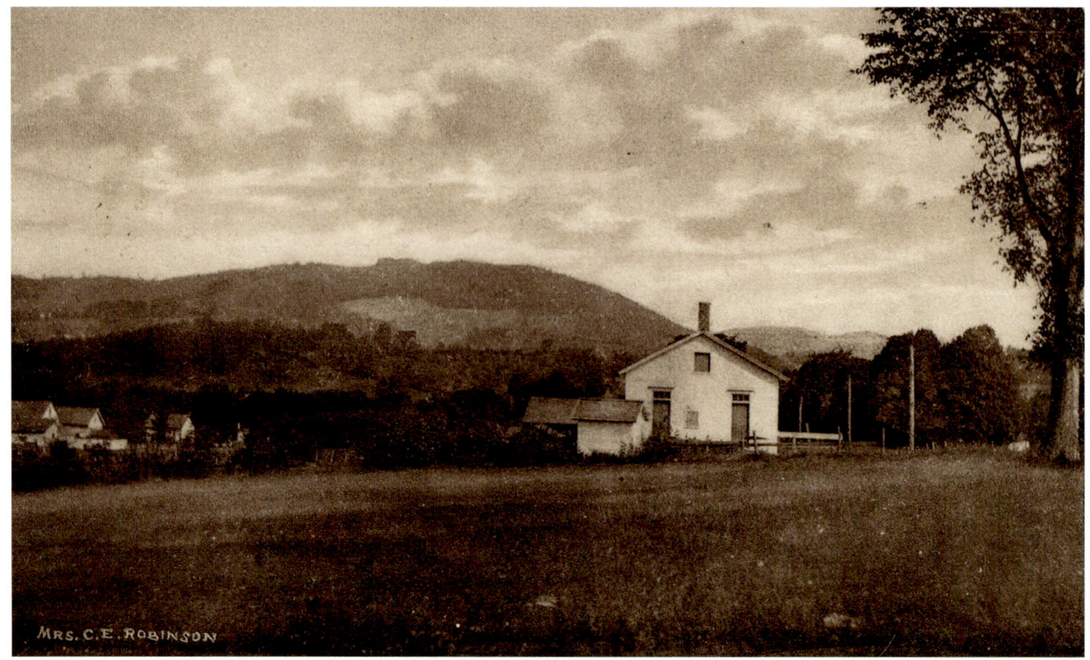

CANAAN: In the area of Falls Village, the first Beebe School stood on a hillside at the edge of town. As with the fate of many schoolhouses, it burned down. The present building was constructed in 1843, with the modern feature of two entrance doors, one for boys and one for girls. The doors lead to separate cloakrooms, "to protect the sensitivities of the girls, especially the older girls" as they removed their outer garments. Each cloakroom had an entrance into the schoolroom. The last day of school in the building was June 1, 1918. It is now set up as a schoolhouse museum, operated by the Canaan Historical Society. (Above photograph courtesy of the Elliott postcard collection)

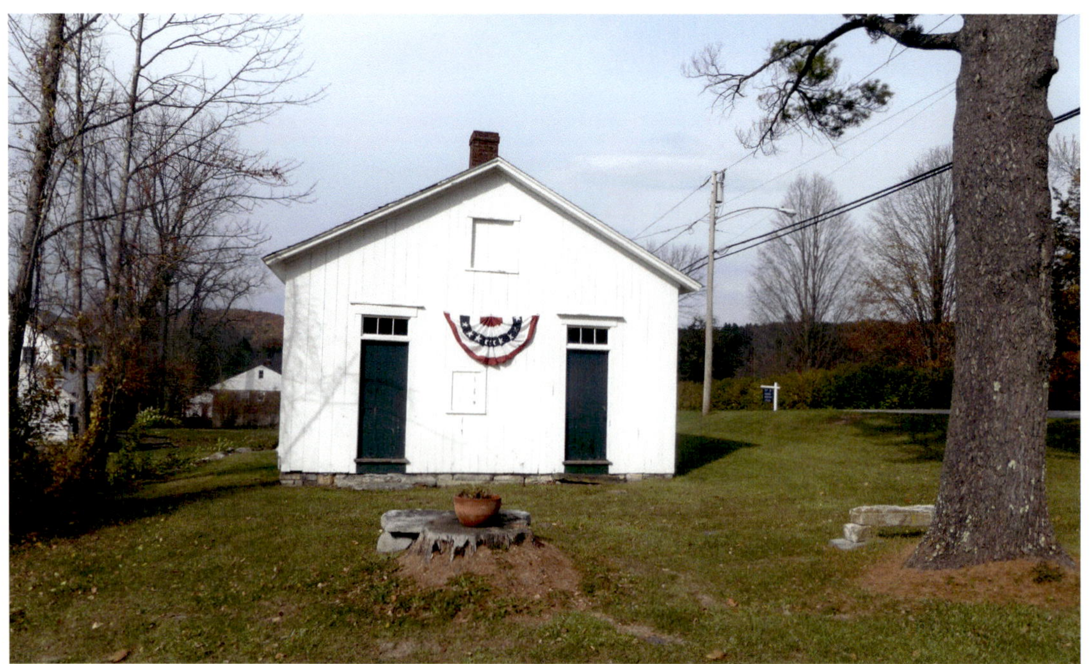

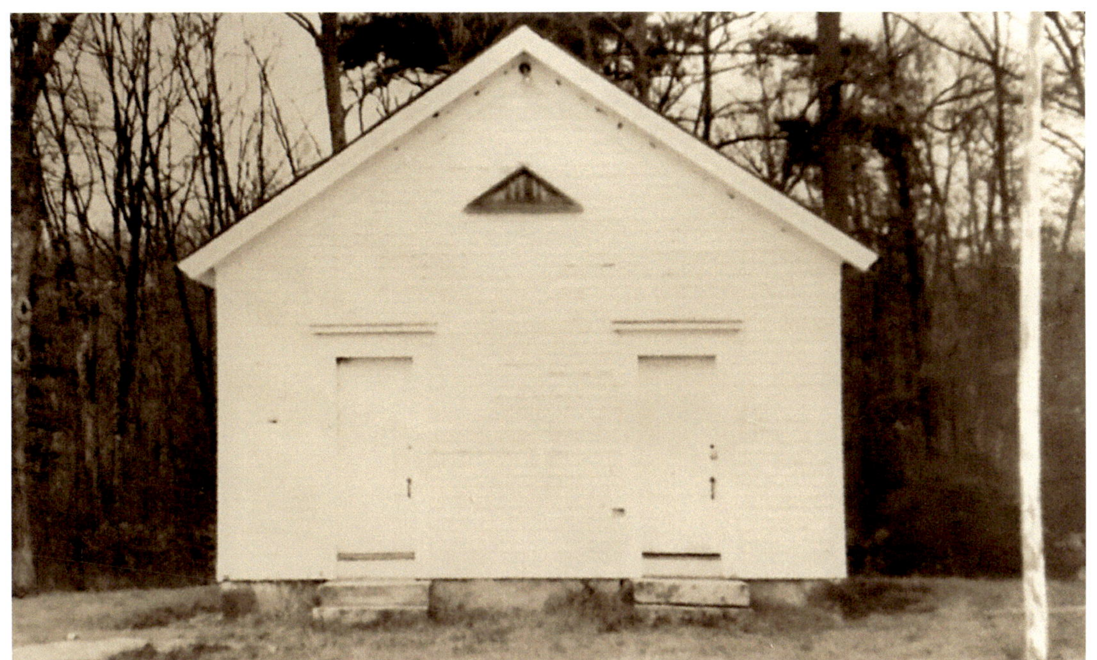

VOLUNTOWN: The Wylie Schoolhouse sits quietly on a triangular quarter-acre piece of land at the intersection of two roads, where it has been since it was built in 1858. Henry Wylie provided the land as long it was used for a school. Even though local consolidation of schools began in 1890, the Wylie School continued as the only town schoolhouse still in use until 1939. Teacher Miss Margaret Tanner taught at the school from 1909 until the school closed. The land was returned to the Wylie family, but in 1970, the school and land were donated to the Voluntown Historical Society. The name of the school, Wylie, is written on a tablet over the door. (Above photograph courtesy of Voluntown Historical Society)

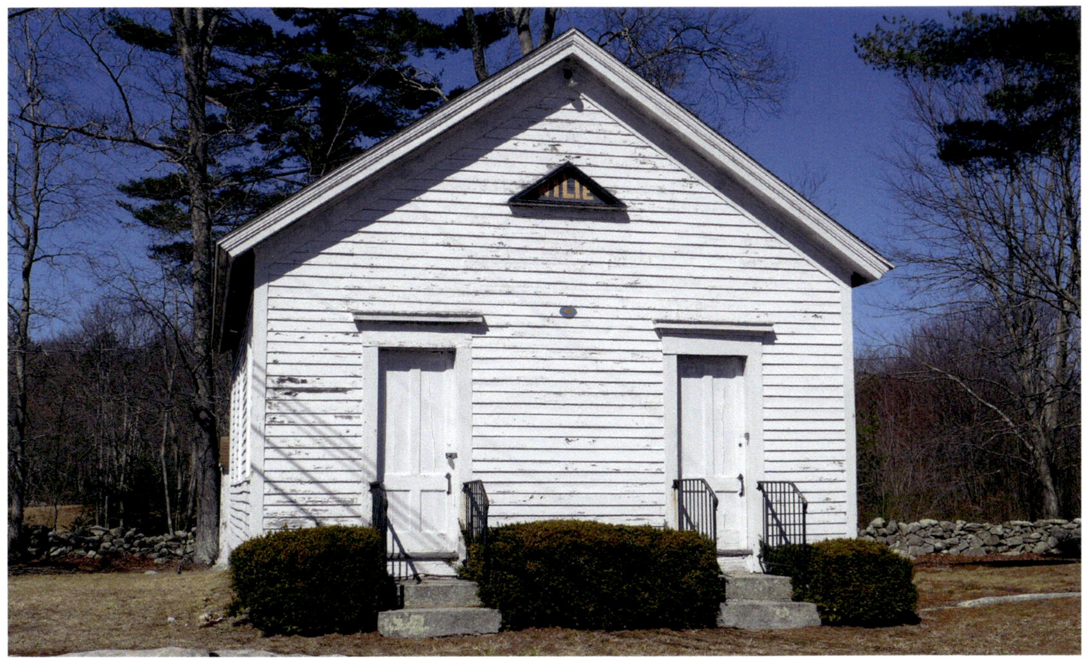

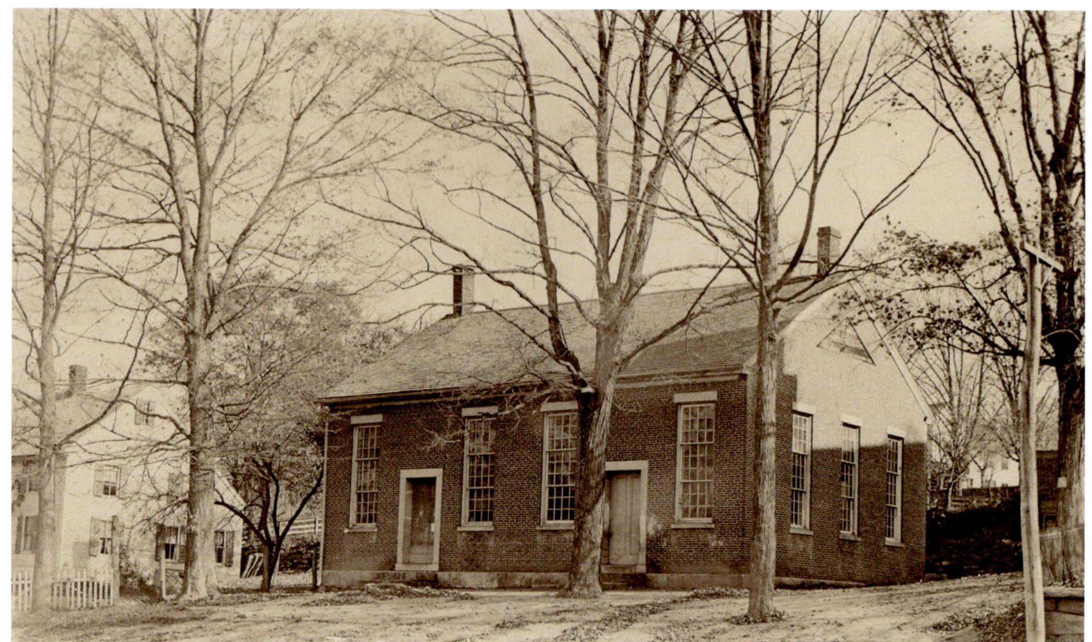

EAST HAMPTON: Known as the Northwest District Schoolhouse, and also as the Middle Haddam School, this unusual building was constructed of brick around 1840. The school builders in Connecticut were becoming aware of the need to have plenty of ventilation and light for the students. The schoolhouse has exceptionally high west-facing windows that let in plenty of sunlight. The two chimneys suggest that this was not made as a one-room school, but as a two-room schoolhouse. This school closed when the new Consolidated School was built nearby and named the Middle Haddam School. The Episcopal Church acquired the old school in 1940 for their Parish Hall and it is still in use. (Above photograph from the Elliott Postcard Collection)

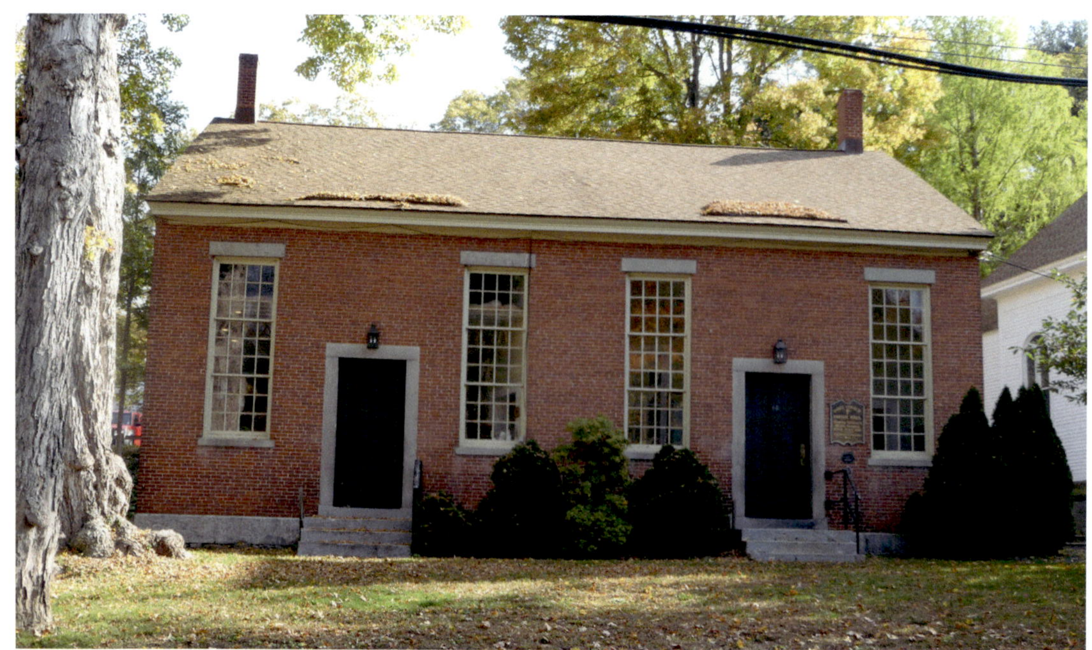

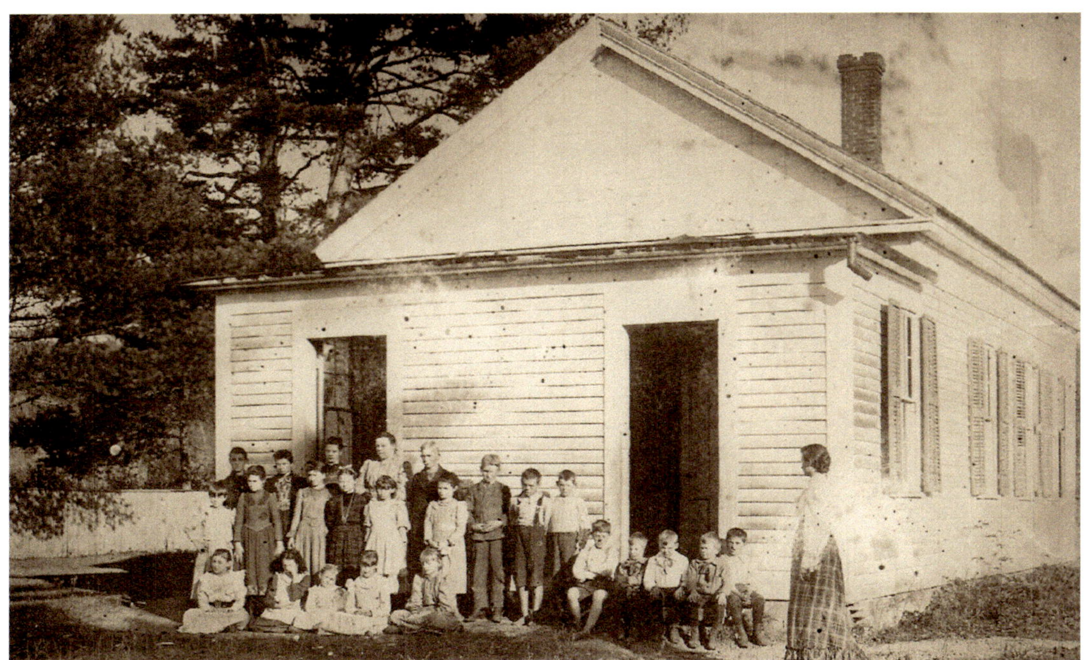

South Windsor: The District 5 Schoolhouse was built in 1862, across the street from a previous school from 1837. The two doors allowed the girls to enter on the left and the boys on the right. The building was used as a school until 1952, when all the students were moved to the Wapping School. Previous attempts to close the school in the 1920s were stopped by the parents because everyone loved the teacher, Mrs. Ernestine Sullivan. In 1952, she was transferred to the Wapping School along with her students. The South Windsor Historical Society owns the old schoolhouse and has turned it into a museum. (Above photograph courtesy of South Windsor Historical Society)

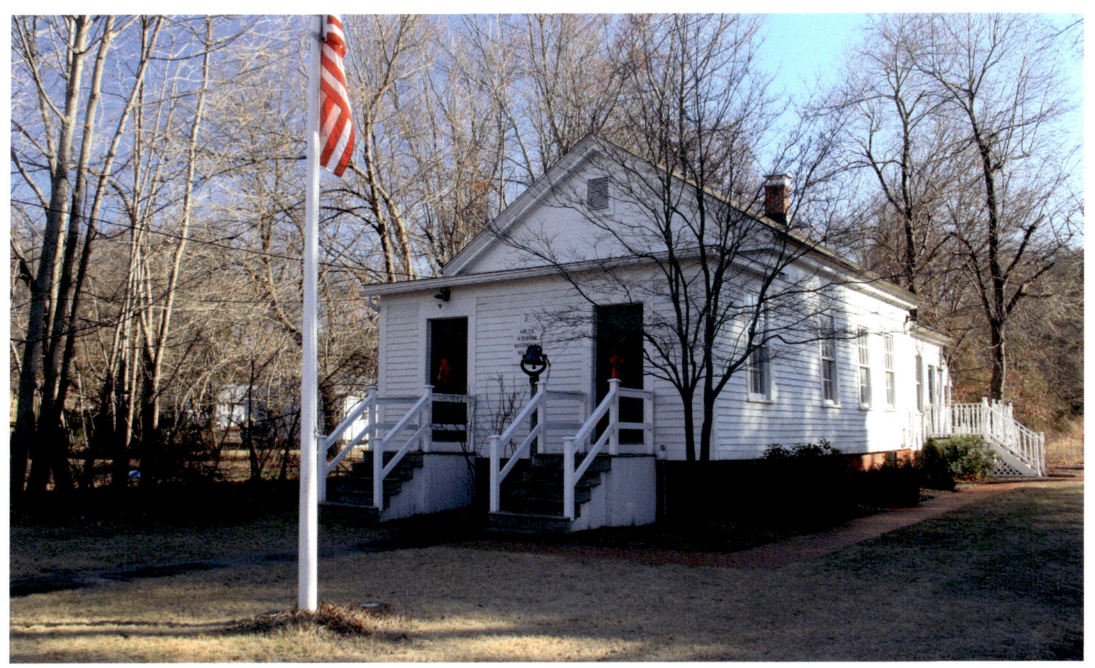

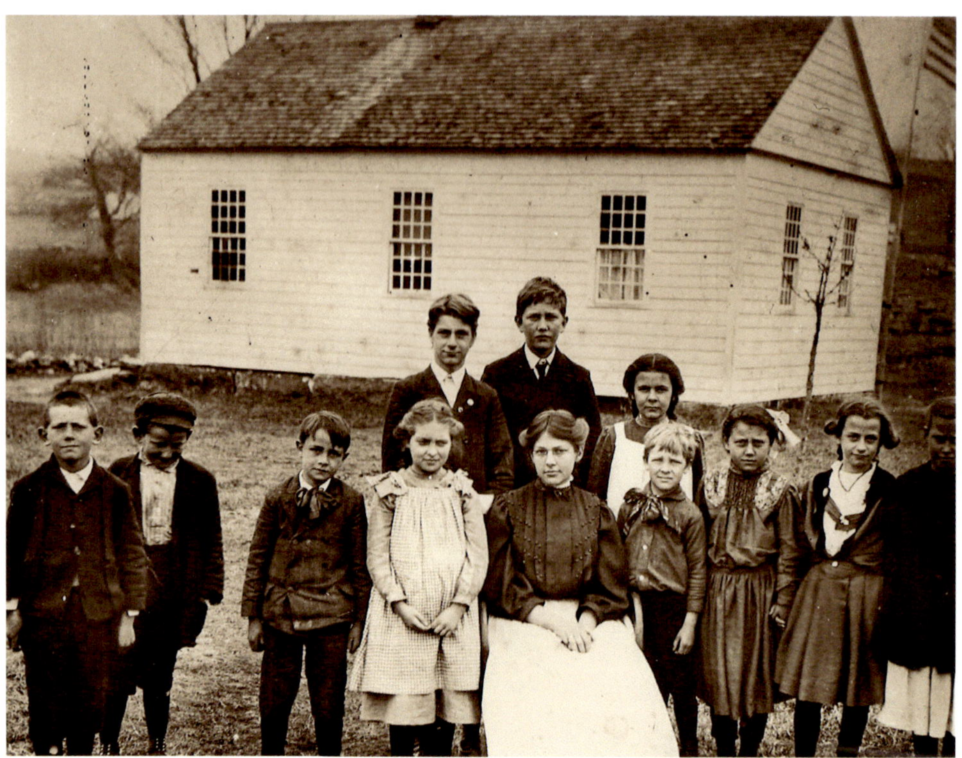

HARWINTON: The First District School, also known as the Center School, was built in 1840, and was originally located at bottom of Center Hill, along the Lead Mine Brook. The school was closed in 1948 when the Consolidated School was opened and all of the one-room schoolhouses were closed. The Lion's Club of Harwinton moved the old schoolhouse onto the property of the Consolidated School in 1972, where it sits on a hillside near the driveway entrance that every student passes daily. Harwinton Historical Society restored the building in 1973, using the original teacher's desk as part of the furnishings. (Above photograph Courtesy CT State Library, State Archives, LS Mills Collection)

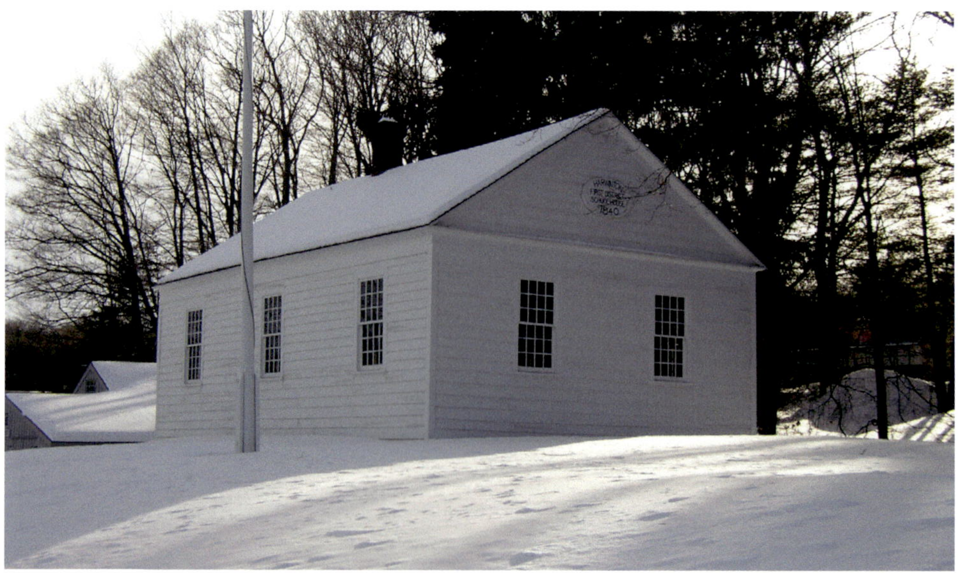

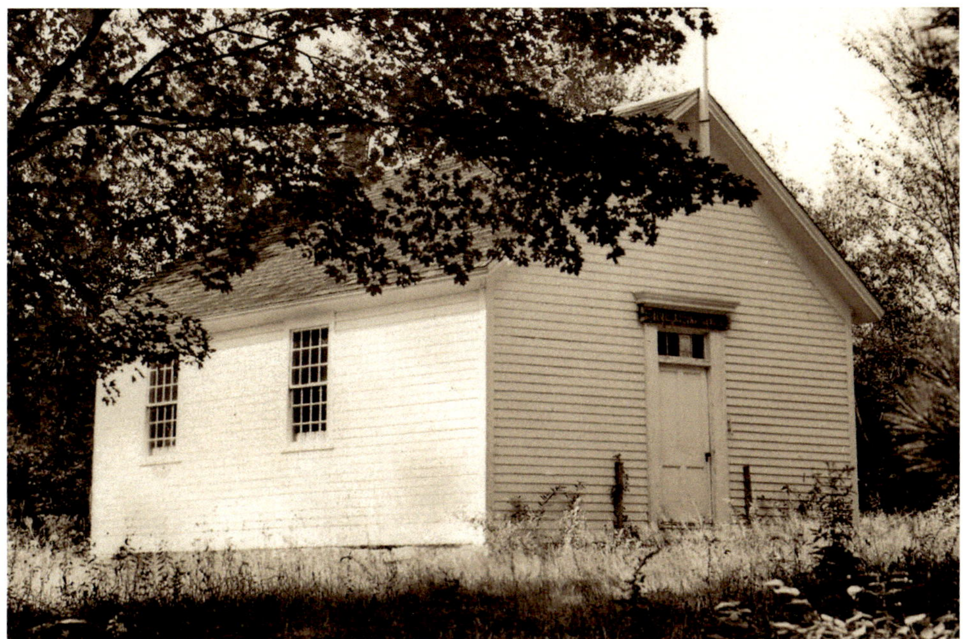

KILLINGWORTH: The Pine Orchard Schoolhouse was built in 1853, replacing an earlier school. The school district was formerly called Nettletown. It was used until 1944 when it was combined with the Lane School. All of the town schoolhouses were sold in 1949 as the students were moved to a consolidated school. The Pine Orchard School was moved in 1950 and converted into a residence in 1970. In 2010, the old schoolhouse was offered to the historical society, as long as it was moved from its location. The school was dismantled and moved to town-owned Parmalee Farm, where it was reassembled. The building is being restored by the historical society. (Above photograph courtesy of Killingworth Historical Society)

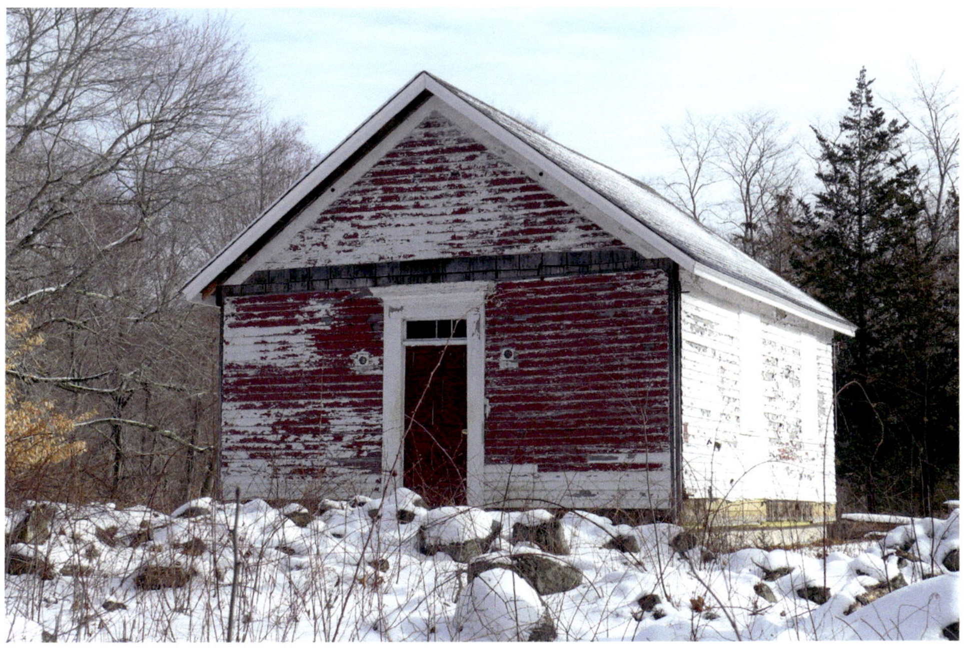

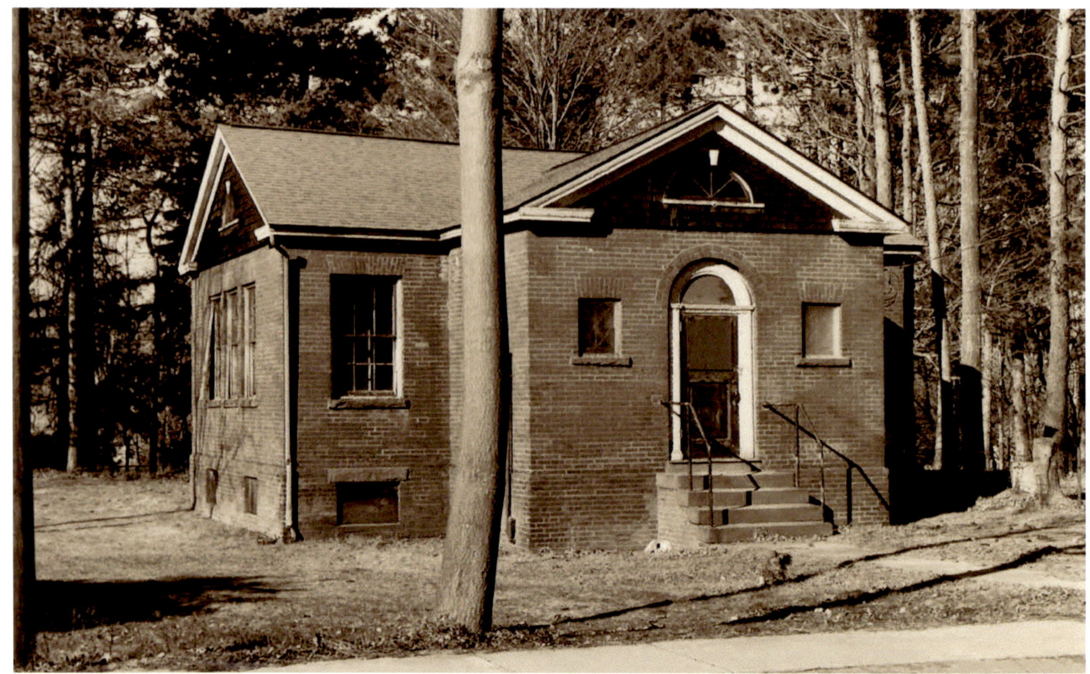

WINDSOR: The Stony Hill School, which was the Second District School, was built of brick around 1856. It was moved across the road in 1899 and rebuilt into the colonial revival style, a style that was made popular with architects due to the 1893 World's Columbian Exposition, where it was featured. The school was closed in 1969, because the road became dangerously busy for the children when it was widened to four lanes. The Friends of Stony Hill School restored the schoolhouse as a historic site in the 1990s, with their first open house event in October 1998. (Above photograph courtesy of the Elliott Postcard Collection)

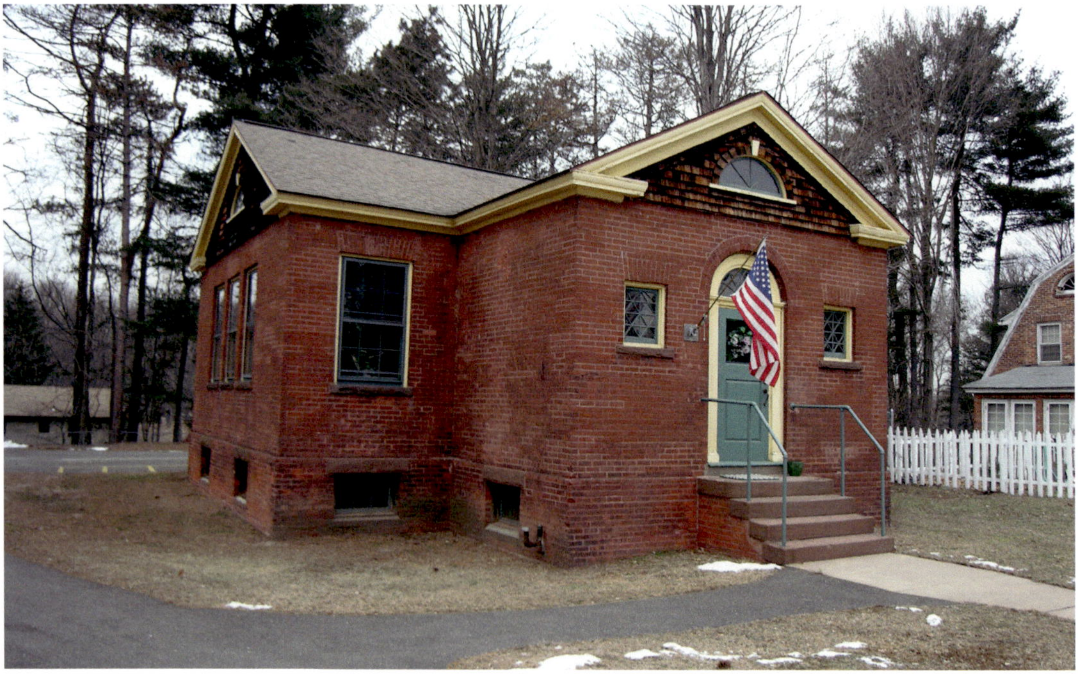

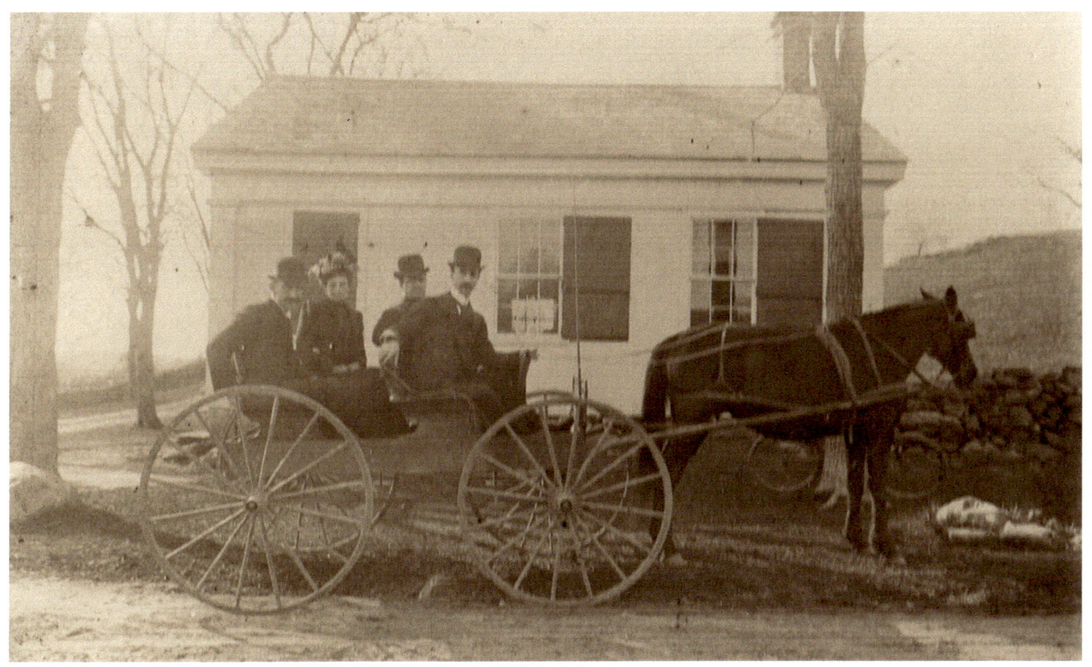

WATERTOWN: The Nova Scotia School House was built in 1853, at a busy intersection. The school was closed at the end of the school year in 1929. It was sold and used as a home and later as various businesses. During the 1970s, the decision was made to save the building and to revert it back to a schoolhouse condition. The building was disassembled and moved to the center of town. Reconstructing the building to a mid-19th century building included the Lions Club Old Fellows, the UNICO Club, and the Watertown Historical Society. The building was opened in May 1993, as a museum operated by the Watertown Historical Society. (Above photograph courtesy of Watertown Historical Society)

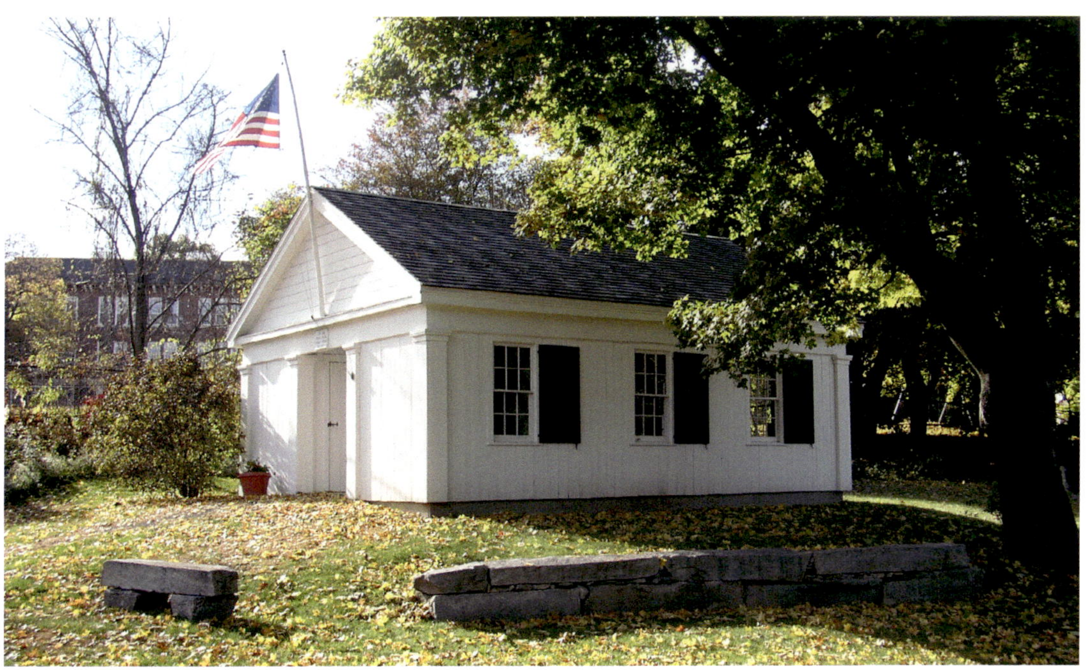

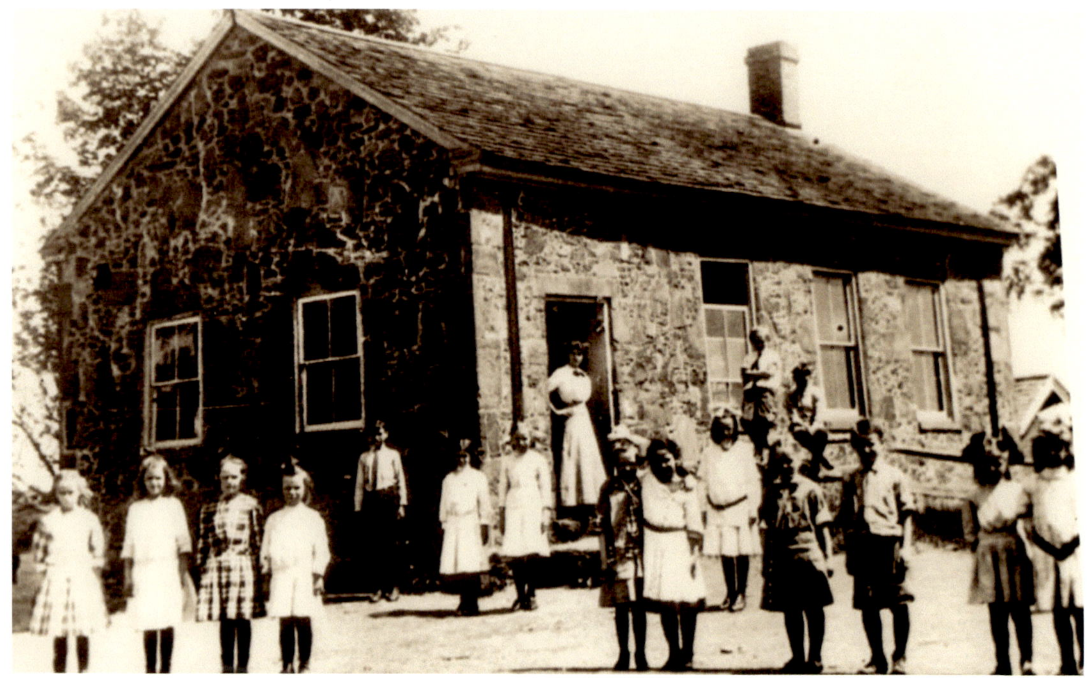

BLOOMFIELD: The Southwest District School was built in 1858 to replace an older building that had burned the year before. It is made from trap rock that was quarried on Talcott Mountain, about a mile away from the school. The budget was limited, but a flourishing local farmer supervised the labor of the town's poor who built the schoolhouse at the final building cost of $288.15. The district school was used until 1923, and then became a library. In 1950, repairs were made by the Wintonbury Historical Society, preserving all the details of the original building. (Above photograph courtesy of Wintonbury Historical Society)

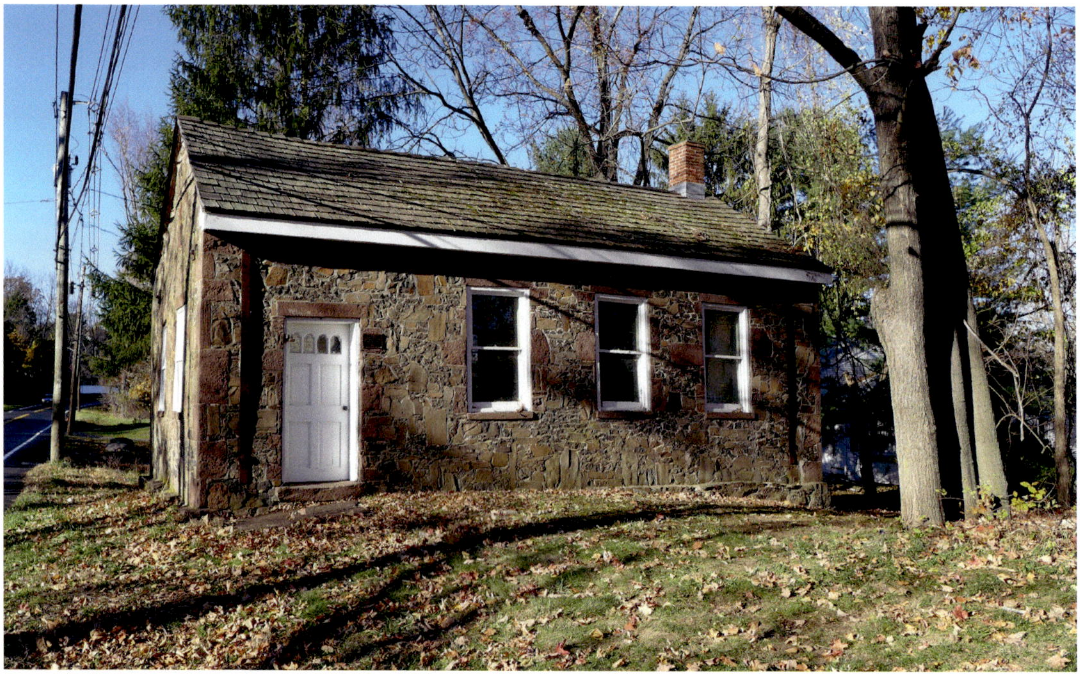

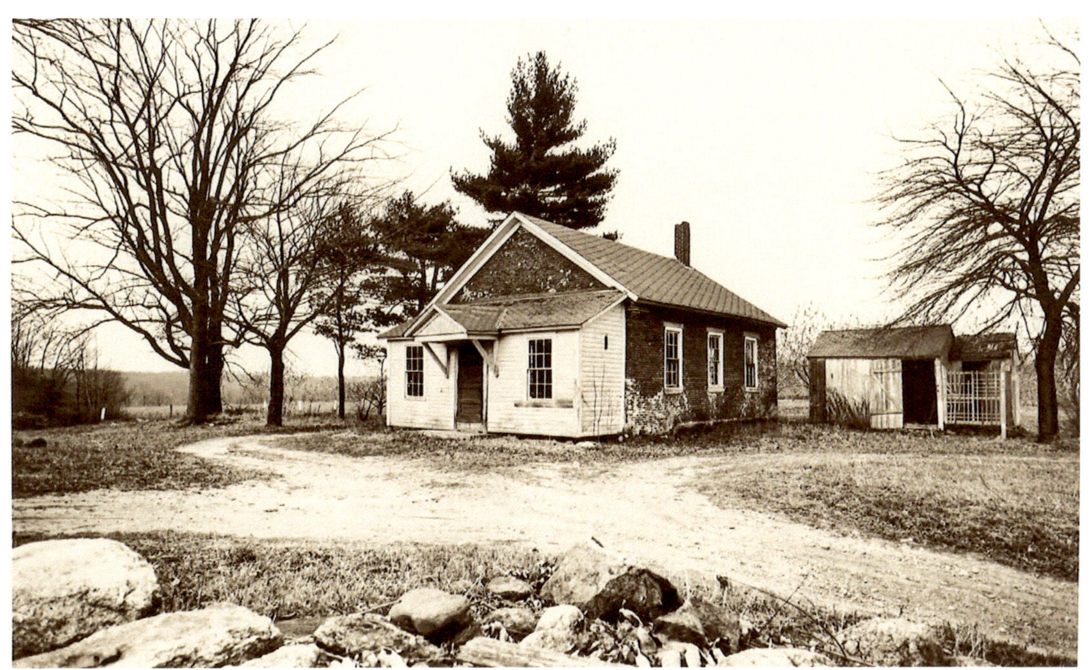

WOODSTOCK: The Quassett School District was organized as early as 1738. The brick school was built in 1854 and used until 1944. Lewis Sprague Mills, who once taught at the schoolhouse, started a fund drive to save the schoolhouse. Hundreds of children saved their pennies to contribute to this purpose. The above photograph was the last photograph of the schoolhouse taken at its original location. Each brick of the Old Quassett Schoolhouse was numbered and removed by hand so it could be put back together in the proper order. In 1953, the school was opened again on the grounds of the new Quassett Elementary School as a living museum. (Above photograph Courtesy CT State Library, State Archives, LS Mills Collection)

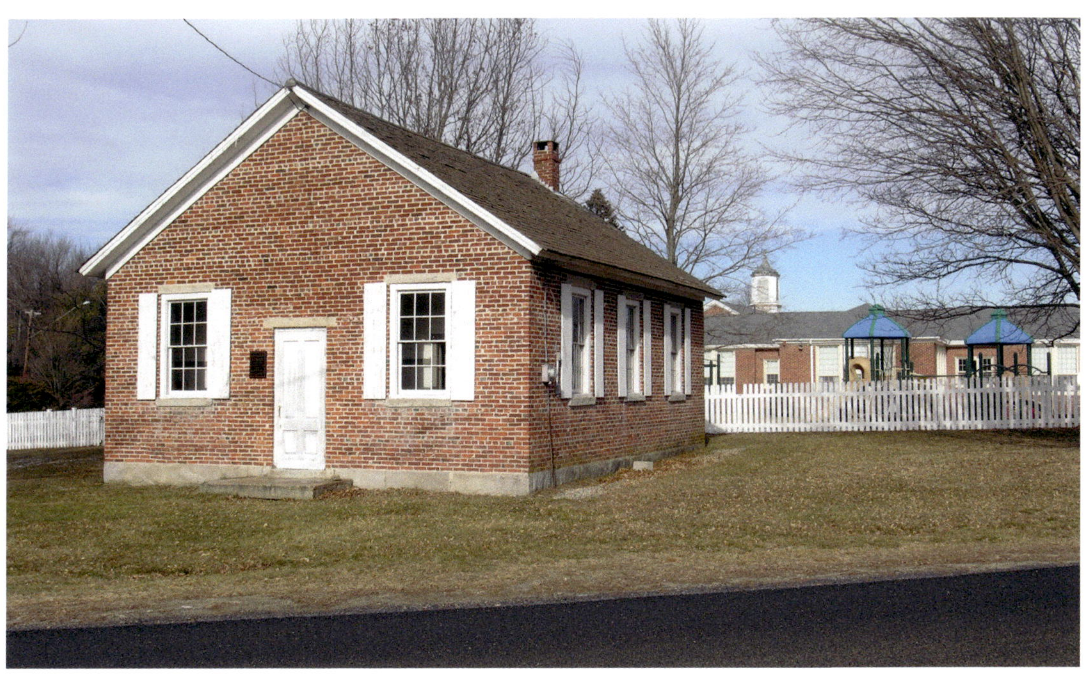

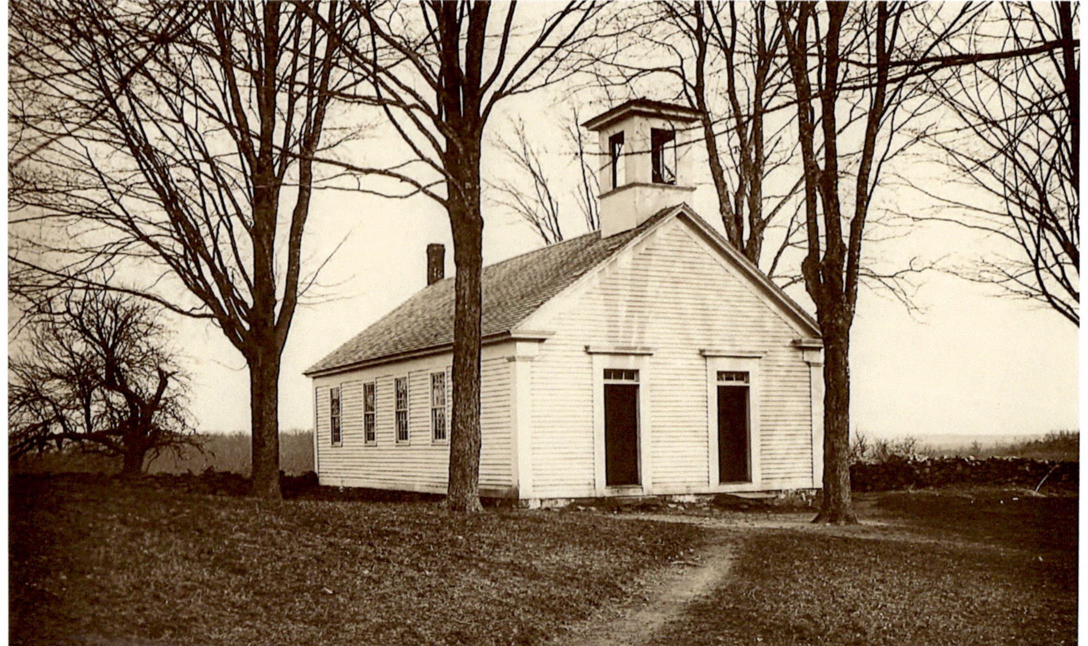

CANTERBURY: The Centre District Schoolhouse, or the Green School, has sat on the Canterbury Green since 1850, possibly earlier. The consolidation of the schools was in 1947 when the Dr. Helen Baldwin School was completed. The schoolhouse was used as the town library until 2001. The Canterbury Historical Society began restoration of the building to return it to an interpretation of an early 20th century district school. Behind the old library shelves, they found the school blackboards that had been hidden for over 50 years. The original bell is still working in the belfry. (Above photograph Courtesy CT State Library, State Archives, LS Mills Collection)

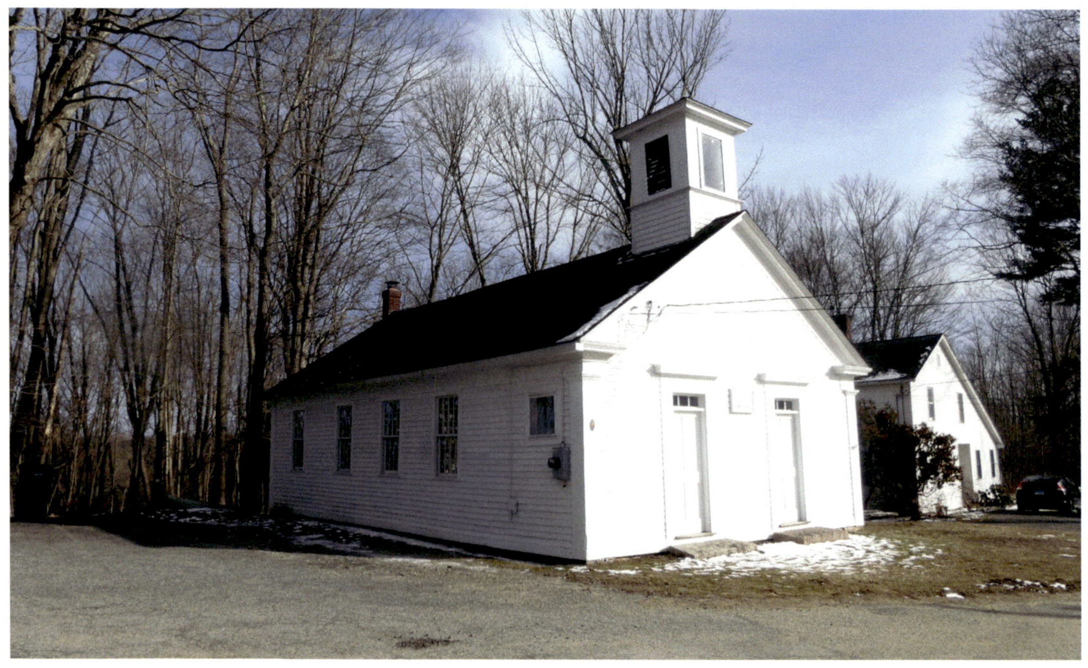

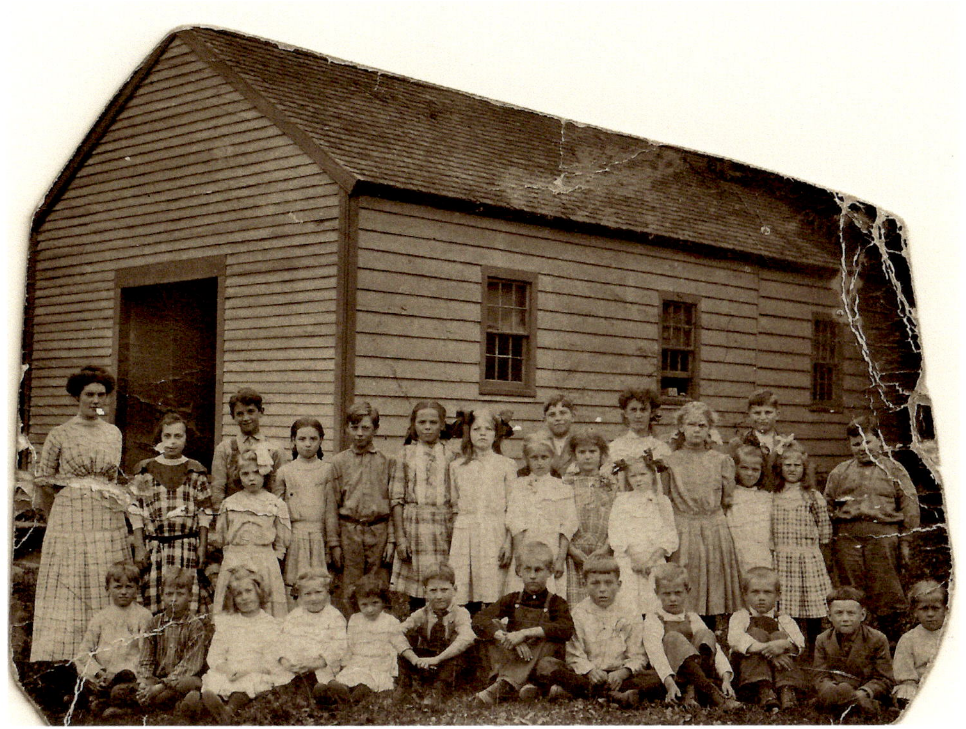

NEW MILFORD: Starting as the Hill District School, classes began in the building in 1843. As the population changed in the mid-1800s, a nearby school in the Pinchgut Plain district was closed and the districts combined into the Hill and Plain District School. The room was heated by a potbelly stove, with wood in the summer and fall, and with coal in the winter. During recess, the children would play across the street in a large field or slide down the huge rock formation behind the schoolhouse. The school closed in 1940. Ruth M. Sullivan donated the Hill and Plain Schoolhouse to the New Milford Historical Society in 1985. (Above photograph courtesy of New Milford Historical Society)

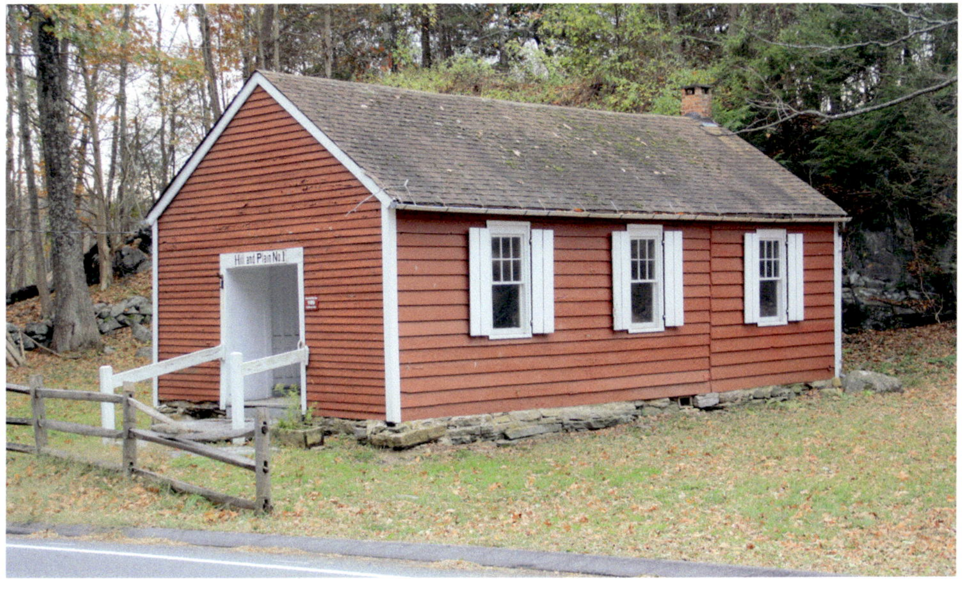

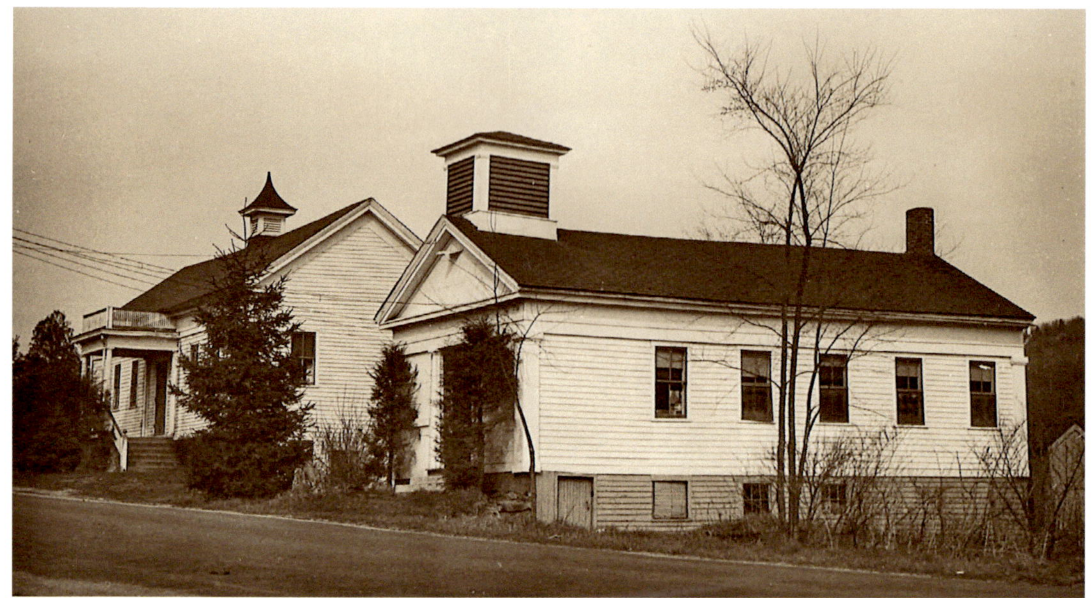

CANTON: South Center School was in built in 1848 as one of the nine Canton school districts. Not only was it used for school, but for prayer meetings, and a popular singing school met there. The school underwent major renovations in 1880, when the building was expanded by 12 feet in length. The school closed in 1941 and the ownership was passed to the First Congregational Church, which sits directly across the street. The Cherry Brook Library was located in the building for 50 years, until 1999. The old school still has its original columns in the front, and a large brass bell in the cupola. (Above photograph Courtesy CT State Library, State Archives, LS Mills Collection)

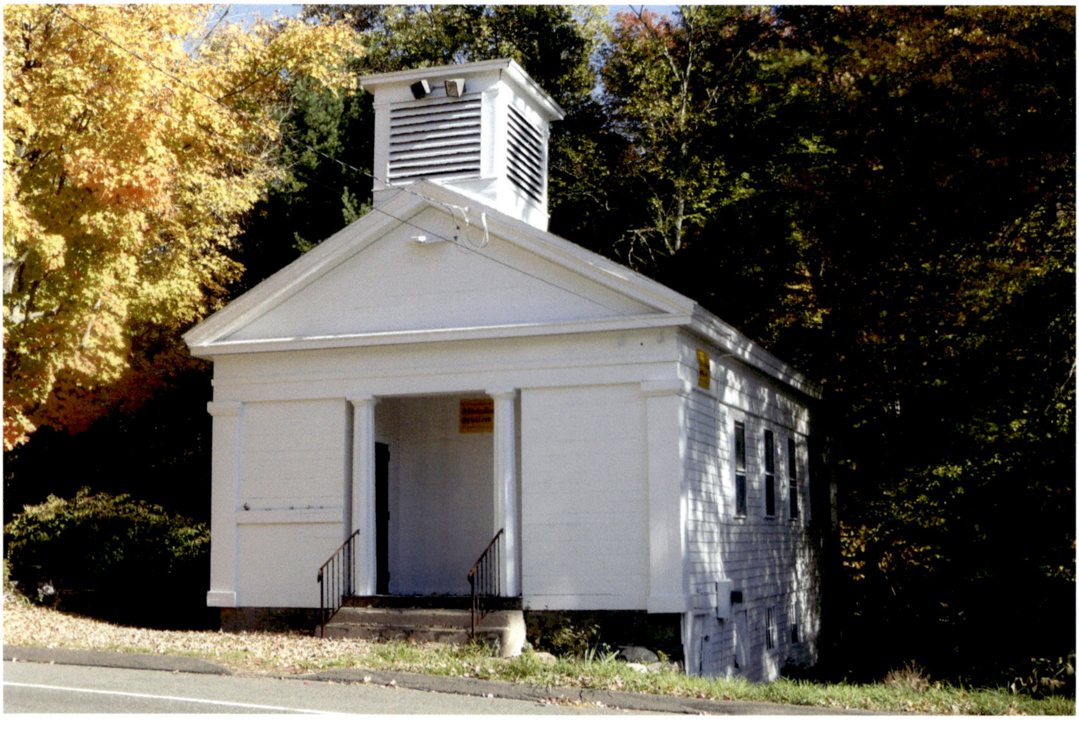

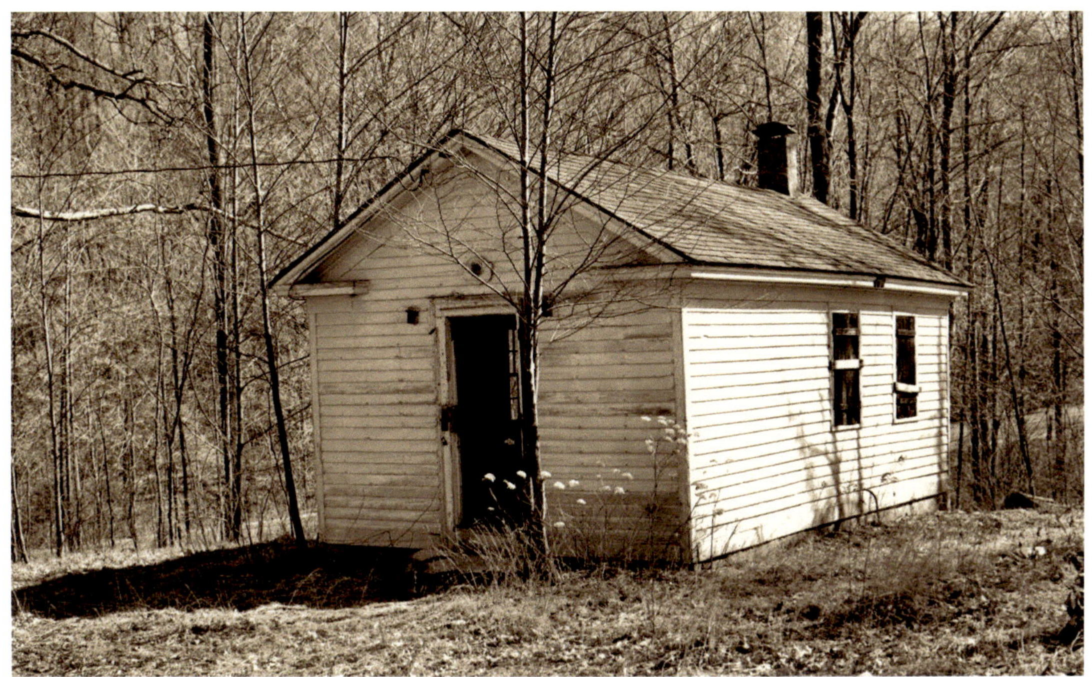

KILLINGWORTH: The Black Rock Schoolhouse was built around 1860, as one of the eight district schools in town. These districts were: Center, Southwest, Chestnut Hill, Union, Land, Nettleton (later Pine Orchard), Stone House, and the Black Rock districts. The Black Rock Schoolhouse was used until 1949. This small schoolhouse was moved from its original location to town property and restored. This is one of the three old district schoolhouses owned by the town of Killingworth, where five more former schoolhouses still exist as a part of a residence or business. (Above photograph courtesy of Killingworth Historical Society)

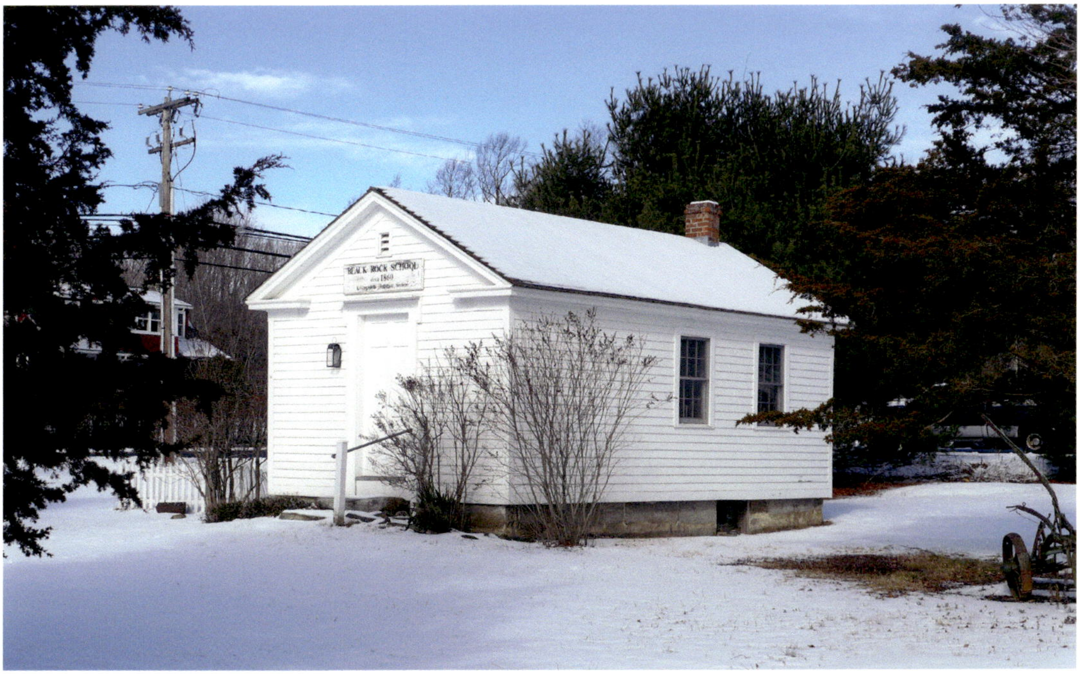

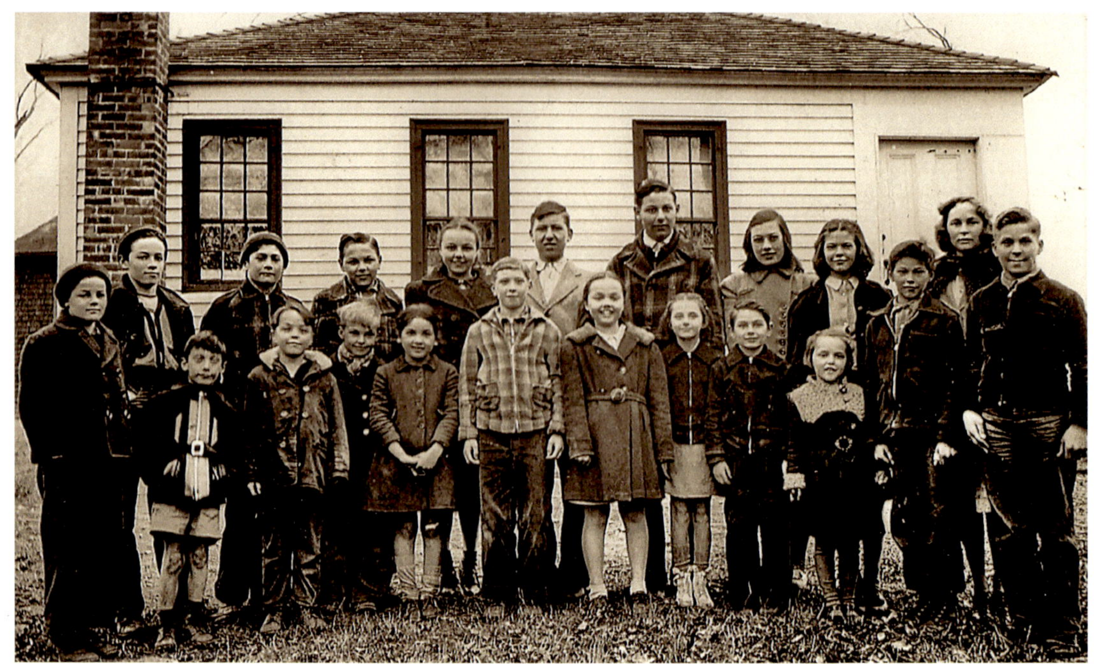

LEDYARD: The Meeting House Hill School was the 5th District School in Ledyard, built around 1857 near the town Meeting House. The school was closed in 1949 when the Ledyard Consolidated School (later to be called the Ledyard Center School) opened and signaled the end of the one-room schoolhouses in town. The building was used for meetings and later as a post office. It was saved from a practice fire by the local fire department and moved from its original position near the Meeting House twice. It is currently located at the edge of the fairground. School children and local businesses raised the money to restore the building as a schoolhouse. (Above photograph courtesy of Ledyard Historical Society, Inc., Ledyard, CT)

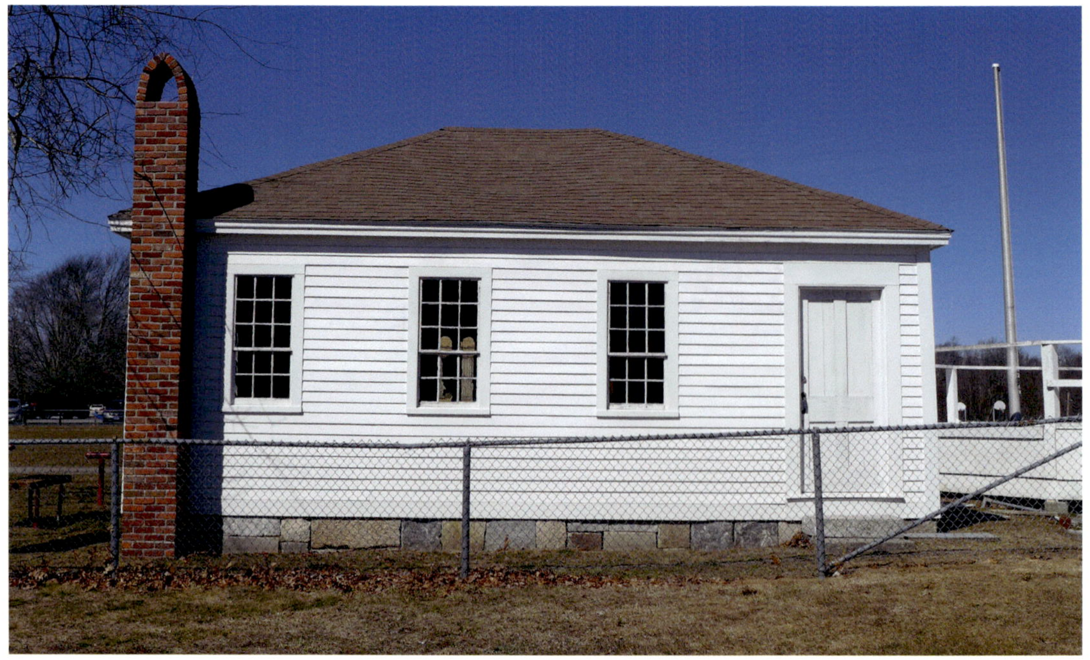

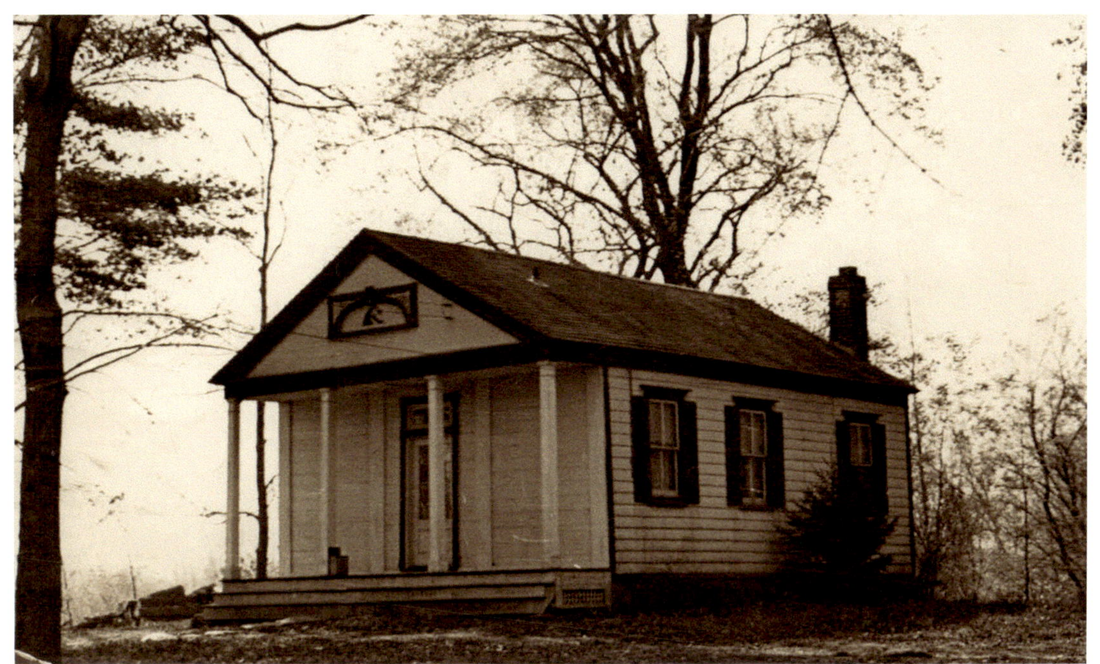

WESTPORT: The building called Westport Academy was a place of education in Westport for over 80 years, run by various organizations and then by the local school district. Westport Academy was the first school to use this schoolhouse, beginning in 1837. Ebenezer Adams ran the school for 30 years. The Greens Farms Academy stepped in immediately and children were taught there from 1867 to 1882. Next came the West Long Lots School, which was open from 1883 until 1898. The Greens Farms School District took over in fall of 1898 and was in operation until the consolidation of schools in Westport. (Above photograph courtesy of WPA Architectural Survey of CT State Library Digital Collections)

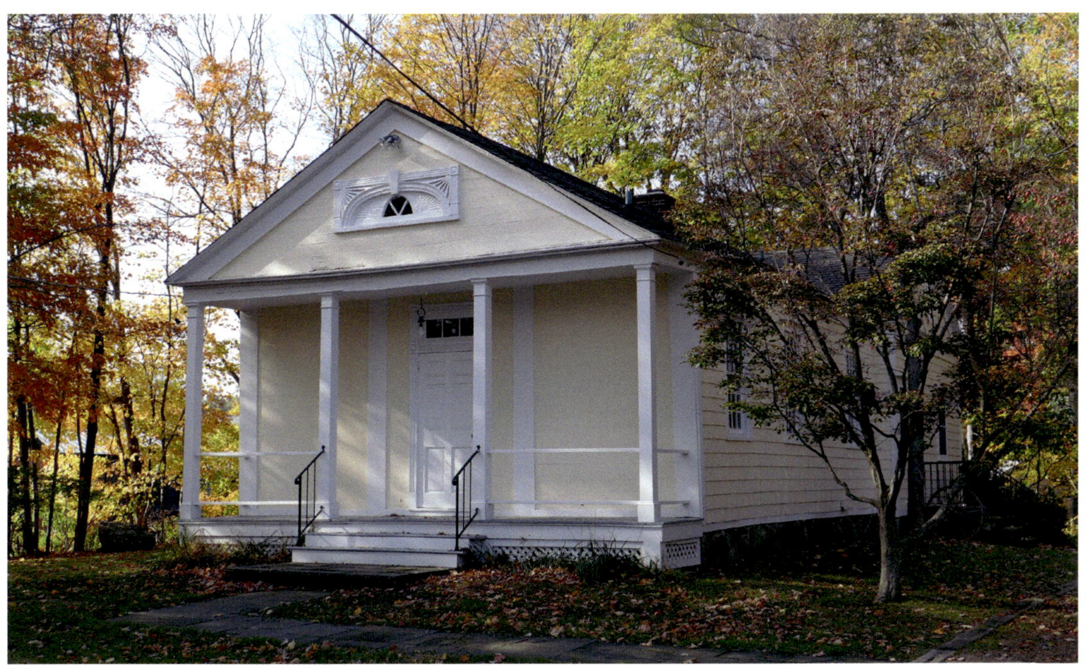

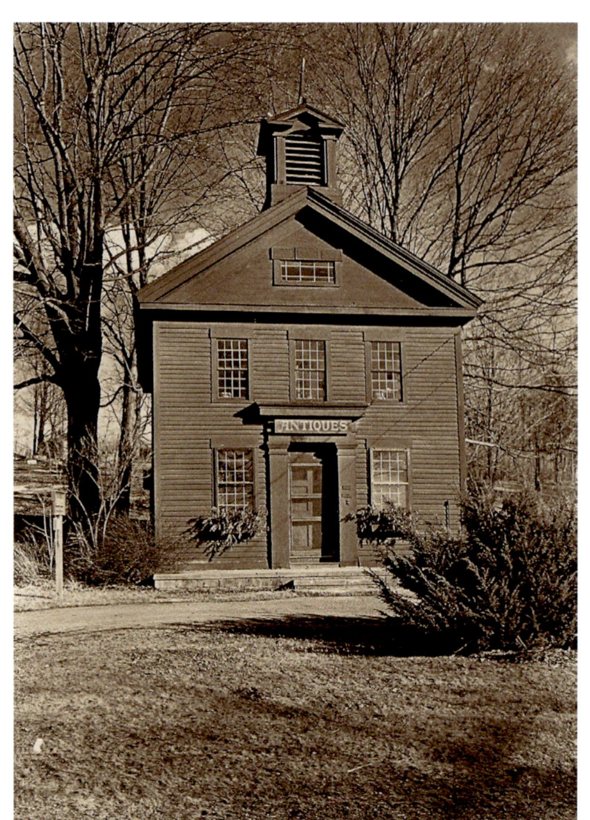

SOUTHBURY: The White Oak District School, a two-story schoolhouse, was built in 1840. While the main floor was used as a school, the upper floor was used for community events until the 1920s when it was needed for a schoolroom. The school was closed in 1941, when the children were on their Christmas break. On January 5, 1942, all the town's students attended the Consolidated School for the very first time. The building was sold and used as an antique shop for many years, and has now been repainted and standing idle under private ownership. (Above photograph courtesy of Southbury Historical Society)

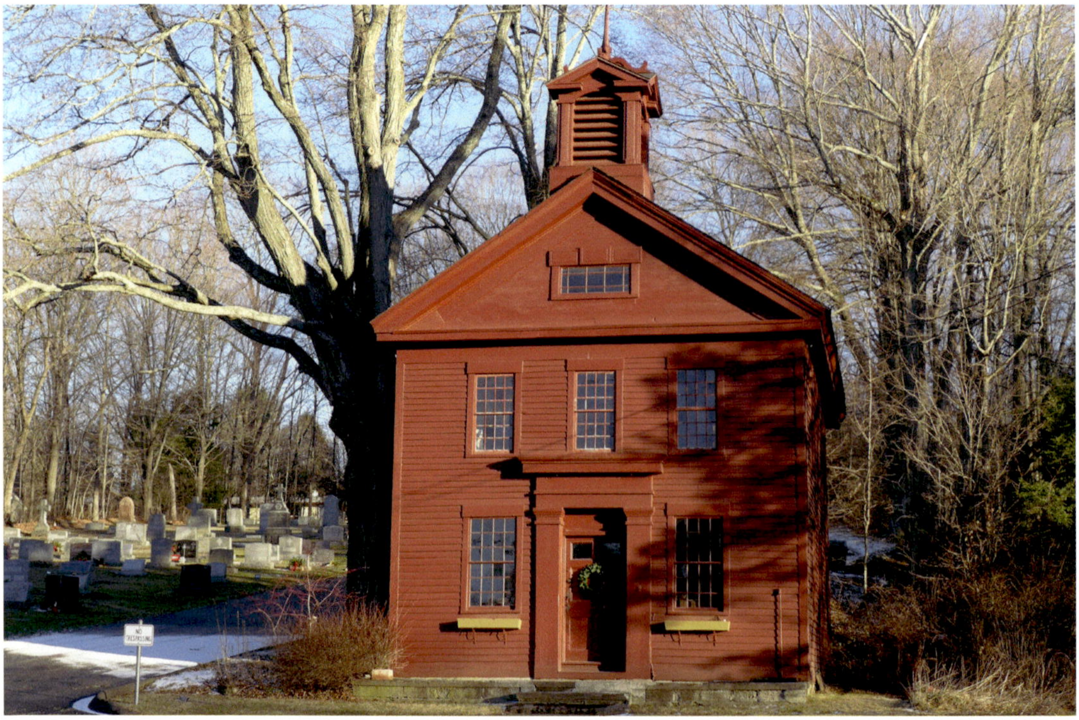

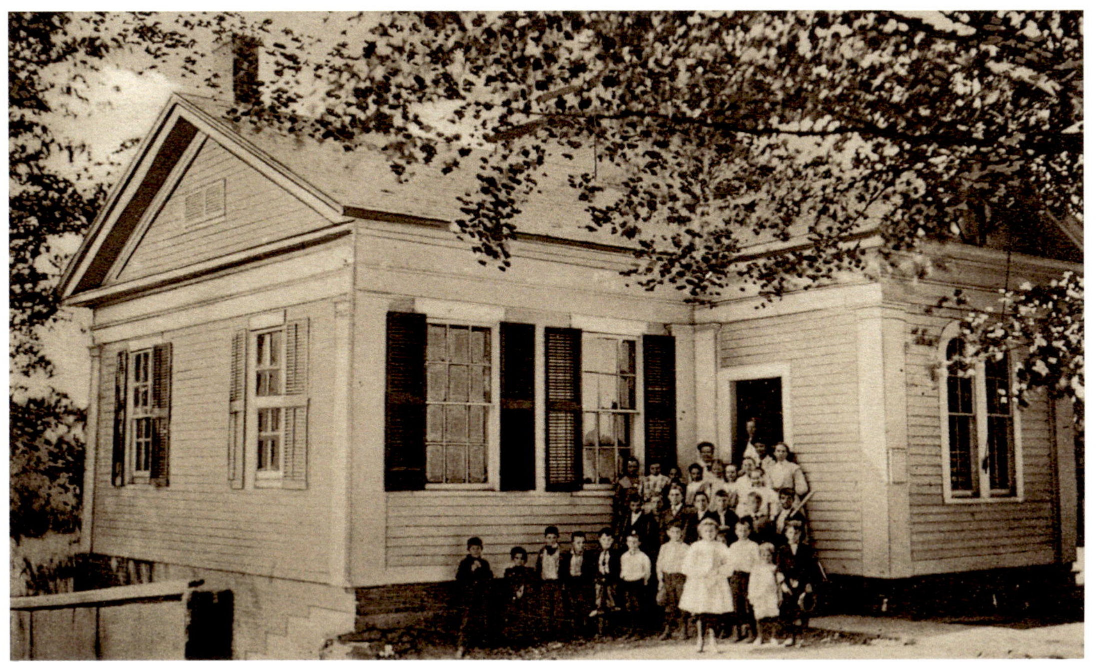

EAST HADDAM: The 2nd District Schoolhouse was built in 1854 in the Greek-Revival style, one of the seventeen one-room schools from the 19th century. The school was also known as the Village School, and the Landing Schoolhouse. The old school sat along the main road through town on one side with a gentle slope to the Connecticut River on the other. The building was used until all of the town's students were sent to the new graded Nathan Hale Ray School in the early 1920s. The 2nd District Schoolhouse has been meticulously restored, keeping the original character intact. The building is currently the private residence of the former Connecticut State Senator Chris Dodd. (Above photograph courtesy of the Elliott Postcard Collection)

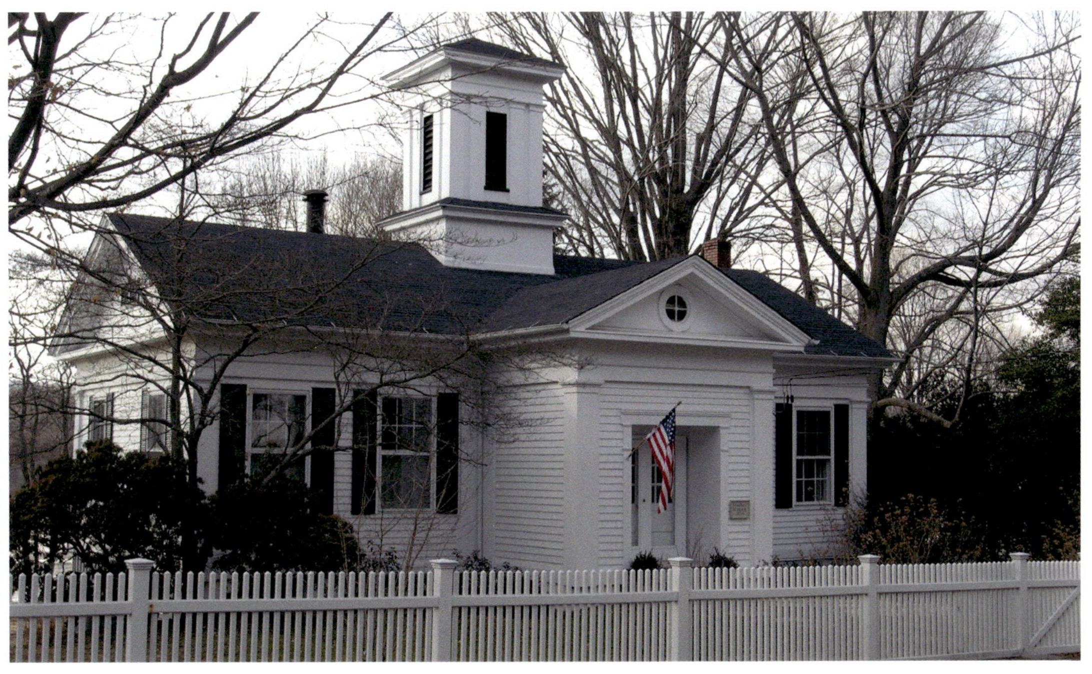

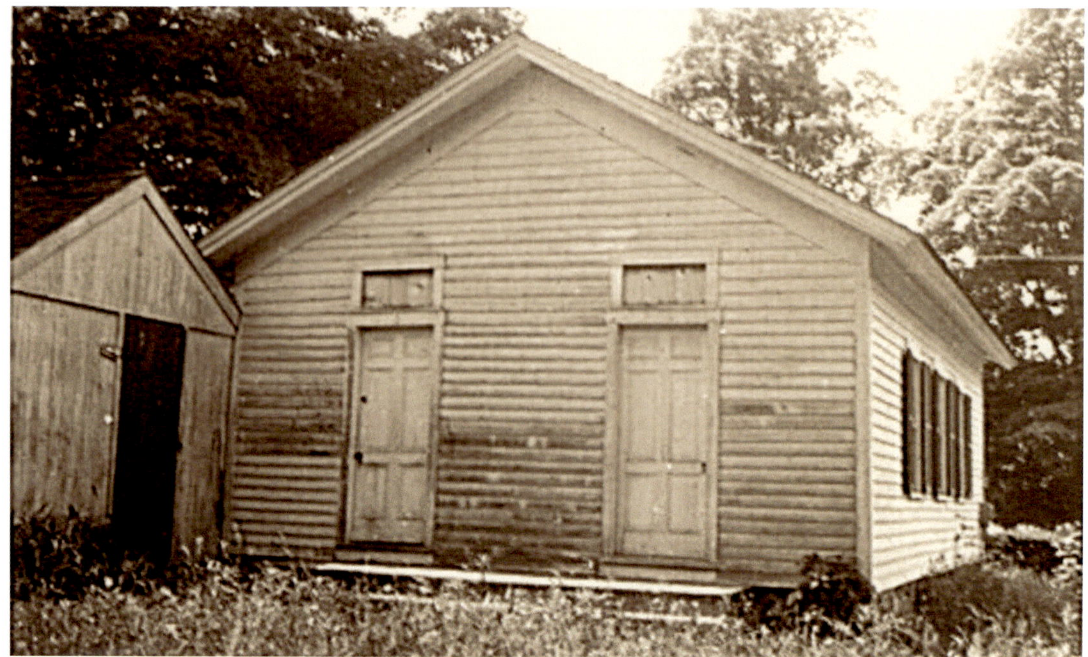

NEW FAIRFIELD: The exact date when the West Centre Schoolhouse was built is unknown, but it was likely built around 1860. The school was used until the consolidated school opened its doors on January 13, 1941. Of the seven original schoolhouses in town, the West Centre School is the only surviving school building that was not sold, and still belongs to the Board of Education. In 1970, the New Fairfield Historical Society was given permission to restore and maintain the building, to be used as a museum. Now known as the Little Red Schoolhouse, children from the local schools visit to see what school was like in the old days. (Above photograph courtesy of the New Fairfield Historical Society)

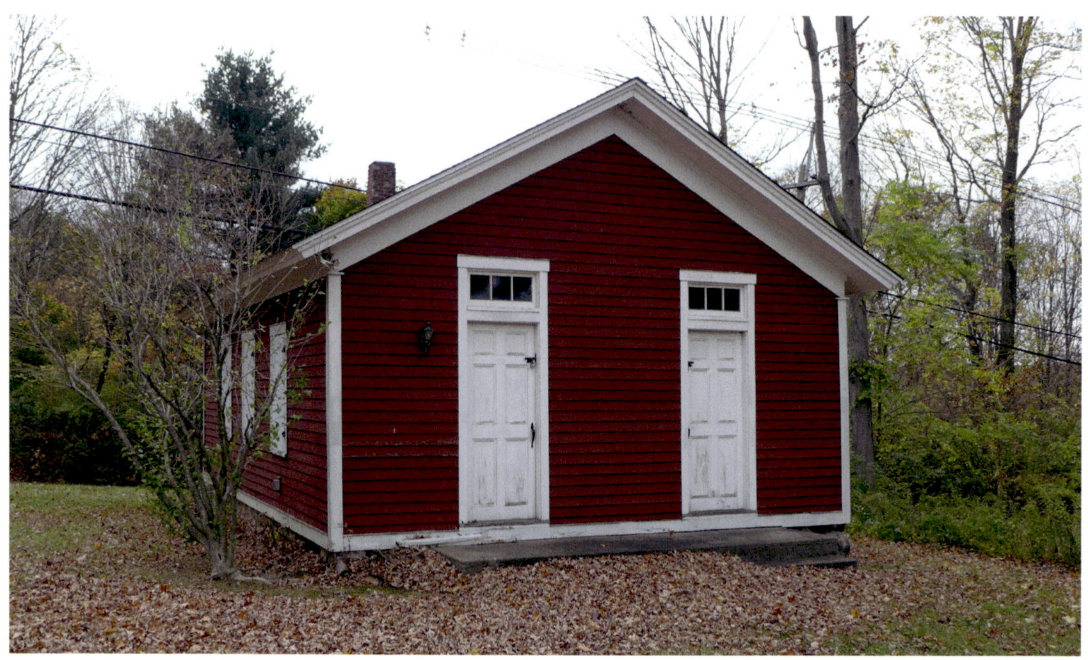

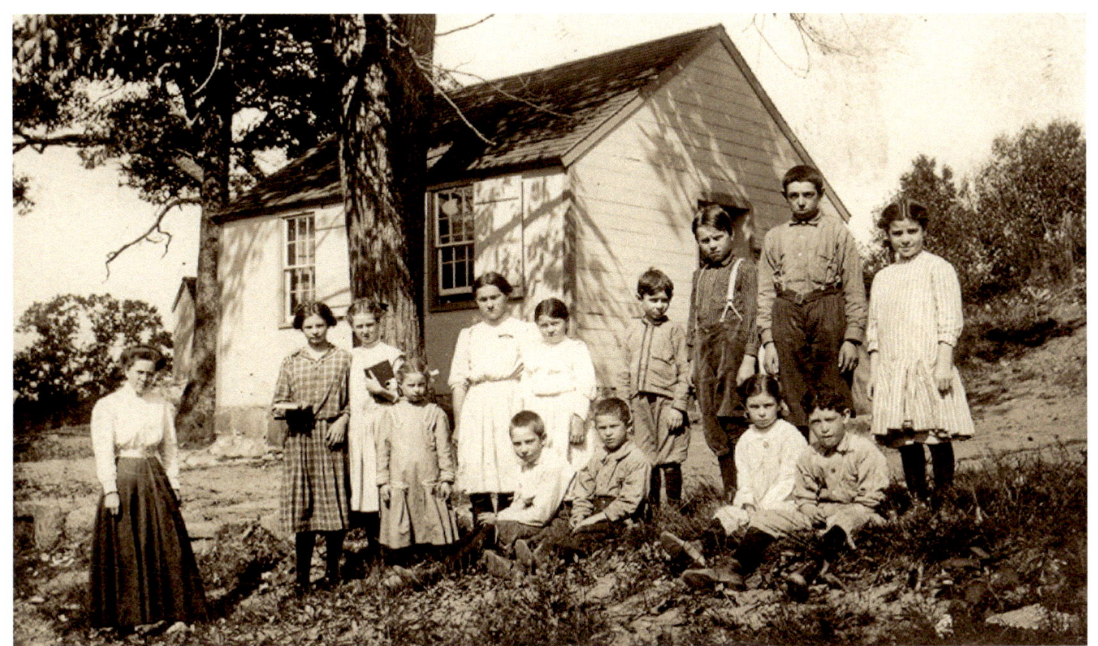

NEWTOWN: Middlegate School District began as the old Bear Hill District with a small schoolhouse along the Newtown-Bridgeport Turnpike in 1783. The name was changed in 1802, when the road became the Newtown-Bridgeport Turnpike and the school was near the middle tollgate. The Middlegate Schoolhouse was built in 1850 and used through 1922. It was sold and used as a house for a while. The building was offered to the historical society as long as it was moved from its location. The old schoolhouse was carefully moved to the grounds of the modern Middle Gate Elementary School in 1973. After restoration and painting, the Middlegate Schoolhouse was once again ready to received visits from young scholars. (Above photograph courtesy of Newtown Historical Society)

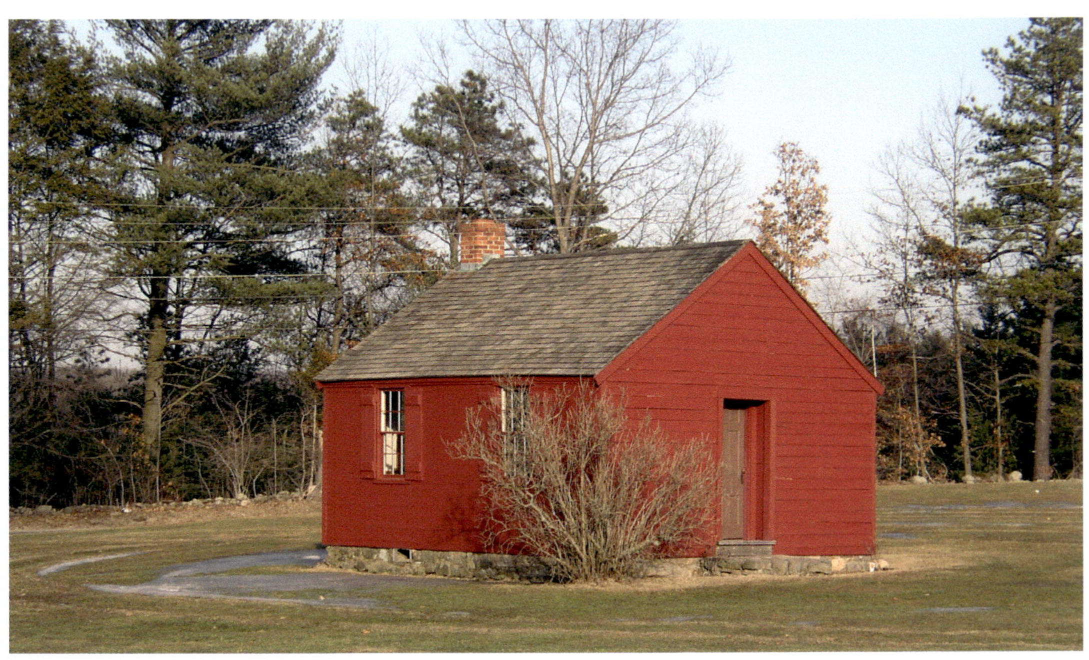

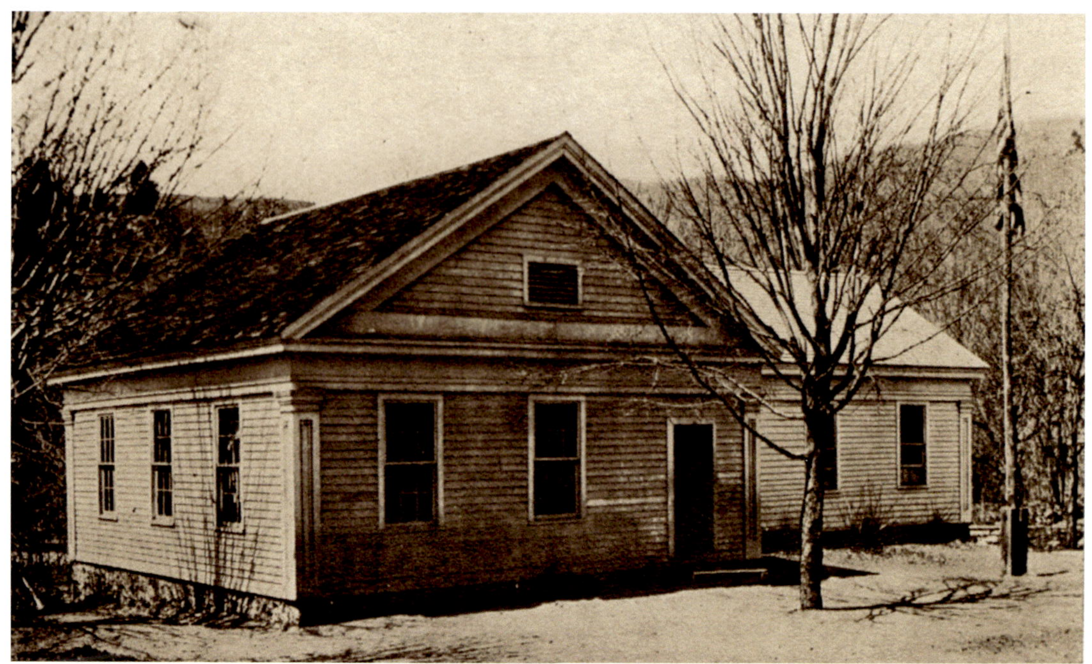

WEST CORNWALL: The District 15 Schoolhouse was built in 1845 on a piece of land between the road and the Housatonic River, just south of the covered bridge. The building was enlarged in 1900, adding another classroom. One student remembers the hurricane of 1938 when the floodwaters reached the bottom of the covered bridge and lapped along the side of the school. The District 15 Schoolhouse closed in 1938 and the children were all sent to the Cornwall Consolidated School the next year. The Hughes Memorial Library moved into the schoolhouse in 1940, where it served the community for over 70 years. (Above photograph courtesy of the Elliott Postcard Collection)

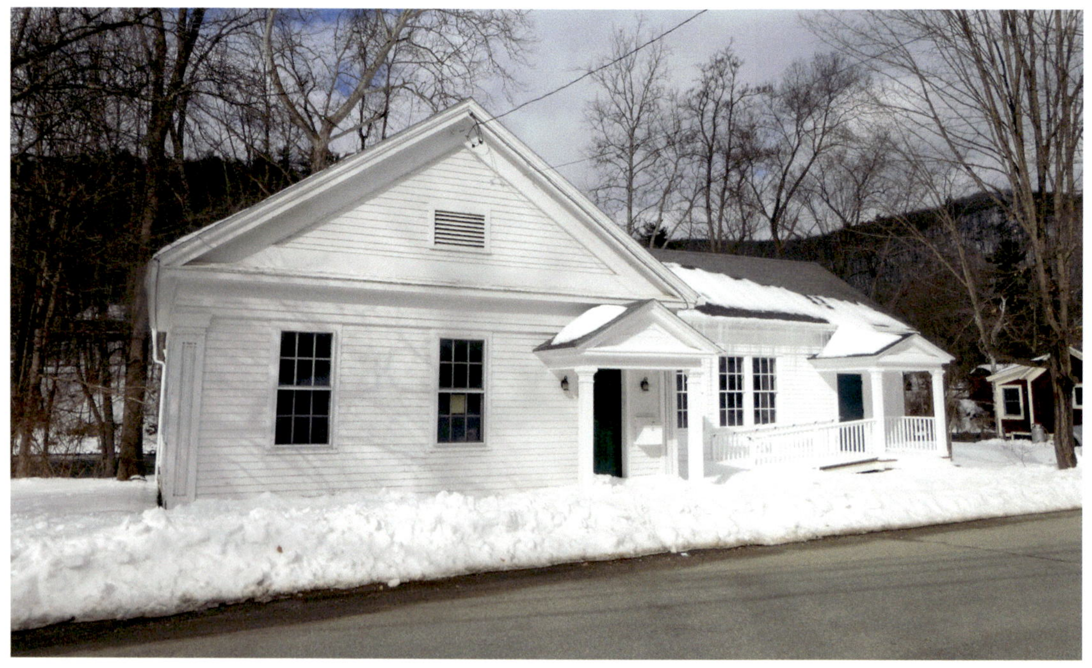

4

Transition to Consolidation, 1861-1909

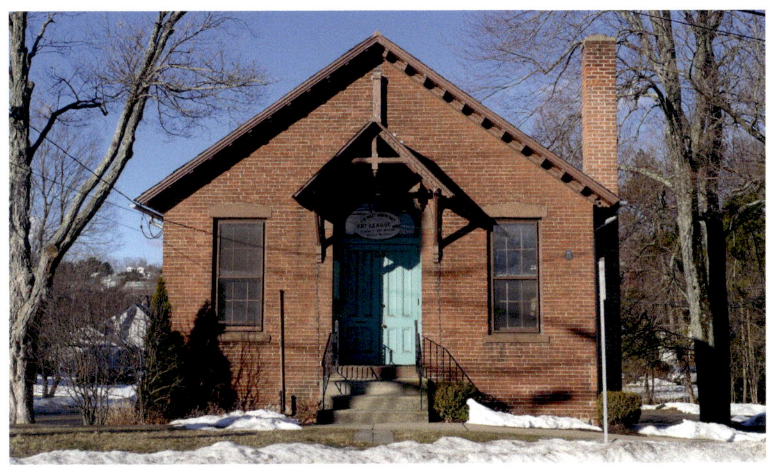

In the 1860s, the district school system came to an end. The state directed the towns to take control over all of their local schools, including the hiring of a superintendent and the selection of a board of education to oversee the schools. Some of the smaller or rundown schoolhouses were closed and the children were moved to better schoolhouses.

As early as 1866, there was some consolidation of the students into larger schools, especially in larger towns. Two-room schoolhouses or larger structures were not uncommon. By the 1890s, the law required the schools to be open 180 days a year. All students were required to spend 60 days of each calendar year in school. By the end of 1899, there were no new one-room schoolhouses being built.

The Old West School (above) was built in 1878, in West Hartford. At the time, this brick school was a shining example of a safer school building for the students. It even had a basement and a heating system. The building has been used by the West Hartford Art League since 1936.

Due to the Consolidation Act of 1909, Connecticut passed a law the required the towns to consolidate their students into large, modern schools, where grades would be separated into classrooms. No longer would one teacher teach all eight grades at the same time. It took many years to completely close the one-room schoolhouses because of their remote locations. The last little schoolhouse closed in 1967, bringing to an end an over 200-year history of one-room schoolhouses in Connecticut.

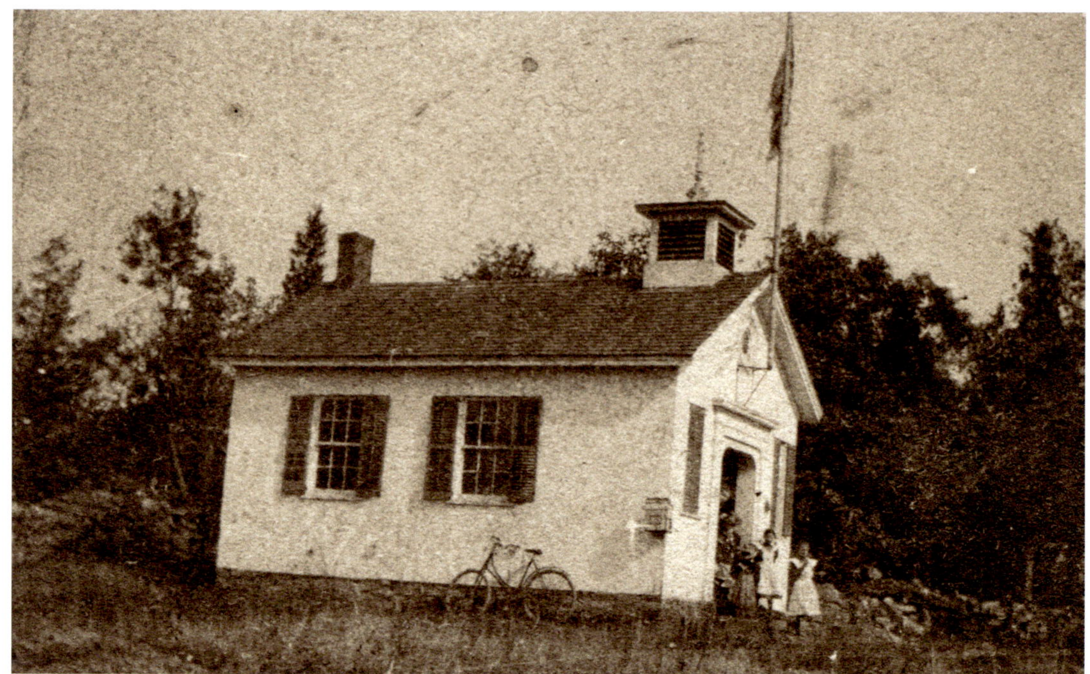

SHELTON: The Trap Fall Schoolhouse was built about 1872 to replace an earlier building. The school was closed in June 1905 due to lack of students in the area. The last teacher was Miss Mary MacDonald, who taught there from 1901 until it closed. She rode her bike to school daily and parked it alongside the building, as you can see in the photograph. For a while, the old school was used as housing for farm laborers, and later as a storage shed for the Bridgeport Hydraulic Company. The building was moved to the grounds of the Shelton Historical Society and restored. (Above photograph courtesy of Shelton Historical Society)

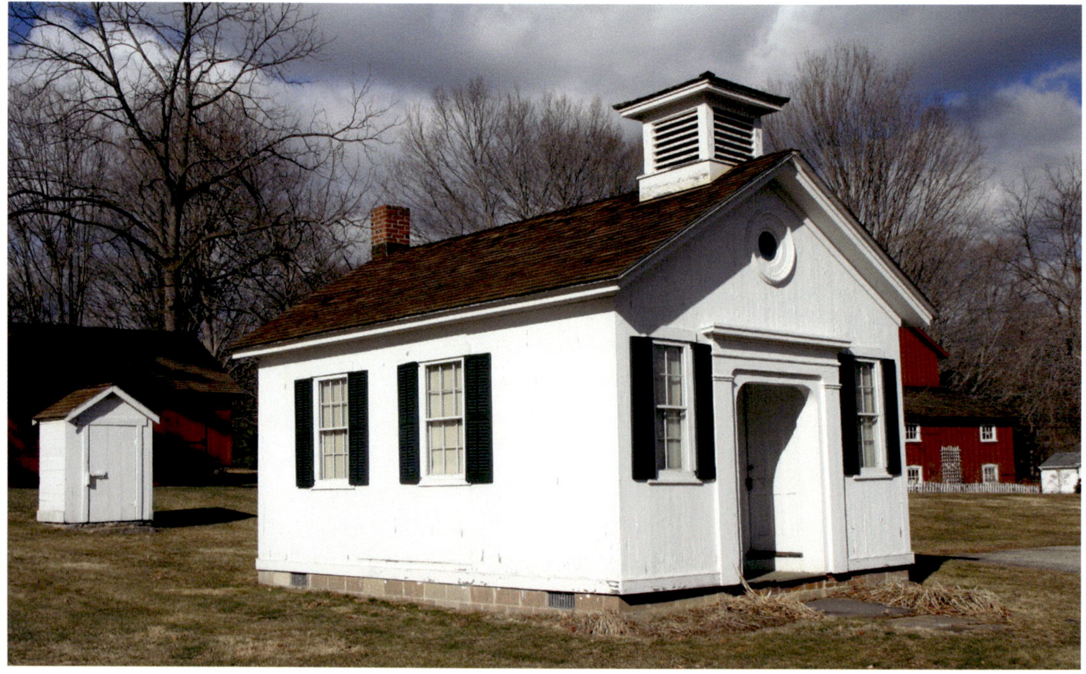

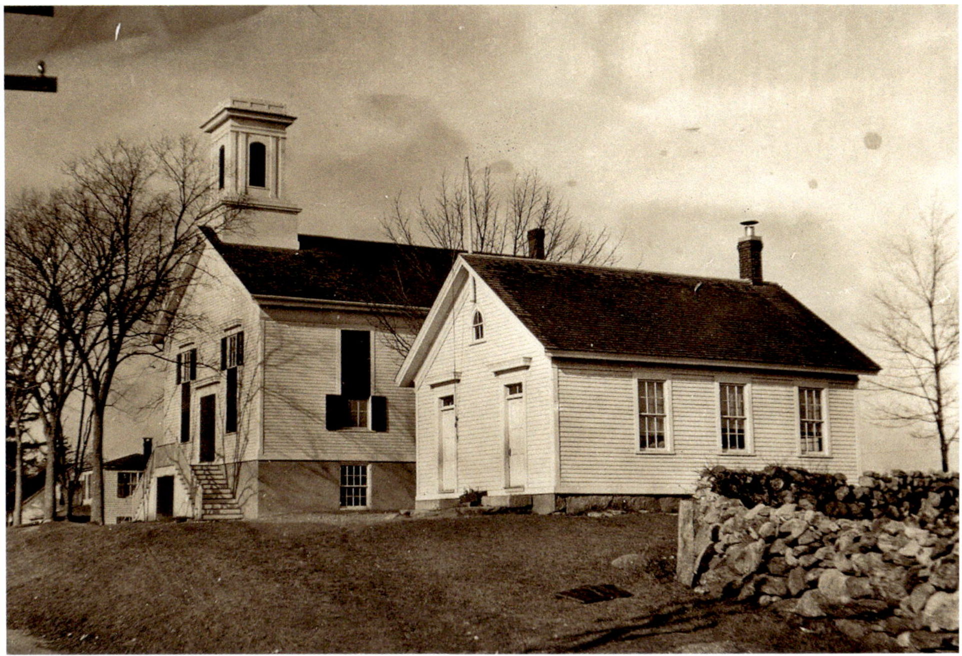

LEDYARD: The District #2 School in the Gales Ferry section of Ledyard was built in 1868 on Hurlbutt Road. Squire Ralph Hurlbutt first donated the land for a schoolhouse in 1750 for an early school. Through the years, the 1750 school was replaced by another school building in 1804. The current schoolhouse has a coved ceiling and a very rare curved blackboard at the front of the room. The school was used until 1927, when a larger two-room schoolhouse was ready for students. The school is owned by the Ledyard Historical Society. (Above photograph courtesy of Ledyard Historical Society, Inc., Ledyard, CT)

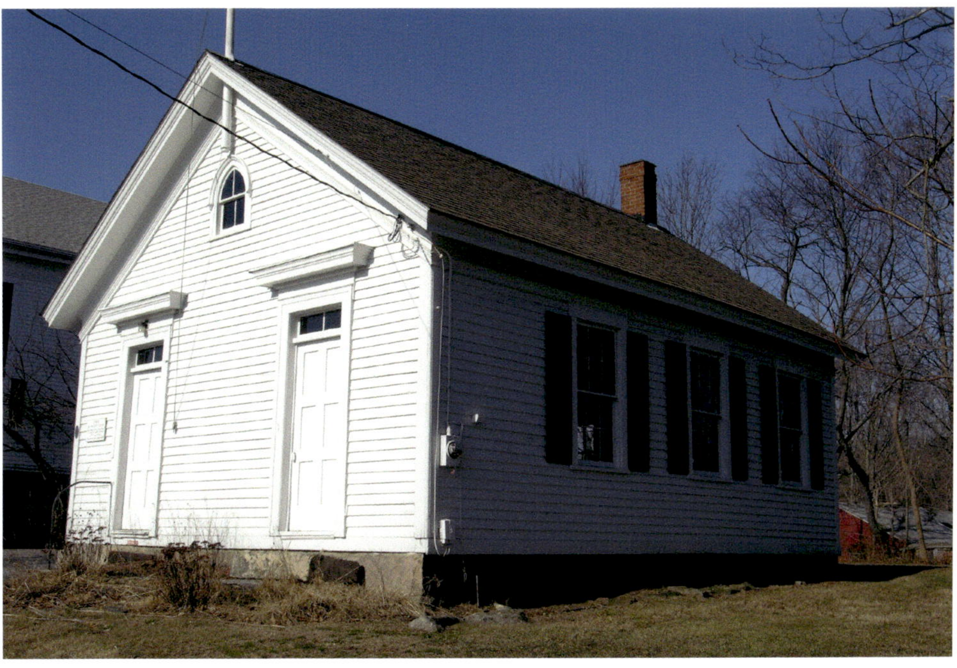

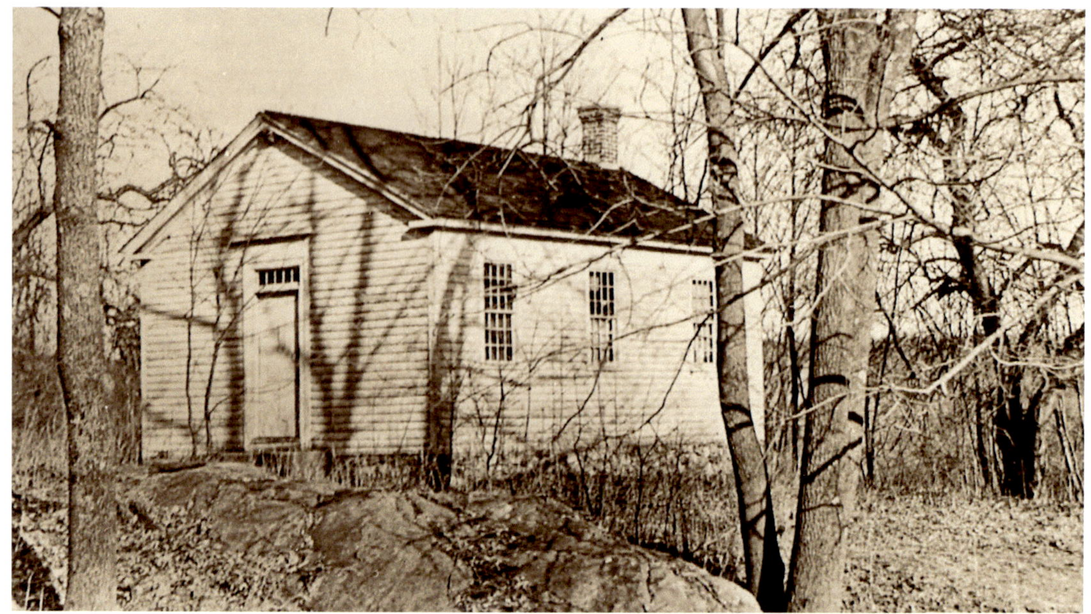

MORRIS: The Mill Schoolhouse was built in 1861 in the Mill District, three and a half miles southeast of the town center. In 1910, the building was moved a short distance out of the way as the Morris Reservoir dam was being built. It continued to be used as a school until 1915, and then sat vacant for almost 25 years. The schoolhouse was moved in 1939 to be part of an apple cider mill. In 1981, it was moved next to the old Morris Meeting House where it was renovated and restored to the way it looked in 1911, based on old photographs. (Above photograph Courtesy CT State Library, State Archives, LS Mills Collection)

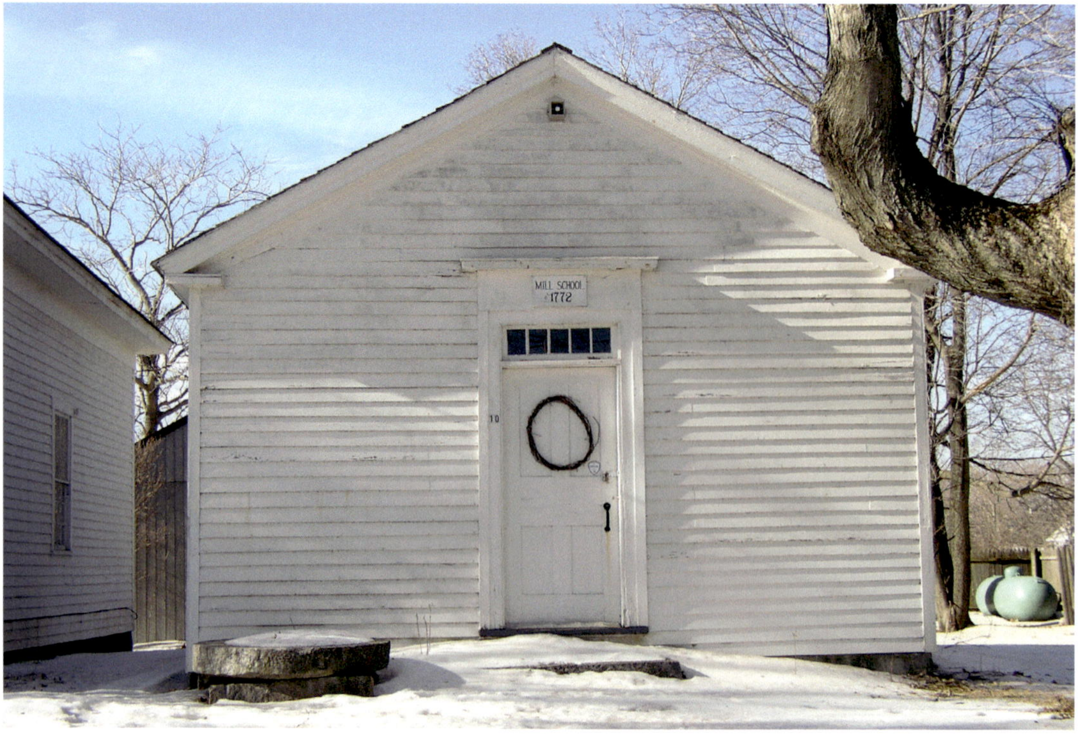

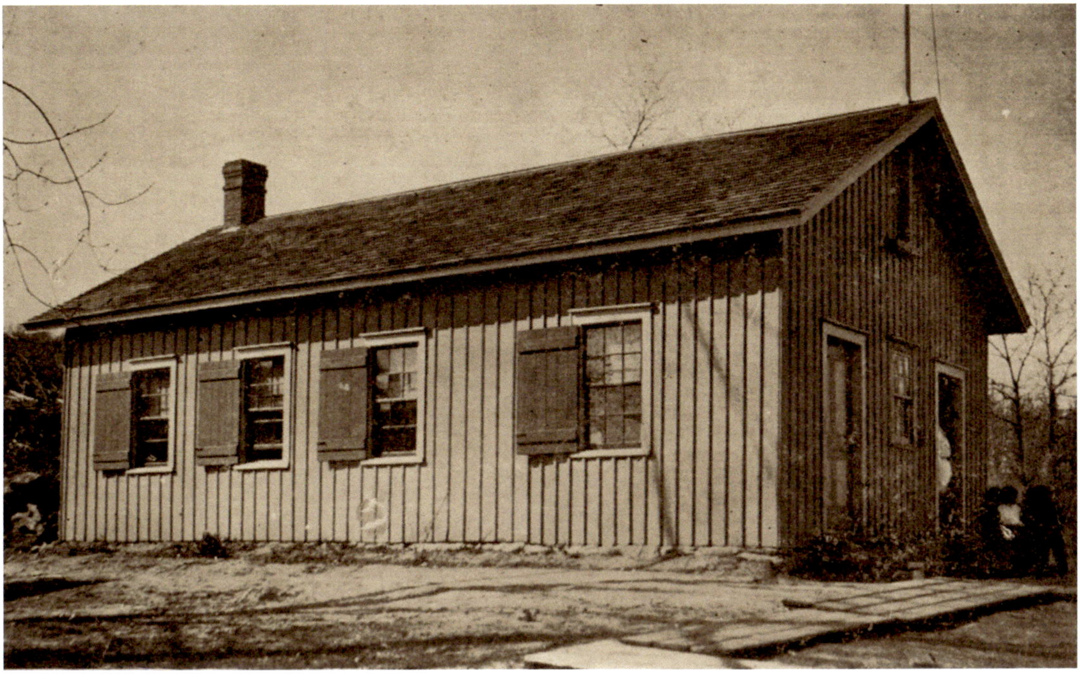

DANBURY: The King Street School built in 1888, on the corner of King and South King Streets, and was large enough to hold 30 students. Since there was no well or water source, drinking water had to be brought in for the students. One year, the parents got together to build a playground. The school was closed in June of 1939. Thirty-three years later, owned by the town of Danbury, the old schoolhouse was moved to Rogers Park, near the Charles Ives Homestead. The building is scheduled for renovations with the Danbury Historical Society. (Above photograph from the Elliott Postcard Collection)

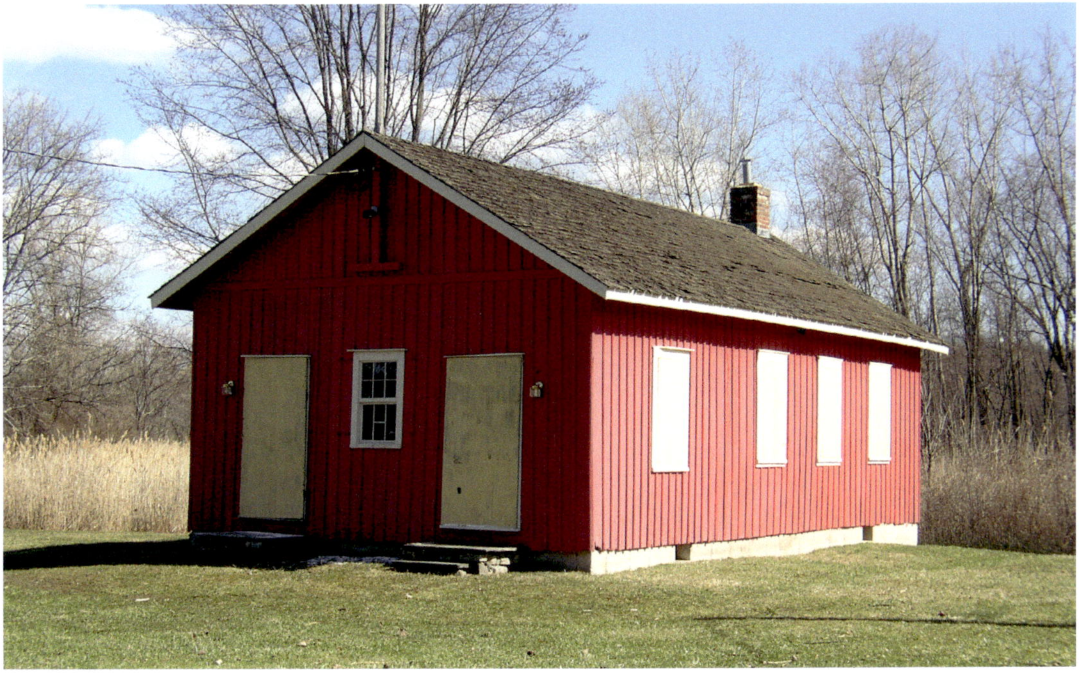

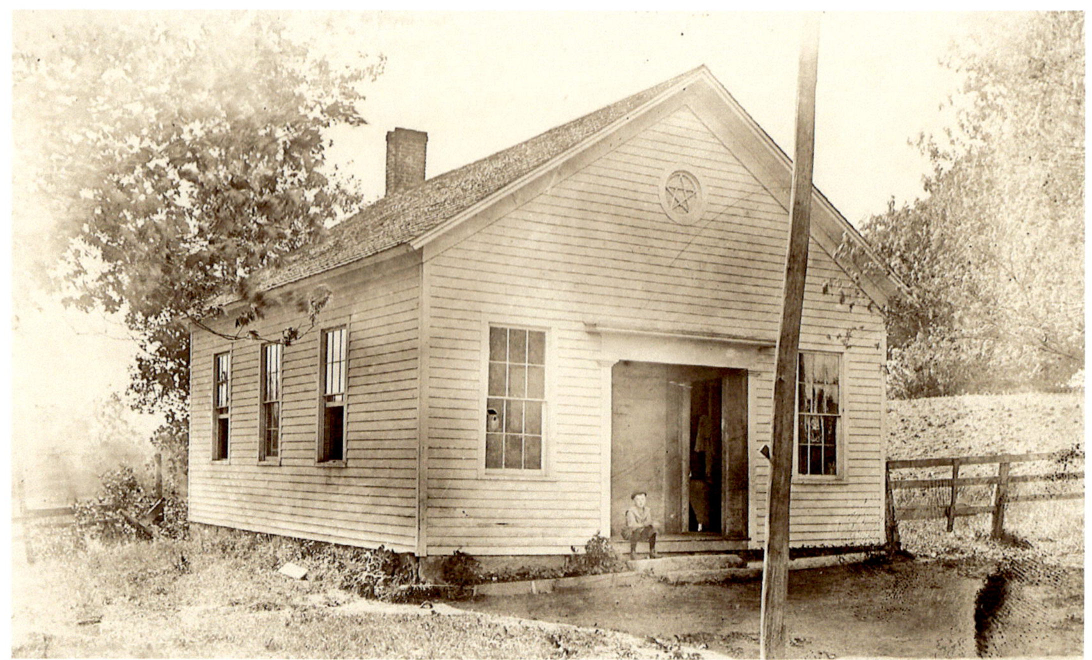

BETHLEHEM: The District #1 schoolhouse, also known as the Center School, was built around 1865, replacing an earlier school from 1832. The school sits across the street from the town green, where it was moved in 1912. Several of the nine school districts were consolidated, causing the closure of this one-room school in 1914. All students were moved to the newly constructed modern school in 1926. The District #1 schoolhouse was used as a library until 1968. The Old Bethlem Historical Society purchased the building for $1 in 1991. While removing paneling to restore the building, they found the old blackboards with original assignments still visible. (Above photograph Courtesy CT State Library, State Archives, LS Mills Collection)

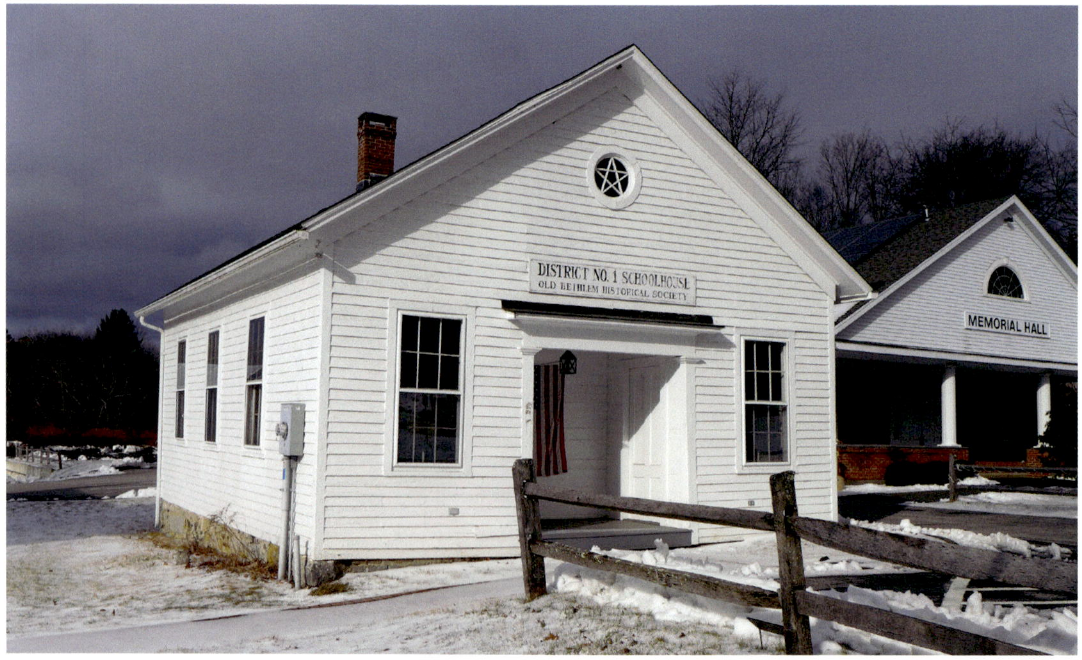

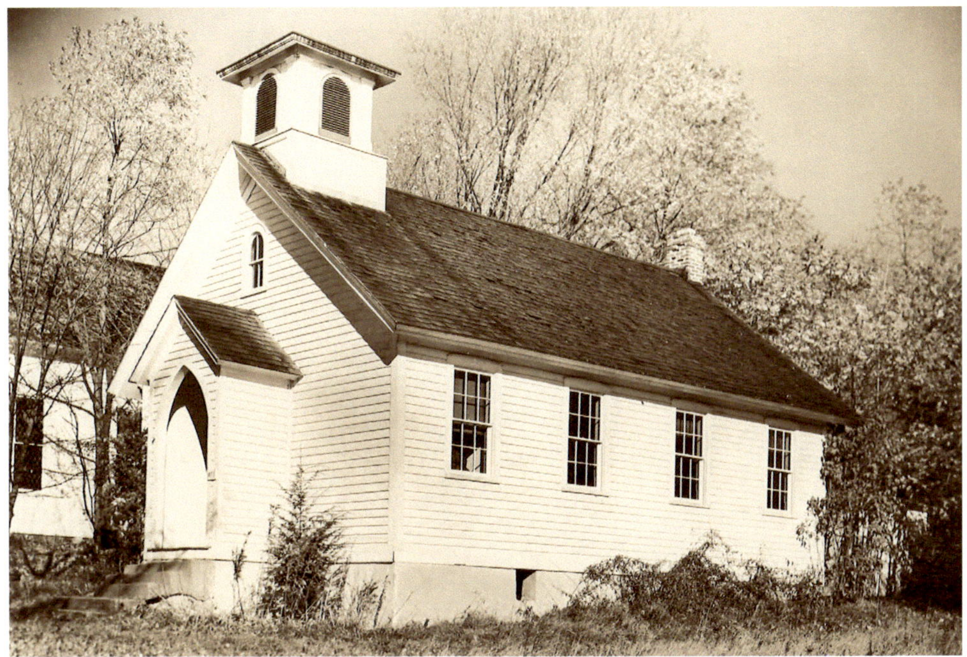

CANTON: The North Canton school district's first schoolhouse was a log cabin built in 1750. The second school, the Little Red Schoolhouse, was constructed in 1859 and had two fireplaces. In 1872, the school was moved south of the North Canton Methodist Church, and a new white schoolhouse was built in its place at the fork of the road across the street from the church. When the road was widened in 1927, the old Little Red Schoolhouse was demolished so the pictured school could be moved next to the church, where is still stands. The building now belongs to the church. (Above photograph Courtesy CT State Library, State Archives, LS Mills Collection)

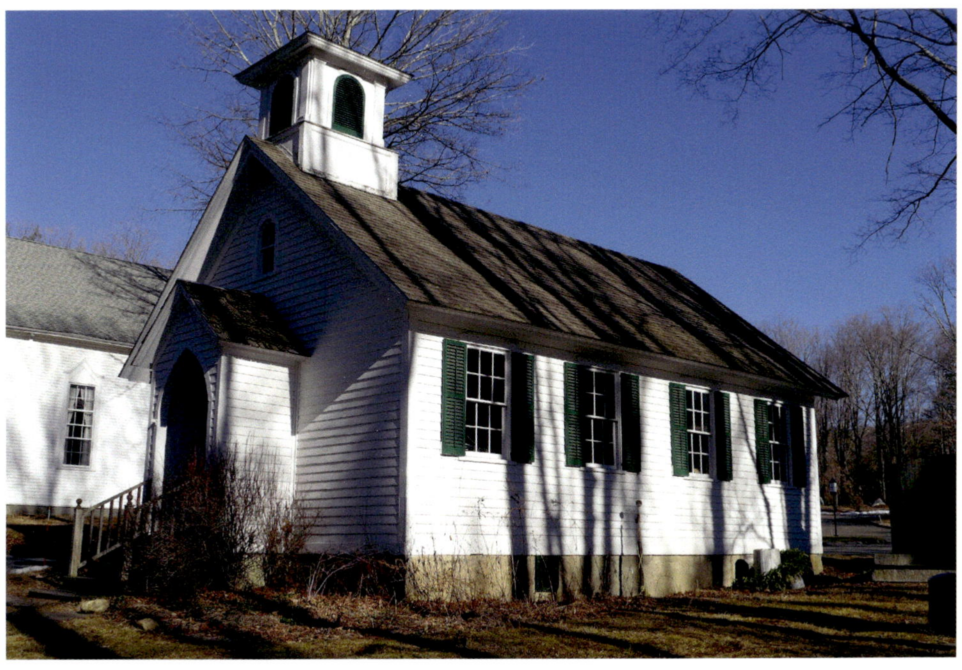

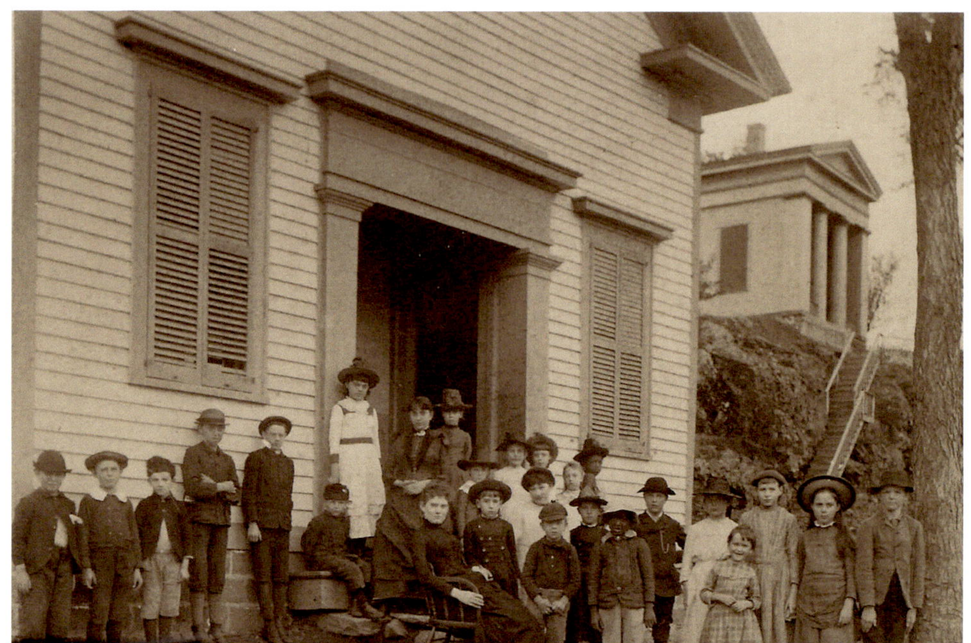

WOODBURY: The 2nd District School, known also as the South Center School, was built in 1867 at the base of a bluff with the imposing Mason's King Solomon's Lodge towering above. Fourteen school districts were spread throughout the town during the 1800s, with three schools on Main Street located a mile apart. The students departed the South Center Schoolhouse in 1899 to join the new Mitchell School that consolidated all of the town schoolhouses. The school was restored thanks to several grants and a lot of hard work from volunteers. Woodbury Historical Society opens the school for students and visitors several times as year. (Above photograph from the H.K. Somerset Collection, courtesy of Woodbury Public Library, Woodbury, CT)

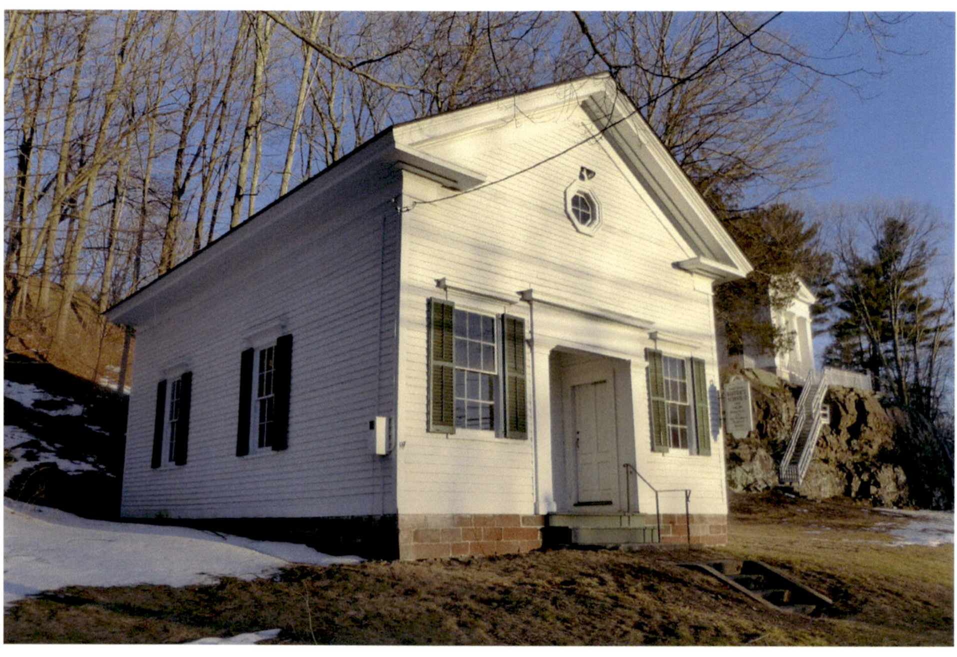

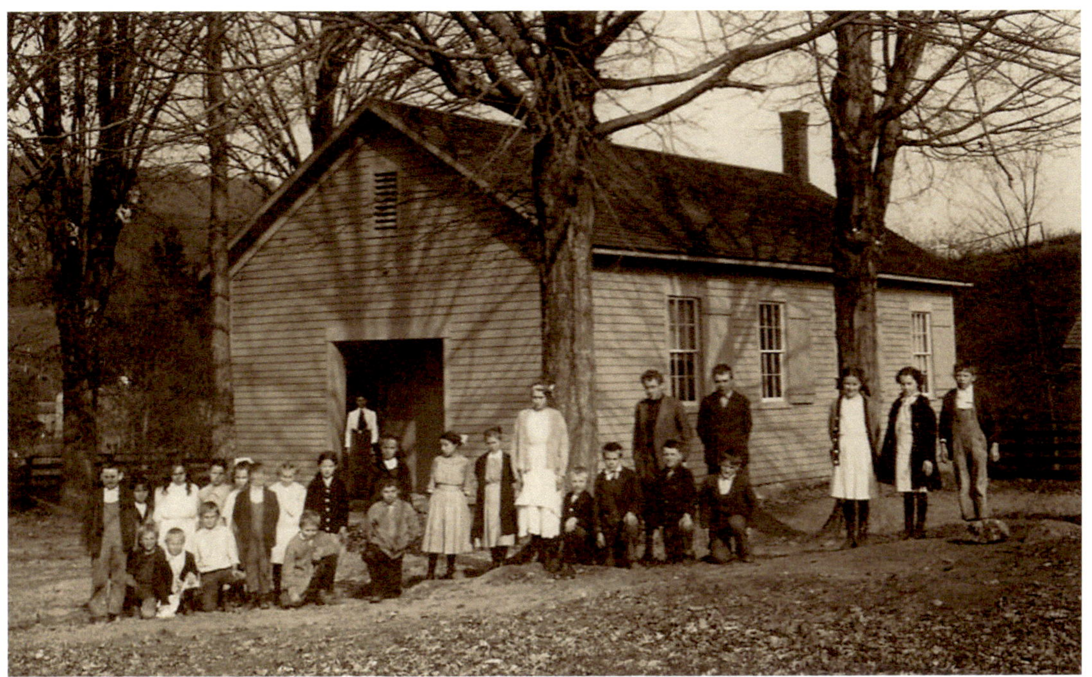

NEW MILFORD: The Northville area of the town purchased the land for the schoolhouse in 1862. Two entranceways allowed the boys and girls to access separate cloakrooms. The room had blackboards all around and a woodstove in front of the teacher's desk, which was raised on a platform. The schoolhouse was shut down in 1955 when New Milford's consolidated school opened. The local fire station used the building for storage for a time. While the town owns the building, Northville Schoolhouse Committee oversees its usage. (Above photograph courtesy of the New Milford Historical Society)

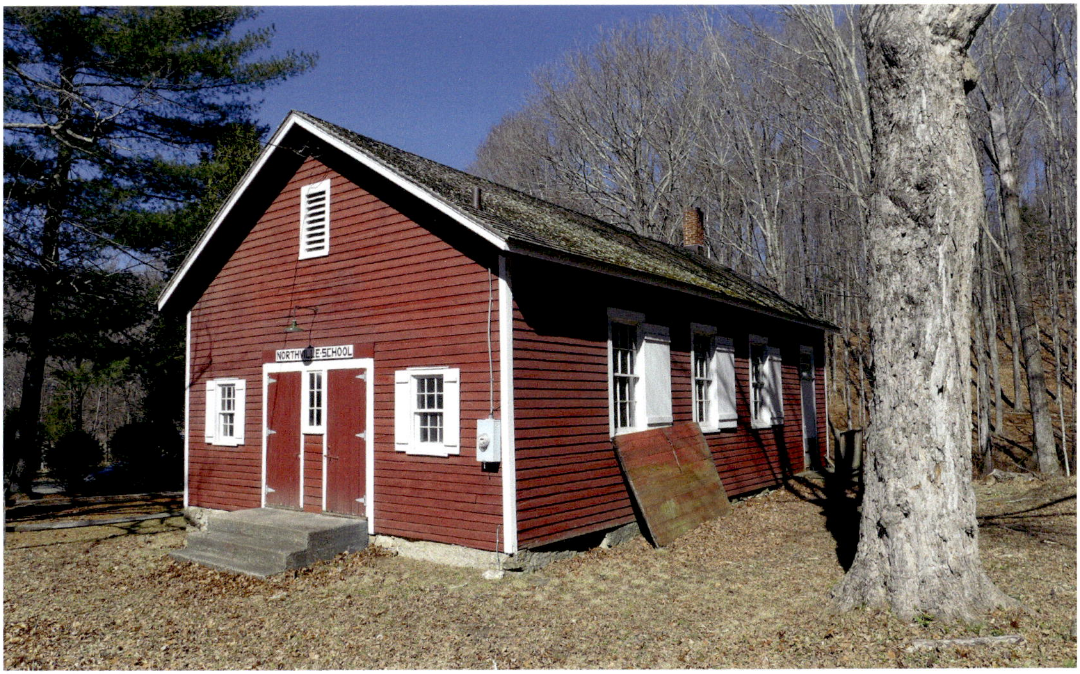

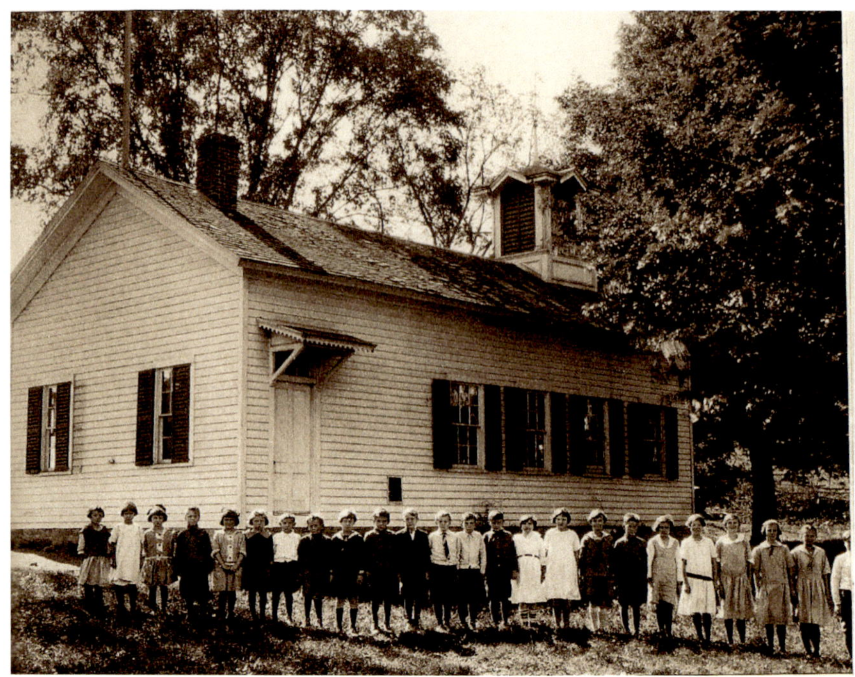

BETHEL: The land for the Plumtrees Schoolhouse was donated in 1866, with the school opening the next year in 1867, as one of five school districts in town. In 1881, the cupola and a four-mile bell were added to call the students to school. The bell could be heard up to four miles away. As the population increased, the school needed to be enlarged to hold 24 students in 1884. The school closed in 1957. During 1962, the building was reopened for kindergarten classes. In 2009, the newly renovated schoolhouse was opened as a museum. (Above photograph courtesy of Bethel Historical Society)

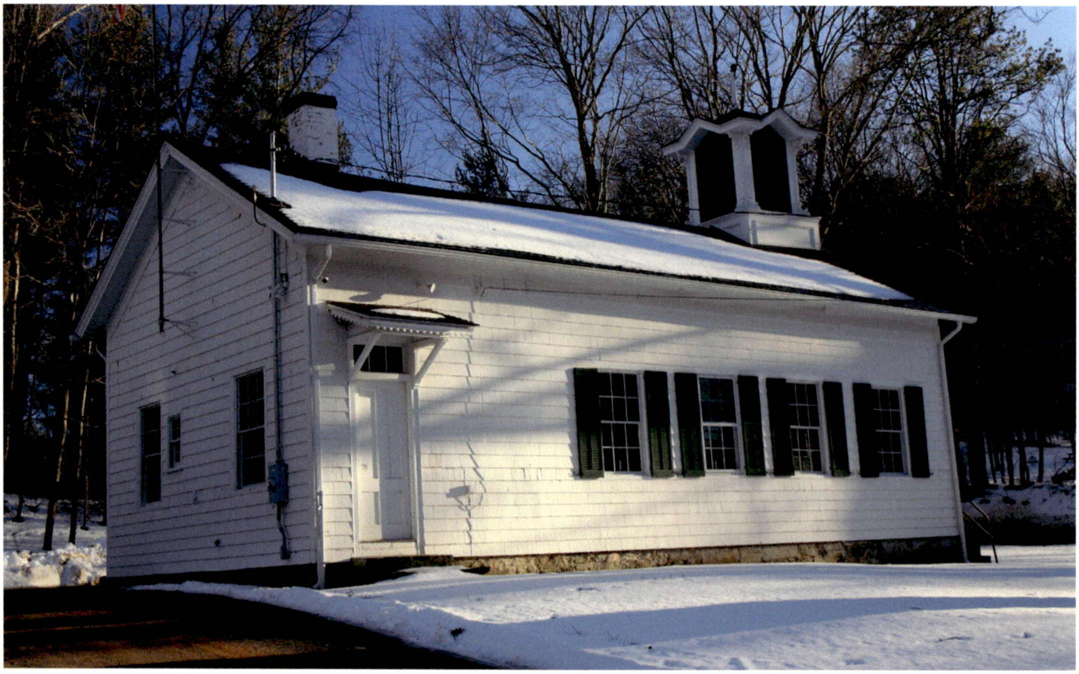

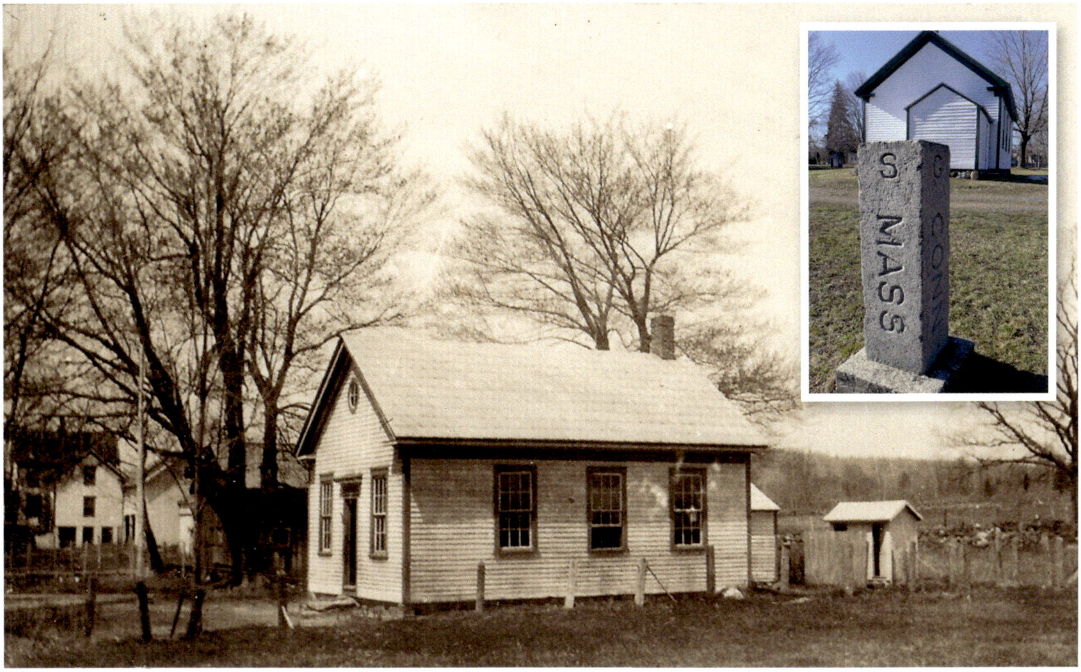

GRANBY: The Cooley School was built in 1878. Years later, the often disputed state border was changed and the outhouse ended up in another town and state—Southwick, Massachusetts. The school was closed in 1948, and 24 years later, it was given to the Salmon Brook Historical Society. The schoolhouse and outhouse were moved onto Historical Society property in 1980. After three years of negotiations, the granite state-line marker was given to the historical society and placed between the school at the original distance from the outhouse. (Above photograph courtesy of the Salmon Brook Historical Society, Granby, CT)

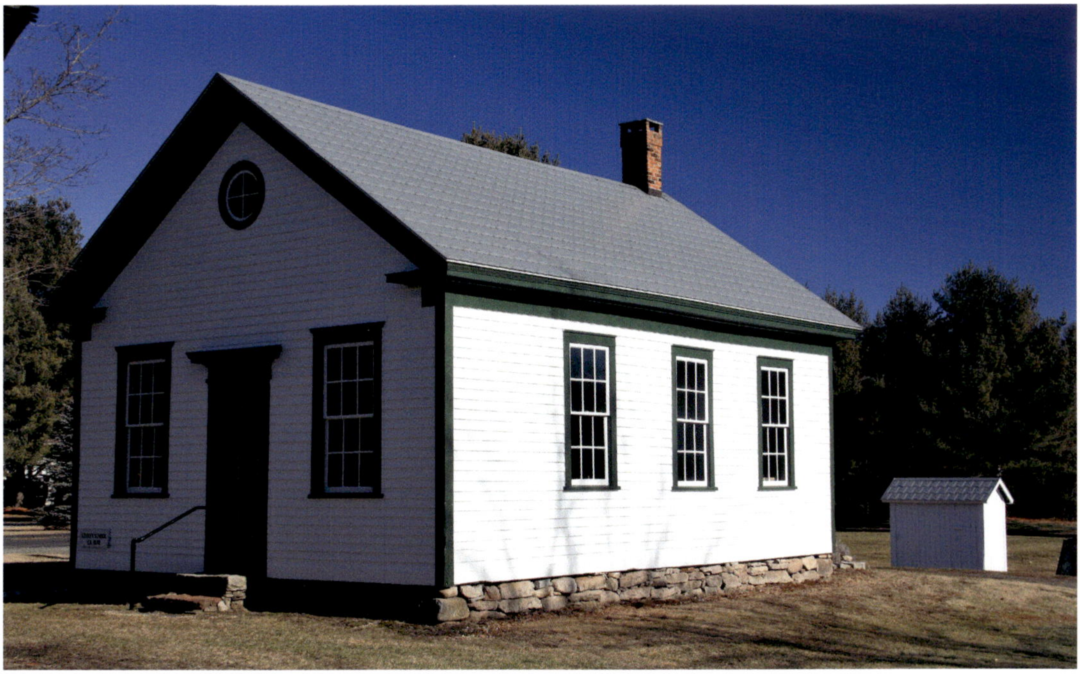

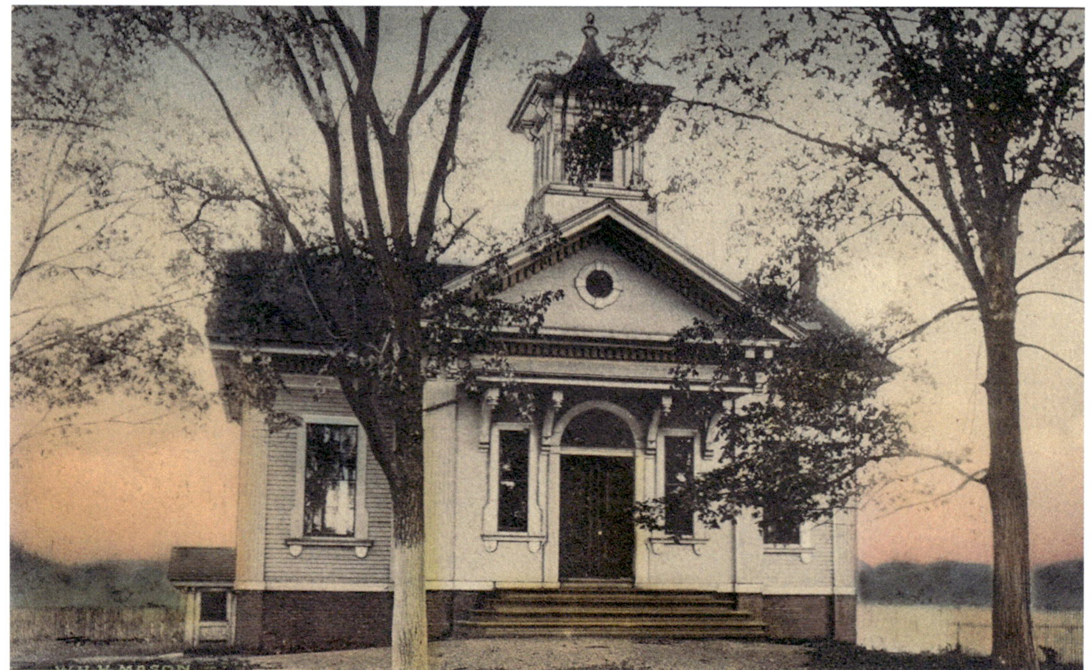

WINDSOR: The Bell Schoolhouse was built to replace the old 1827 5th District School building, which burned down the previous year. Built in 1871, this wealthy area decided on the Italiante design, a new architectural style popular in the United States during the late 1800s. The school was named after the bell that was donated by neighbor General William S. Pierson, who was a civil war soldier. The school closed in 1935. This old school building, a private residence, is still an impressive sight after all these years. (Above photo courtesy of the Elliott Postcard Collection)

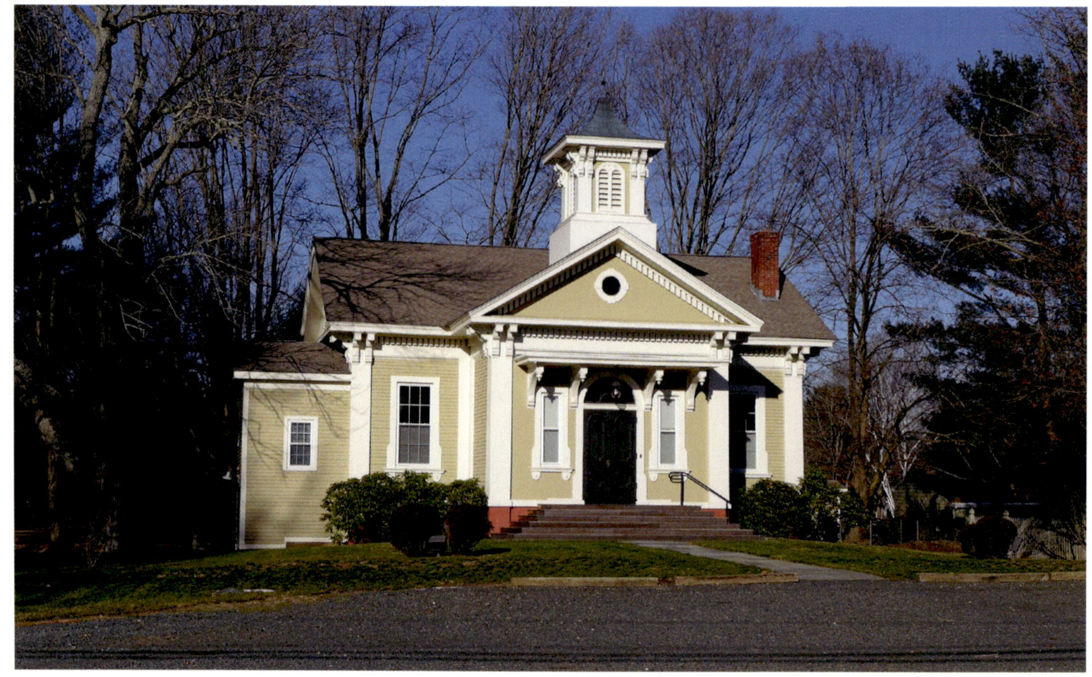

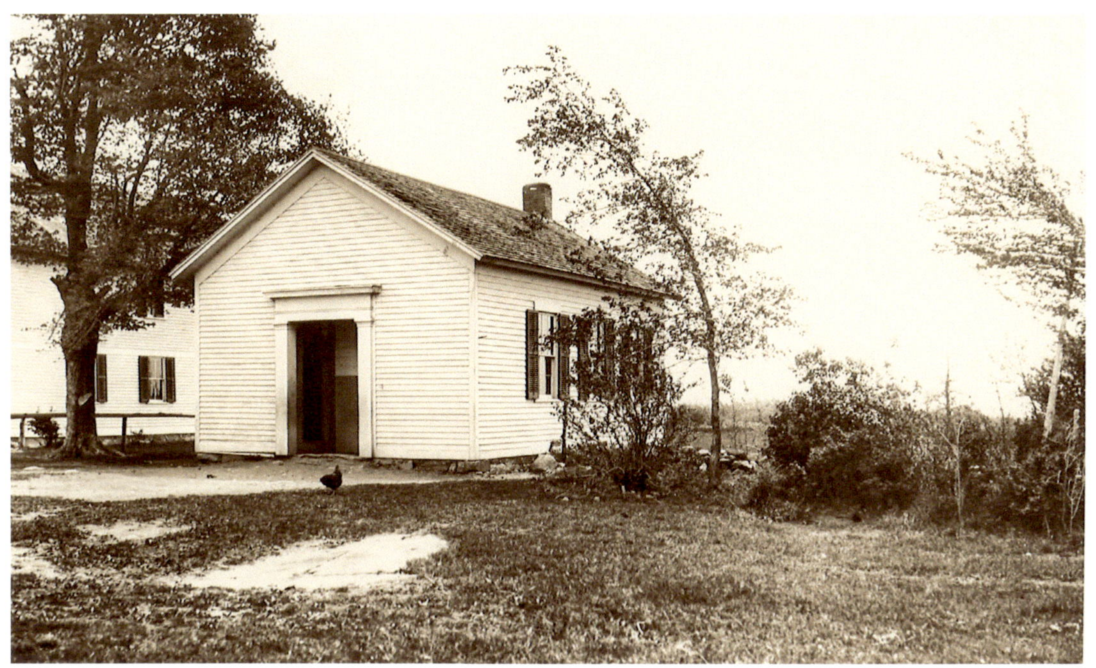

PROSPECT: The Center School stands across from the town green where it was built in 1867 after the previous schoolhouse on Schoolhouse Lane burned down. The location was not ideal, being on the top of a bare hill where the cold winds whipped around in the winter. The school was used until 1936, when the Community School was built. The building was then used for different purposes by the town: for a while it was the town hall and during World War II, a telephone center for the civil defense. The Prospect Historical Society refurbished the building as a schoolhouse museum. (Above photograph courtesy CT State Library, State Archives, LS Mills Collection)

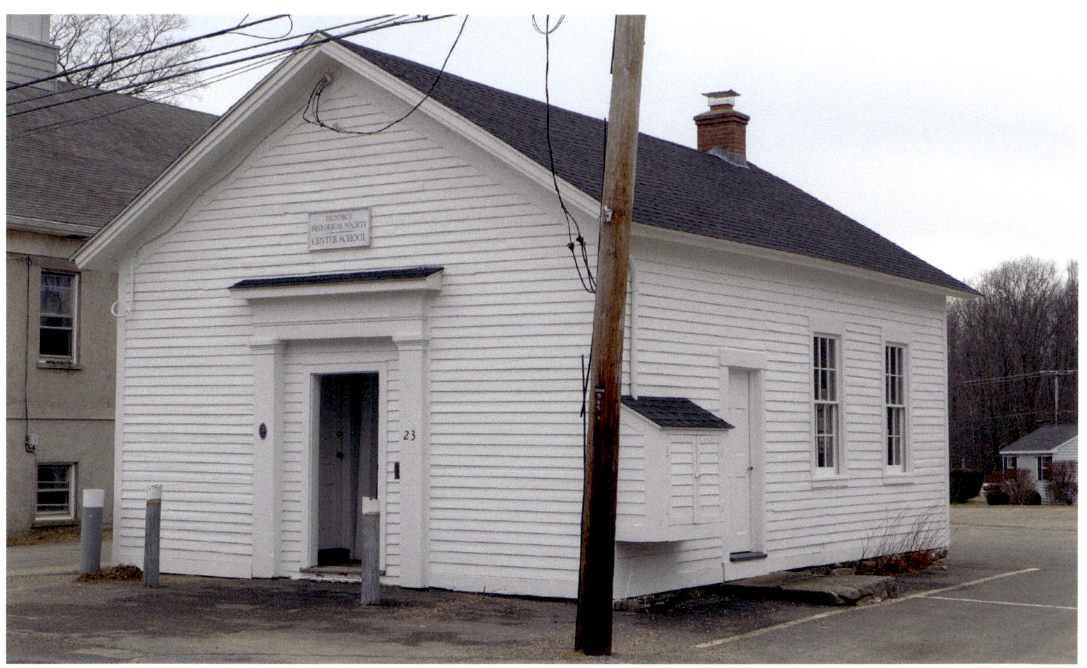

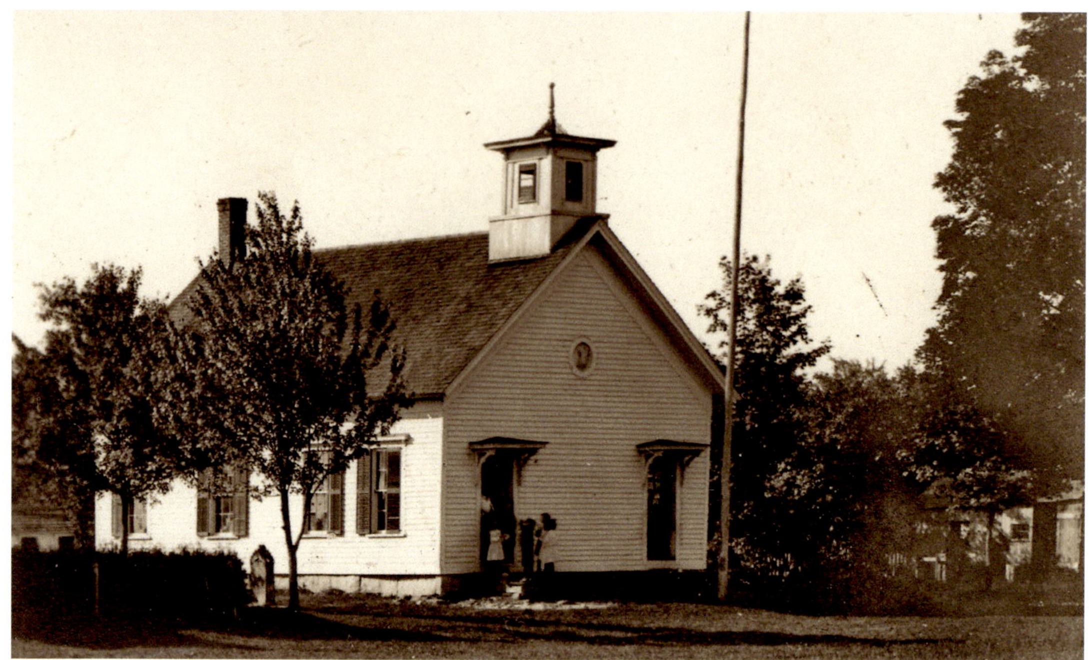

HEBRON: The Center Schoolhouse was built to replace a two-story 1828 schoolhouse, which burned down in 1882. The new building was constructed in 1883 as a two-room school, and was Hebron's largest schoolhouse at that time. As the school population changed, several smaller schoolhouses were closed and their students were sent to the Center School. It was used until 1949 when the new consolidated school was built. The school building became a Hebron historic property on February 3, 2006. The aged school bell pealed in celebration. The Center School is owned by the Jones-Keefe-Baston American Legion Post 95. (Above photograph courtesy of the Elliott Postcard Collection)

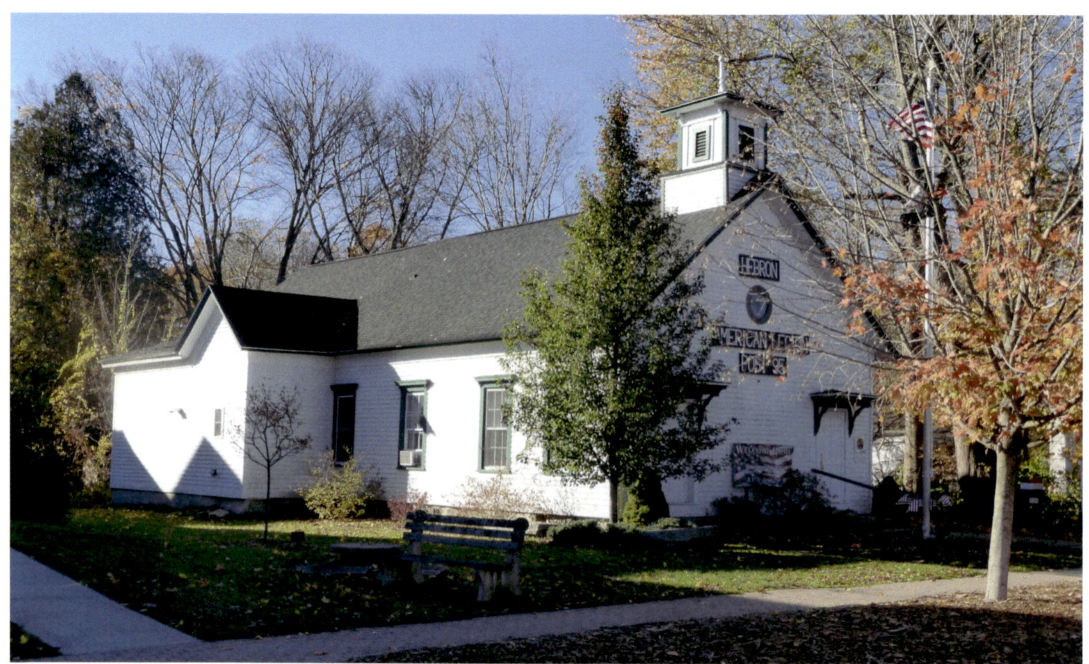

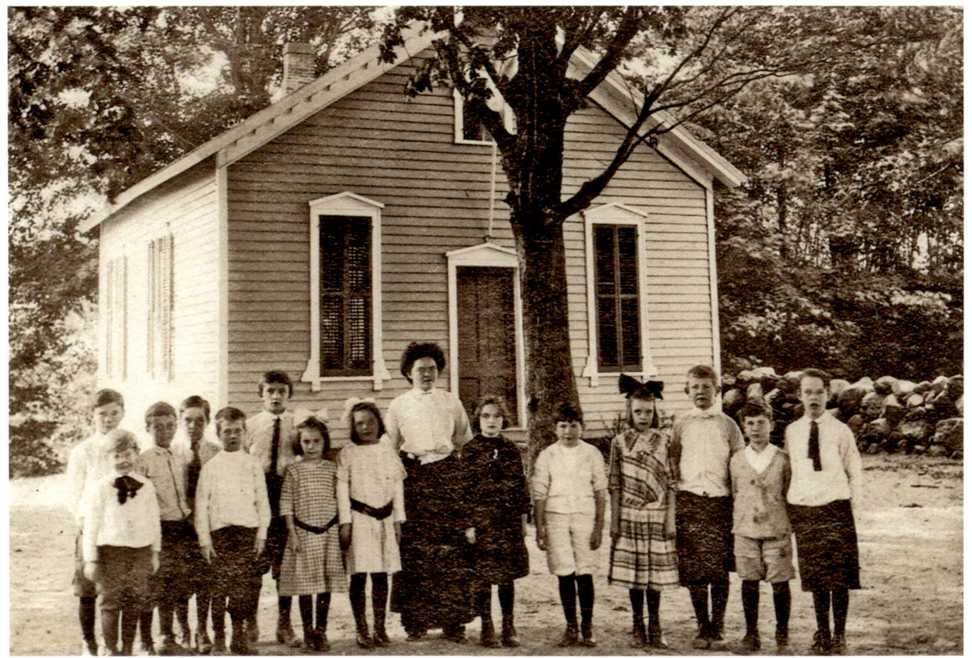

NEW CANAAN: The Carter Street School was constructed in 1868. The last teacher of the school, Mary J. Kelly, attended the same school in the 1890s. She earned her teaching certificate and returned to instruct the neighborhood students for 47 years. When the town tried to close the schoolhouse to send the students to a modern school, the parents objected. The school was closed in 1957 when Miss Kelly retired. The photograph shows the students with Miss Kelly as the new teacher in 1911. The historical society acquired the schoolhouse in 2003, and have kept it in pristine condition, looking exactly as Miss Mary J. Kelly left it. (Above photograph courtesy of The New Canaan Historical Society)

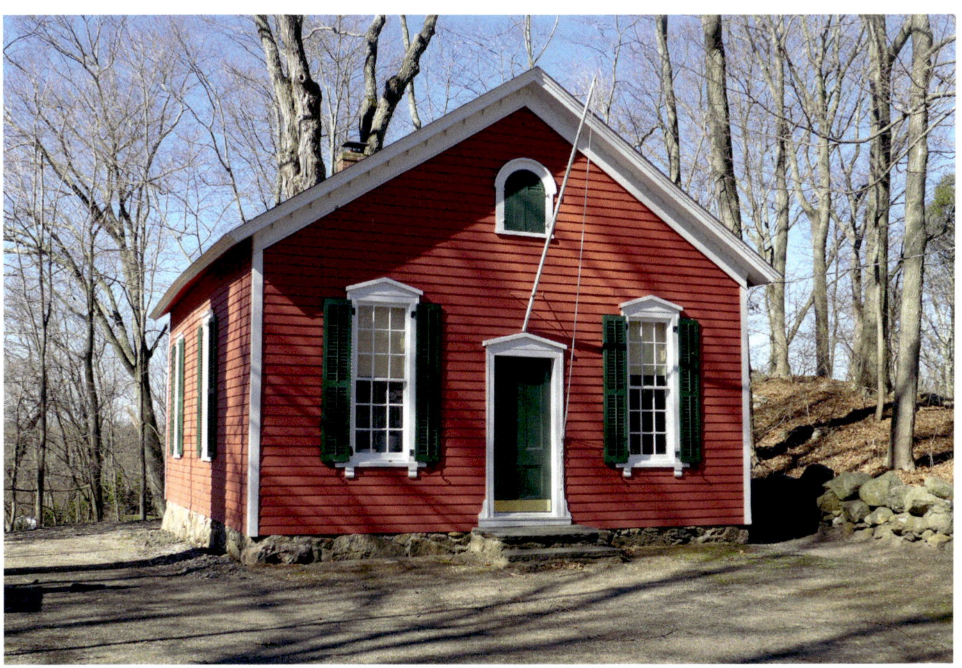

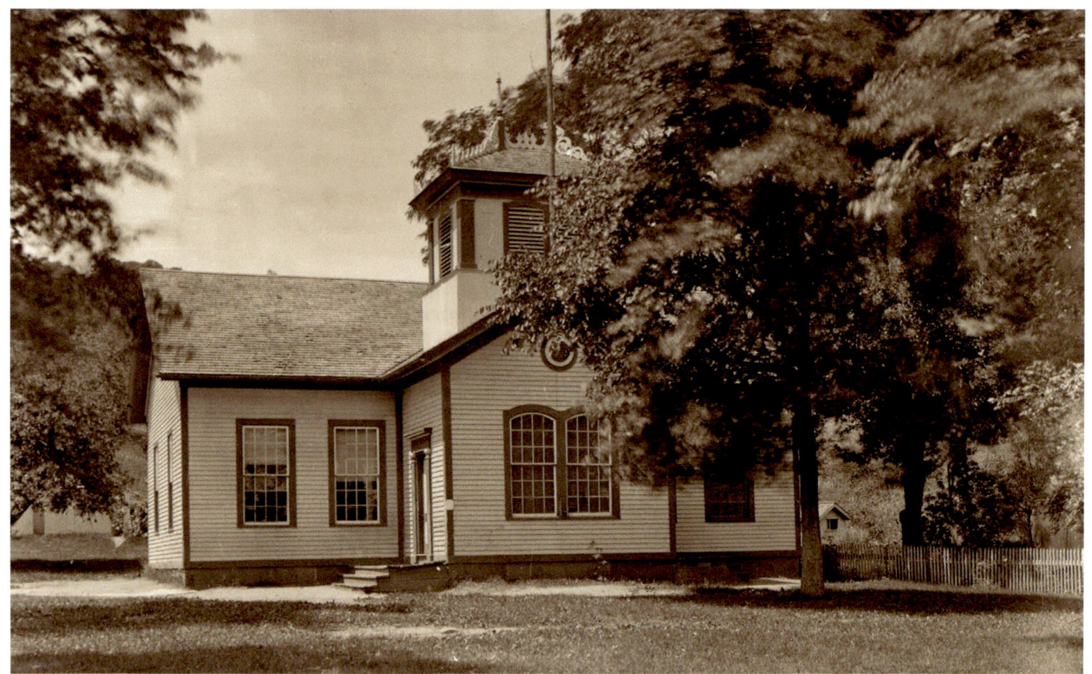

HADDAM: The First District School, also known as the Haddam Center School, was a two-room schoolhouse that was built in 1866, to replace an older, smaller, school. The town boasted of fourteen school districts in 1814. Several of these school buildings still exist as homes or have been converted for other uses. In the early 1950s, a new elementary school was built and most of the small schools closed down. The First District School, now known as the Old Schoolhouse Meeting Place, is the home of the Haddam Senior Center. (Above photo courtesy of the Haddam Historical Society, Haddam, CT)

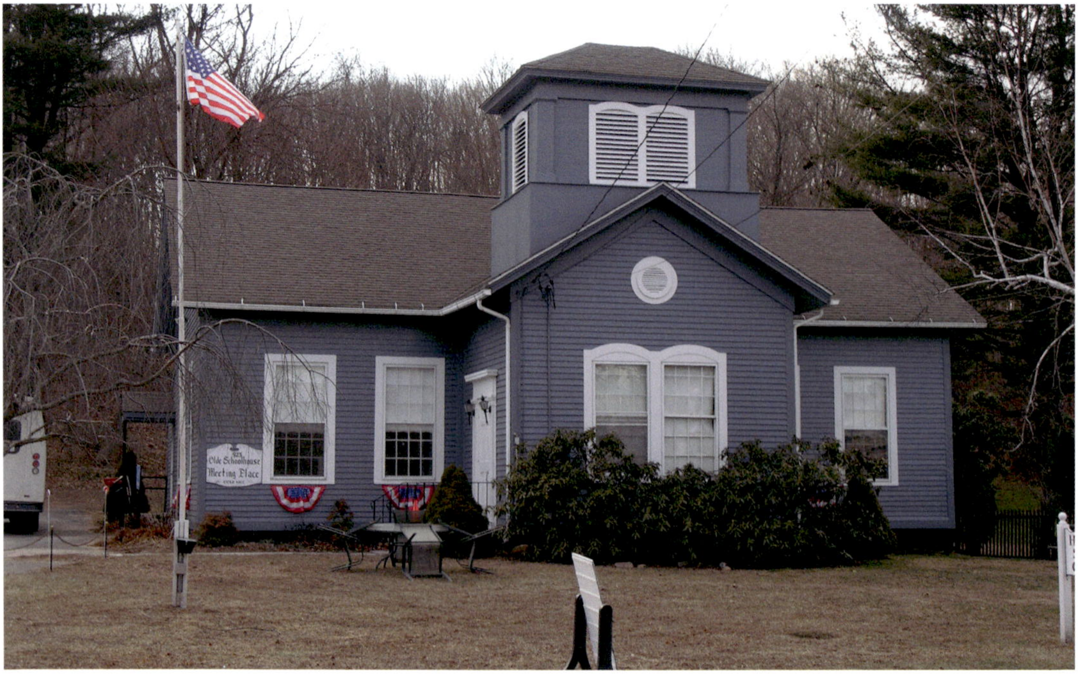

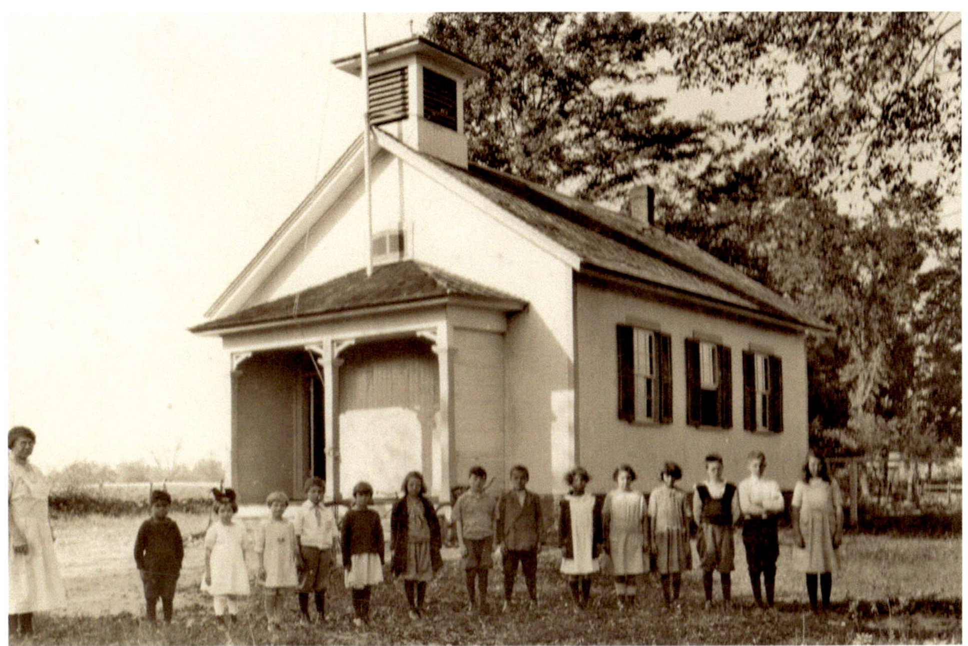

WOODBRIDGE: After the first South School burned down in 1876, a new building was constructed the following year using the same foundation. The school was used until 1928, when the students were sent to the consolidated school. Still a town building, it became the first official firehouse of the area. The fire chief carefully placed the bell in storage. The school was turned over to the Amity and Woodbridge Historical Society in 1973. The restoration committee carefully restored the schoolhouse based on old photographs and an old floor plan from 1877. The bell was recovered from the town storage barn and once again hangs in the school belfry. (Above photograph courtesy of Amity and Woodbridge Historical Society)

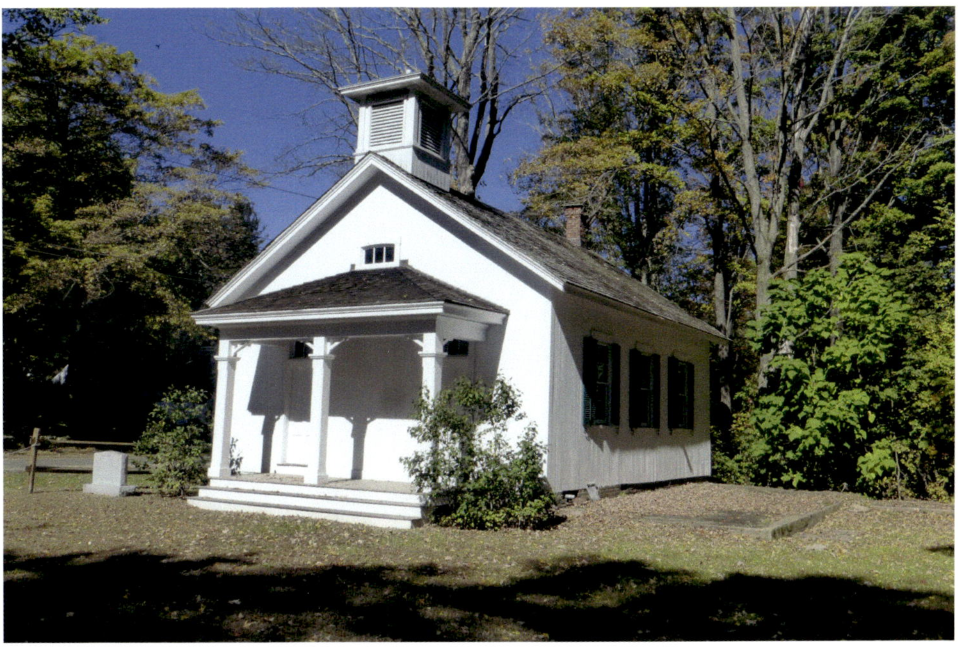

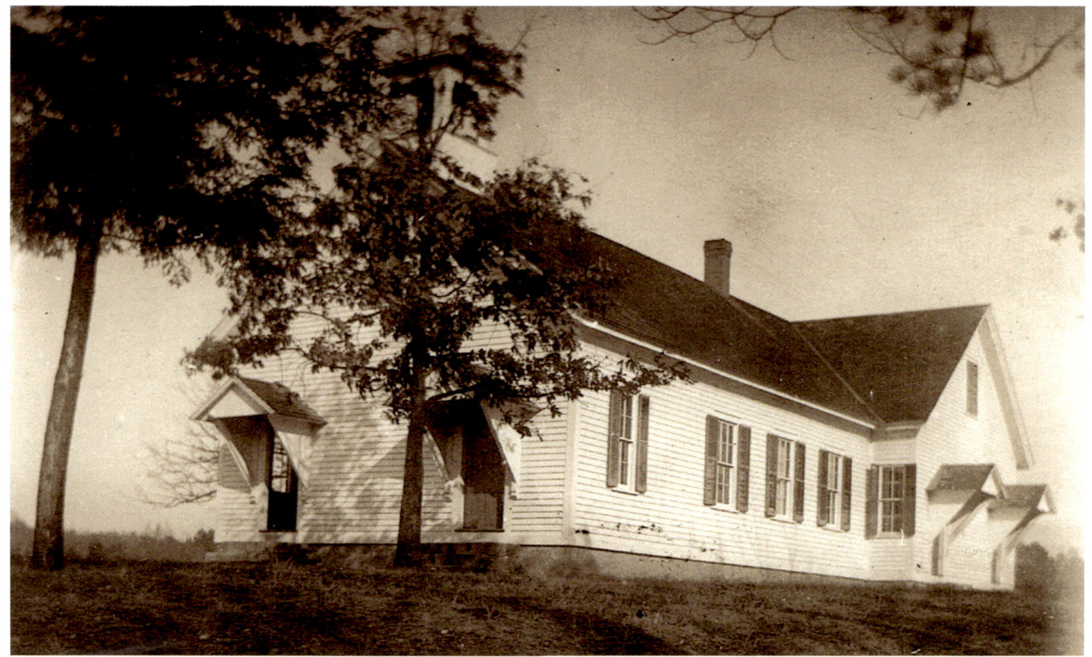

GLASTONBURY: Built as a one-room schoolhouse in 1889, the 17th District School, later to be called the Neipsic School, expanded to a two-room school in 1900 for the fall session. The updated classrooms were supplied with maps, dictionaries, and reference books. The school visitor recorded in 1901 that "The pupils of the two rooms have earned and mounted a bell which can be heard throughout the district." During 1936, lavatories were installed in the school building. The new modern Eastbury School opened next door and signaled the end of Neipsic Schoolhouse in the fall of 1949. The building now houses a branch of the Glastonbury Library. (Above photograph courtesy of Glastonbury Historical Society)

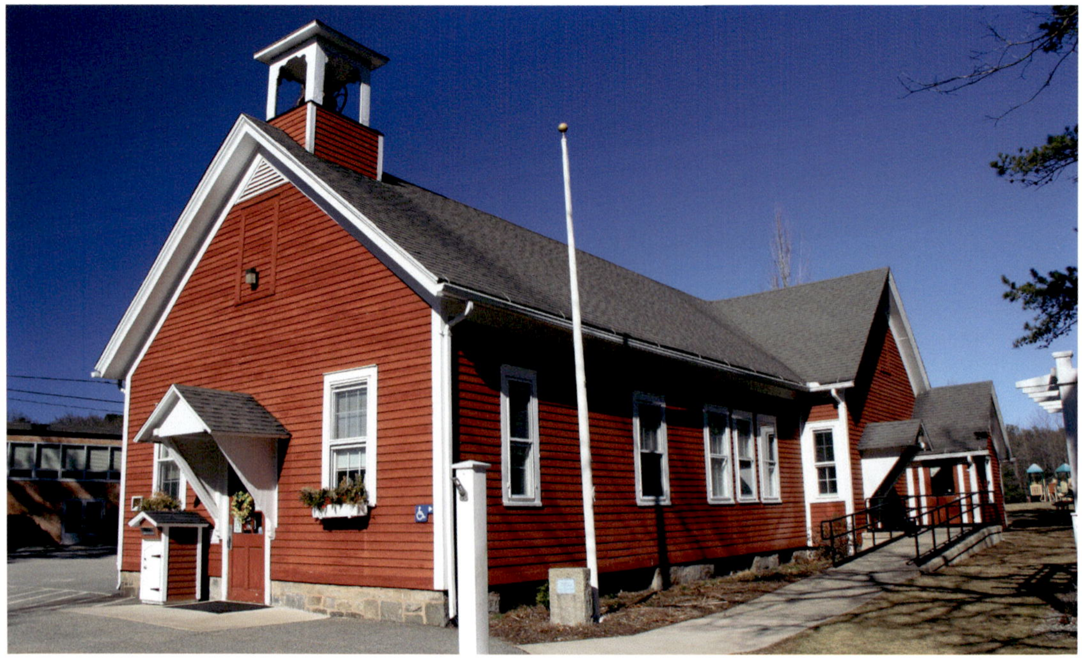

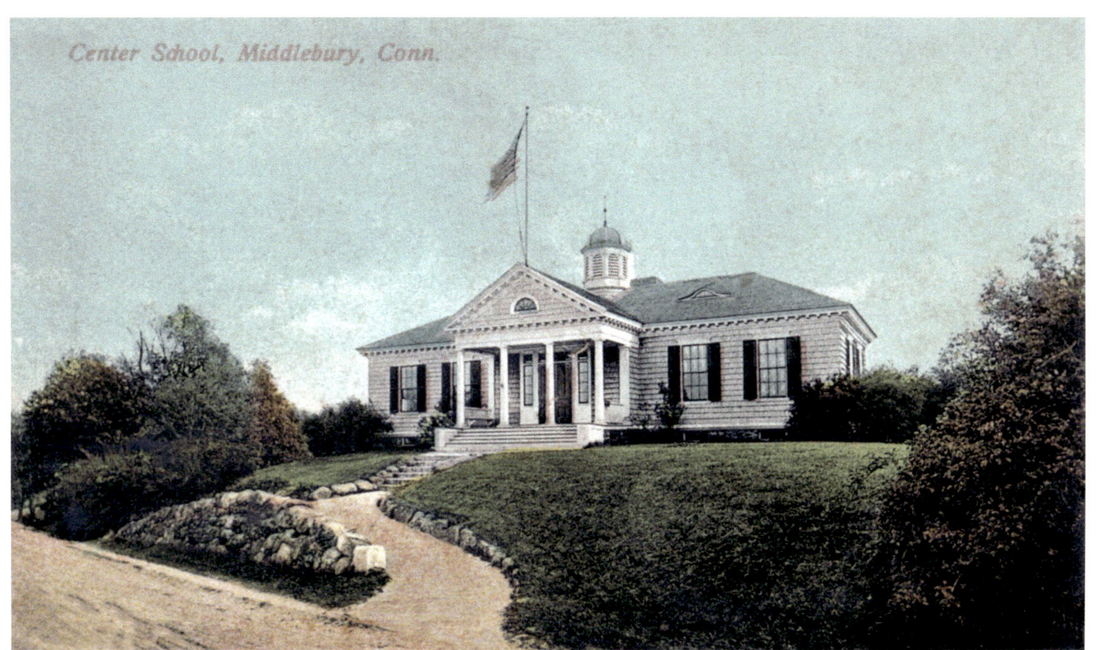

MIDDLEBURY CENTER SCHOOL: This beautiful two-room schoolhouse was built in 1897 and sits on a hill overlooking the valley. The style, design, and landscaping were meticulously created to enhance the location. Students from the nearby aged Union Academy were transferred to this new schoolhouse. The school was used until 1932, when the consolidated Shepardson School was built across the street. The Center School building was used for a while as the town library in one room, and housed town offices in the other. Occupied by the Middlebury Historical Society since 1975, the building retains its charm, both inside and out, while the original brass bell still rings in the cupola. (Above photograph courtesy of Middlebury Historical Society, Middlebury, CT)

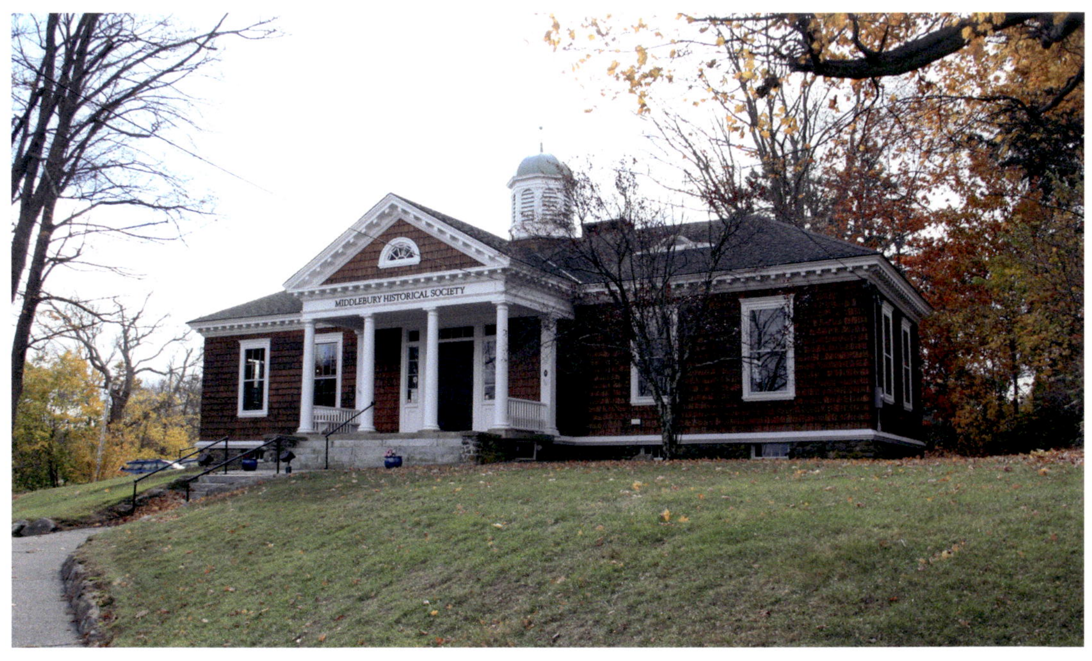

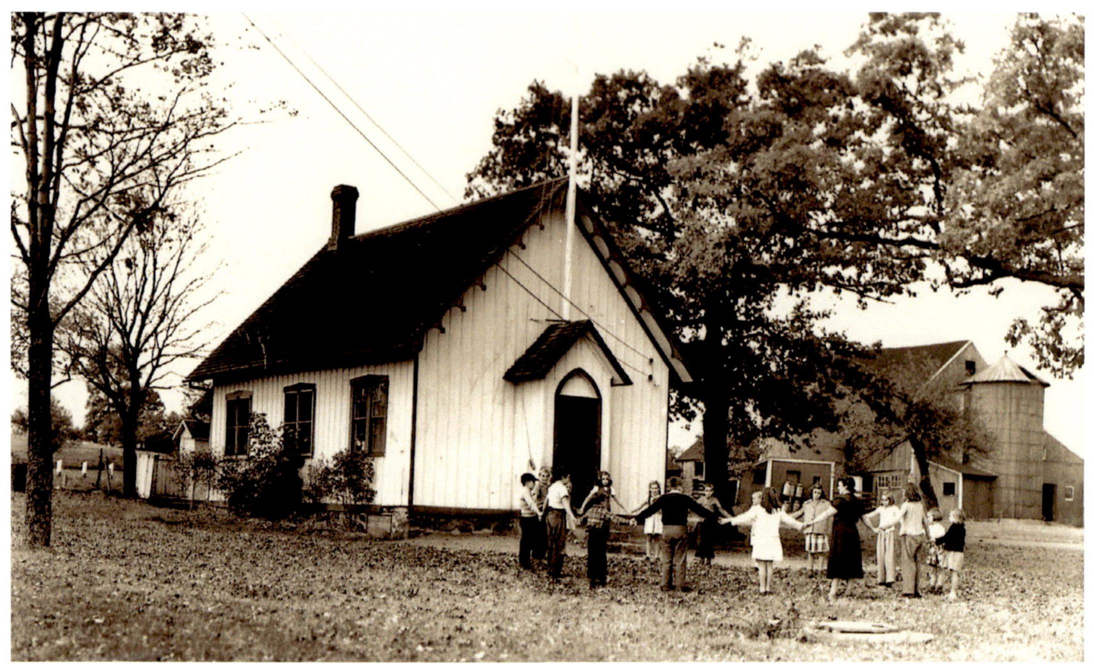

AVON: School #7 is a unique, beautifully designed building, which highlighted all the ideal features of a modern schoolhouse in December 1865. The high ceiling provides excellent ventilation, and the large windows increase the lighting inside the building. In 1927, the name "Pine Grove School" was suggested because of a large grove of pine trees nearby. The school was closed in June 1949 and the students started the new fall term in Towpath School in the center of town. The Avon Historical Society maintains the schoolhouse that is furnished as it was in the early 20th century. (Above photograph courtesy of Marian Hunter History Room, Avon Free Public Library, Avon, CT)

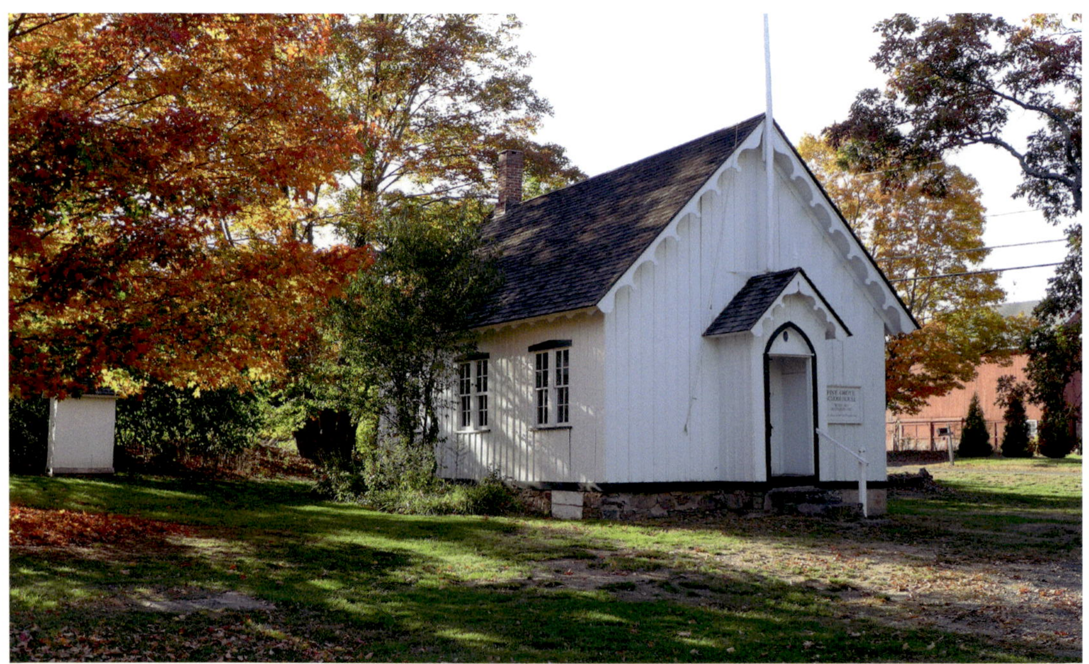

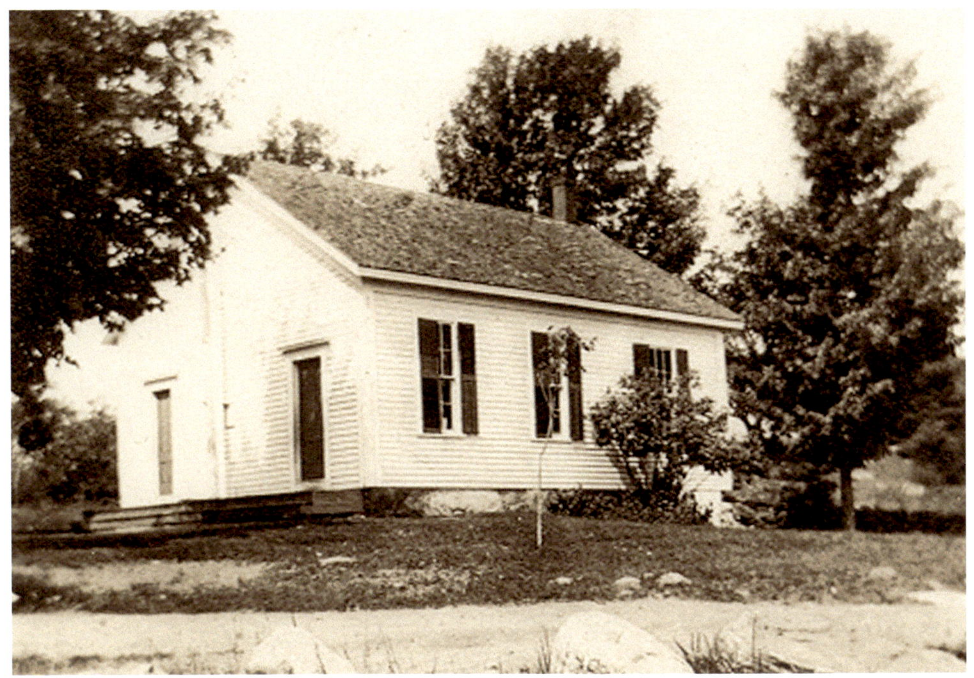

WOODSTOCK: The Red White School, the 11th school district of town, was built in 1873 to replace the "Red Schoolhouse," which burned down on the same site. The old school was painted red and the new school was painted white. The school closed in 1939. This is the only one-room schoolhouse left in Woodstock that has not be converted or moved from its original location. The Neighborhood Mutual Benefit Society used the building until 1969, when it came under the control of the Woodstock Historical Society. (Above photograph courtesy of Woodstock Historical Society)

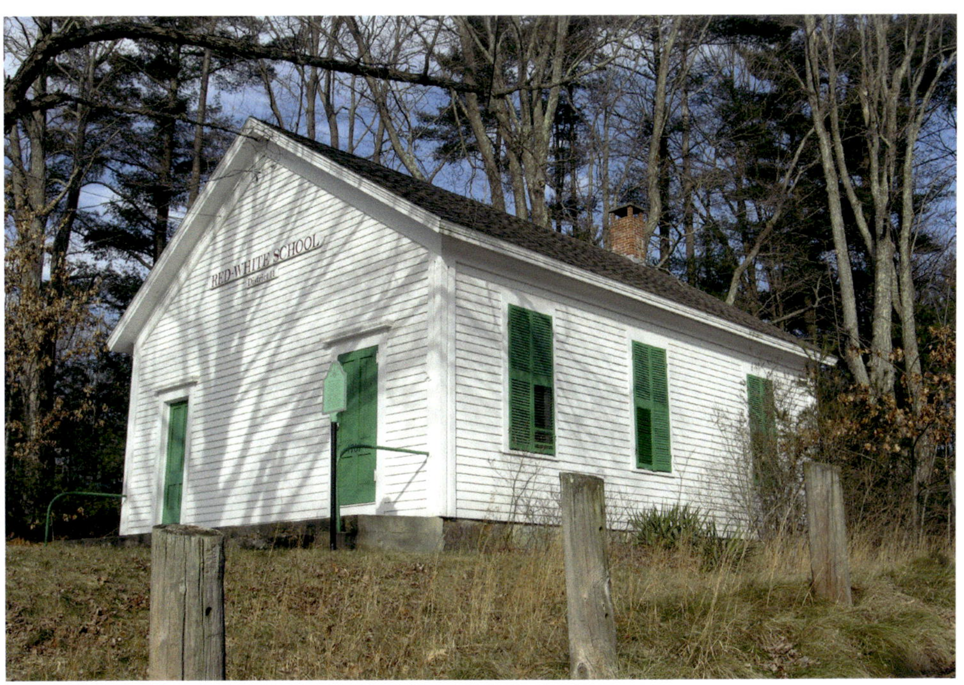

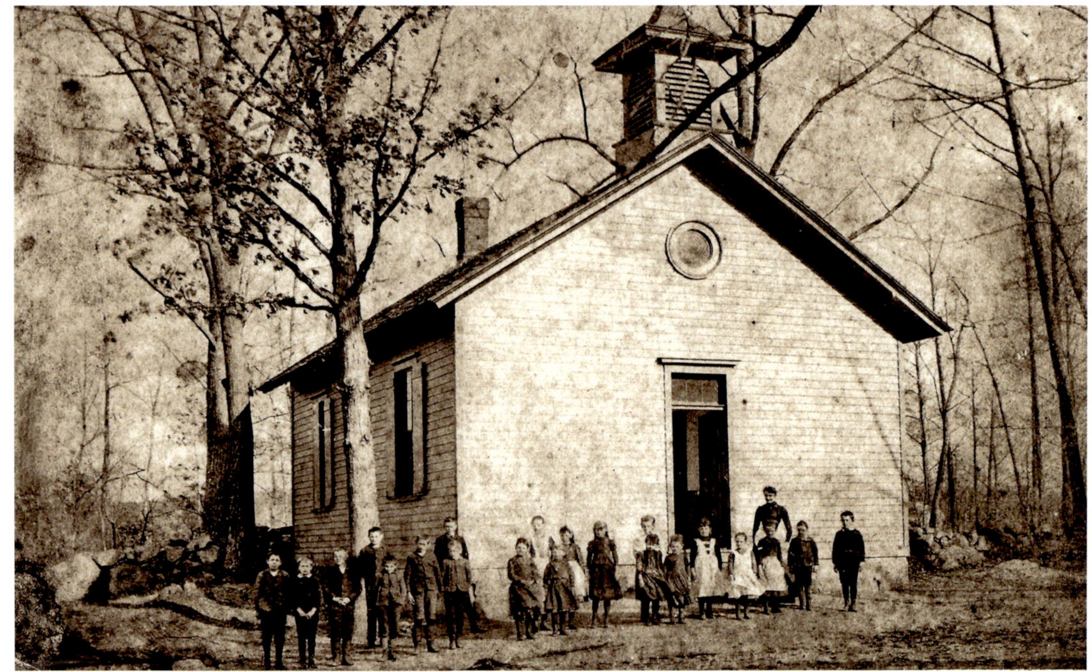

RIDGEFIELD: The Branchville Schoolhouse was built around 1875 in an area once known as "Ridgefield Station District." The area was isolated until the railroad came through, then developed into an industrial community. The school was used until around 1927, when the children were moved to a larger schoolhouse in the village. The Schoolhouse was used for a time as a meeting hall by the Jaycees, and now as a storage place for the town's athletic and Little League equipment. Recently, there have been conversations about restoring the old schoolhouse for use as meetings and events. (Above photograph courtesy of Ridgefield Historical Society)

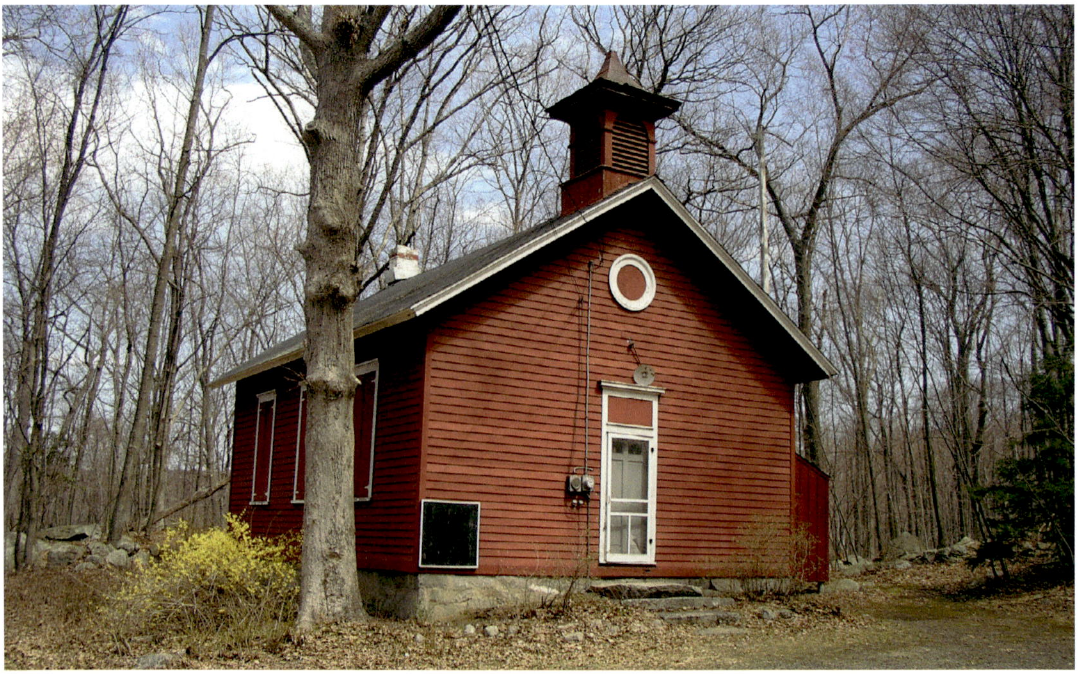

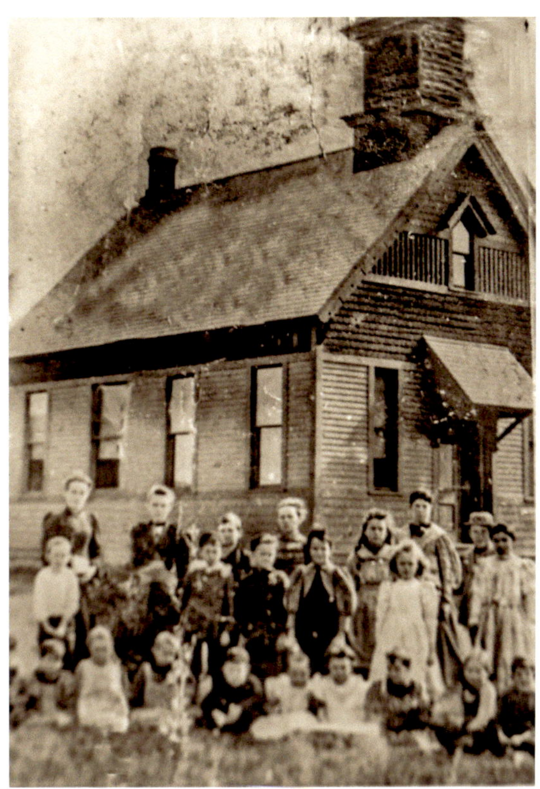

SALEM: The old Salem Center District Schoolhouse was built in 1885, on the town green joining the Congregational church, the Episcopal Church, and the Old Town Hall. At one time, Salem had six districts schools. As the population increased, there were discussions about adding rooms onto this schoolhouse. Instead, in 1940, a new larger three-room school was opened for all of the school districts. The schoolhouse was later used as the Grange Hall. The picture shows a class outside of the new school in 1885. (Above photograph courtesy of Salem Historical Society, Salem, CT)

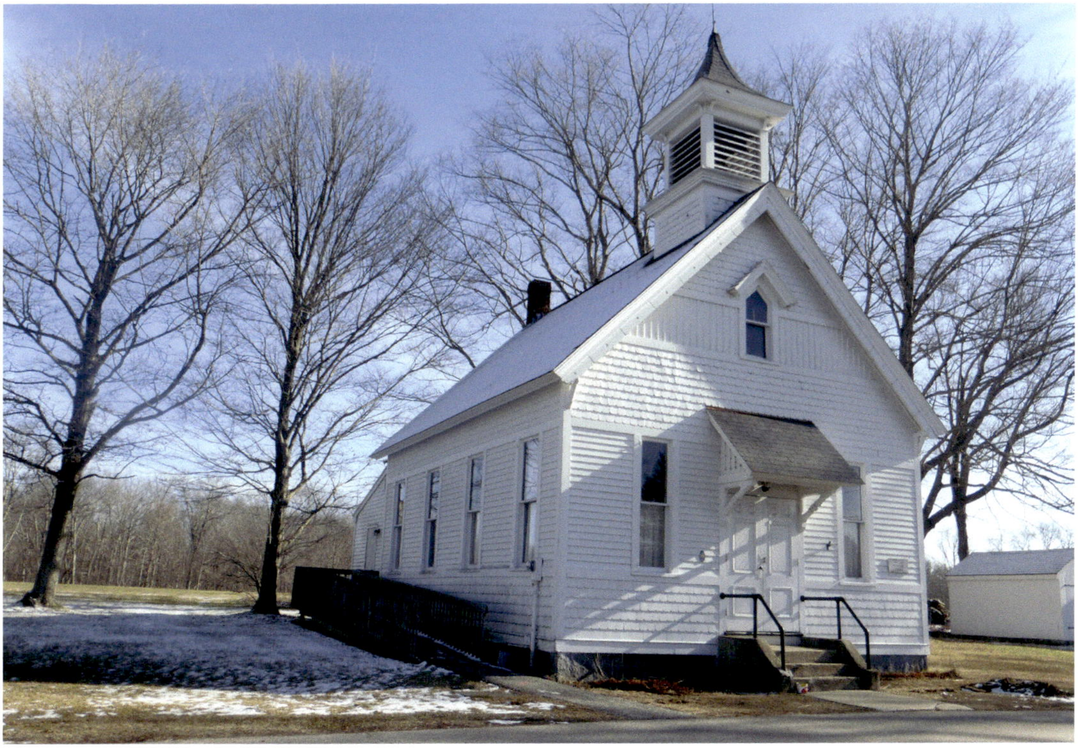

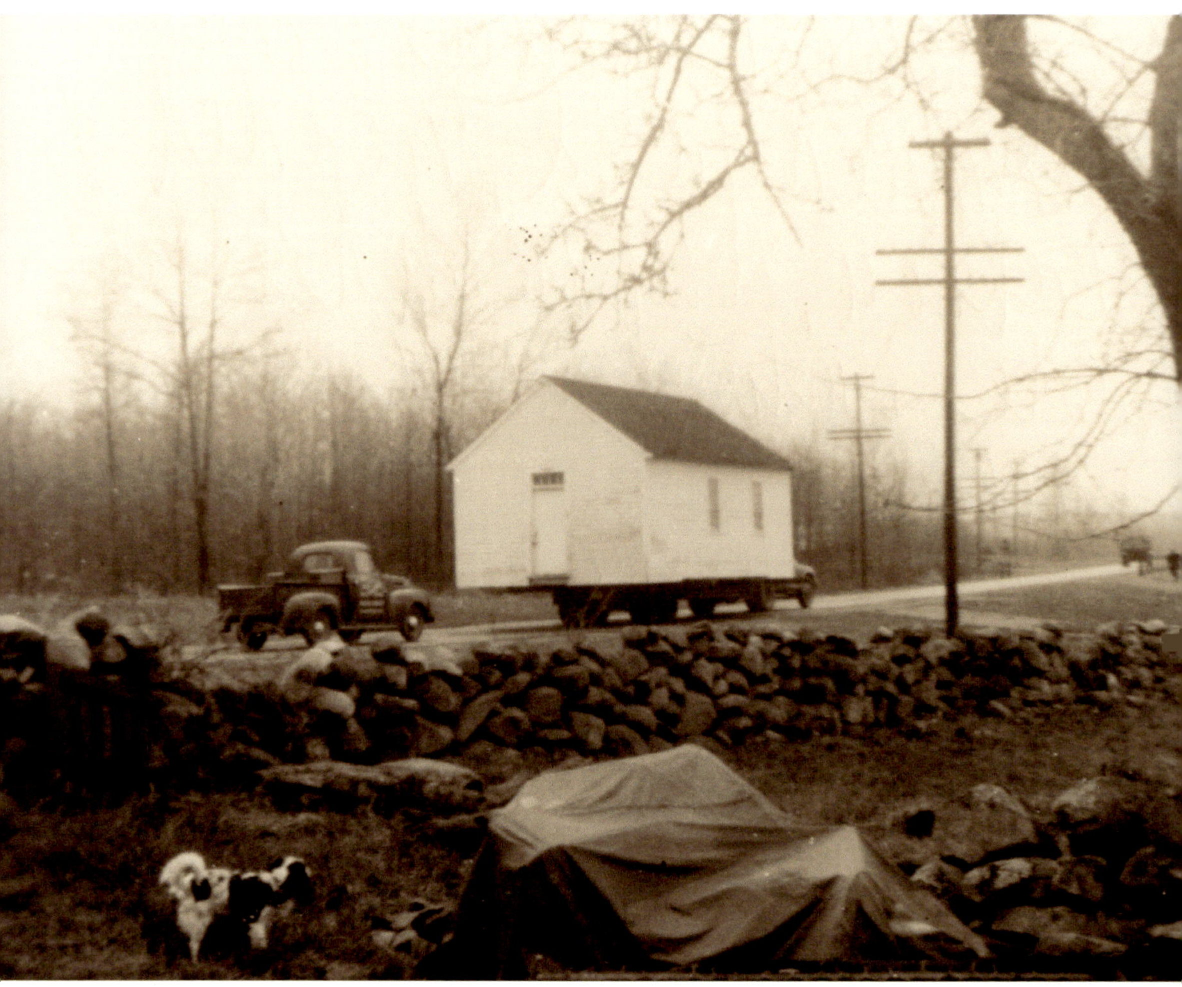

(Above photograph of the Gallop Hill School, courtesy of the Ledyard Historical Society, Inc., Ledyard, CT)

The one-room schoolhouses, left silent after the modern consolidated schools were opened, are now calling us back to visit. Take a moment to find the schoolhouses in your town and support the Historical Societies and towns who keep them alive.